MISSION ACCOMPLISHED

MISSION ACCOMPLISHED

THE ENGAGING MEMOIR OF A
CZECH FIGHTER PILOT FLYING FOR
BRITAIN IN WORLD WAR TWO

FRANK MARES DFM

GRUB STREET · LONDON

Published by
Grub Street
4 Rainham Close
London
SW11 6SS

British Library Cataloguing in Publication Data
Mares, Frank
  Mission accomplished: the engaging memoir of a Czech
  fighter pilot flying for Britain in World War Two
  1. Mares, Frank 2. Great Britain. Royal Air Force – History –
  World War, 1939-1945 3. Fighter pilots – Great Britain –
  Biography 4. Czechs – Great Britain – Biography
  5. World War, 1939-1945 – Personal narratives, Czech
  6. World War, 1939-1945 – Aerial operations, British
  I. Title
  940.5′44941′092

ISBN-13: 9781904943822

Typeset by Pearl Graphics, Hemel Hempstead

Printed and bound by MPG Ltd, Bodmin, Cornwall

Grub Street Publishing only uses
FSC (Forest Stewardship Council) paper for its books.

CONTENTS

I dedicate this book to the memory of my friends with whom
I crossed the border to Poland, sailed to France and finally arrived in
England, where they all laid down their lives in the war against the
Nazis. They are: Albin Nasvetter, Antonin Kašpar, Vladimir Michálek
and Jan Chalupa.

NB: Throughout the book I'll use the English
spellings of their names.

ACKNOWLEDGEMENTS

There are several people I must thank for getting my book published in the form that you see it today. My friend, the late Norman Fendall, to whom I refer in my Introduction, inspired me to put pen to paper in the mid-1990s and then helped me to improve its English. Then Mike George formatted the draft manuscript to include some of my photos and sketches with the aim of getting an English version published, but without success. A version in Czech was published in 1999.

Then after many years of the English manuscript lying on a shelf along came the RAF Harrowbeer Interest Group (<u>www.rafharrow beer.co.uk</u>) from which I met Bernie Steed and some of his colleagues in July 2006. Within a couple of weeks Bernie, acting as my 'agent', had found a suitable publisher – Grub Street. Grub Street moved very fast and here is my book.

I thank Debby Mason who is a personal friend of Lord (Norman) Tebbit of Chingford and risked that friendship by asking him to write the Foreword. I thank Norman Tebbit (former RAF and BOAC pilot) for saying 'yes'. Lord Tebbit had also been the chairman of the fund-raising committee for the Battle of Britain Memorial on Victoria Embankment – for which the Czech Government was a major donor.

I also thank Brian Salt, of the RAF Harrowbeer Interest Group, who scanned my photo and sketch collection in preparation for Grub Street to use.

And finally, to Bernie Steed and Peter Davey, both former military aviators, who spent many weeks meticulously proof-reading the manuscript in order to correct errors and to smooth out the rough edges without losing the flavour of a story told from my heart. I know that Bernie's and Peter's desire for accuracy has meant a great deal of detective work using my RAF pilot's log book and many other sources of information. To my original manuscript they have added a map and tables of my movements, a glossary of terms, and an index.

I thank them all for helping me to say 'Mission Accomplished', for a second time.

FOREWORD

Frank Mares' story, *Mission Accomplished*, is a very personal story – but it is part of a great historical timescape of the mid 20th Century.

Like many Czechs and Slovaks, Mares escaped Hitler's National Socialist War machine as his country, deserted by its friends (including Britain), succumbed without a struggle. Now in the 21st Century, Mares living in his adopted country of Britain can look back with pride at the liberation of Czechoslovakia from the Soviet communist empire and its peaceful separation into the Czech and Slovak Republics which are now part of the free Western world.

In 1938, with four friends, Mares risked everything to fight for his country. They escaped to France where they found themselves abandoned and almost drafted into the French Foreign Legion, although Mares had begun his training to fly, and wanted only to become a fighter pilot to take the war to Hitler's Germany.

He paints a graphic picture of the rottenness of France in 1939; its lack of nerve and will to fight. Escaping the Germans again as France surrendered, Mares eventually arrived in Britain to complete his training and fight with the Royal Air Force.

This is not just a "boys' book about flying and the war". There are some fine descriptions of the life of a fighter pilot – boredom, excitement, danger, fatigue and tragedy. However, I believe what Mares tells us about the British in 1940 will provoke some soul searching today. The welcome he received refutes the canards about the insular class-ridden English. His descriptions of a society independent, self-disciplined and law abiding, stoic and uncomplaining even during the London blitz of 1940-41 which cost over 40,000 civilian lives, will rekindle a sense of pride and raise questions about our country today.

Without men like Mares, Hitler would have triumphed. We should be proud that he adopted our country and that his Czech genes have enriched our British nation.

Truly this is a story which we should read and reflect upon.

The Rt Hon Lord Tebbit CH, PC

INTRODUCTION

It was a typical spring day that found me looking out onto an English garden that was beginning to show signs of life after its hibernation. I was miles away in thought and it was only in the background that I was conscious of the phone having rung – not until my wife announced that the call was for me, did I recover from my reverie.

The call was from someone completely unknown to me at the time and was concerning the old disused airfield, on which at one time I had served, and now was only a matter of a mile or two away from my house. Then followed a meeting on the old airfield and with the aid of a site plan it became possible to recall a whole host of instances from over fifty years ago. A truly incredible walk down a lane, full of memories, had begun.

From this small get-together sprang a relationship that continues to blossom and grow and was probably instrumental in reviving the aims that had lain dormant with me for a good many years, which was to commit the story of a life, my life, to paper. I had planned for quite a long time to place on record the details of an active life that contained a number of twists and turns and it occurred to me that, at the very least, I should set the record down if only for the sake of my children and grandchildren.

Maybe, in telling the story in this way, I would understand myself why it became essential for a Czechoslovakian lad to commit himself to an escape from the possible subjugation of his native land and the enslavement of his personal spirit. I felt that I was not at all ready to be enslaved in whatever disguise it presented itself and it became increasingly clear that plans would have to be made, the successful execution of which, would prevent any such outcome.

In company with four friends who were all of a similar disposition, we set out upon a journey that would provide sufficient excitement to spur us on to achieve our aim. On the way we encountered some spine-chilling, hair-raising and electrifying moments which young men of reasonably tender years were able to assimilate without too much effort. Sadly, I am the only survivor of the events that were undergone over sixty years ago. This book is written from the detailed diaries I kept.

Frank Mares DFM
Sampford Spiney, Devon

CHAPTER 1

BORN TO FLY

I was born free in the Czechoslovak Republic and until the age of six, lived in the small tranquil village of Zamyšel, amongst the forested hills of Sumava in West Bohemia. It was a poor but friendly and happy community of farmers who freely shared their land, tools and food. Life was hard but the inhabitants were content and intensely patriotic. In my early years I was mostly in the care of my grandparents because my father was away in the army and my mother was training to be a midwife.

Apart from religious pictures and ornaments with which these God-blessed people adorned their homes, there was always a portrait of our president prominently displayed. I must have been four or five years old when I came to understand that Tomas G Masaryk was not only our president but also our 'father' and was loved by all. I loved him at the first sight of his picture – an aged man with a kindly smile and a gentle face with wrinkles around his eyes, as if he was perpetually bemused by my presence. The spectacles he wore were pinched upon his aristocratic nose; his drooping white moustache and short beard increased my respect for him. My first reading lesson incorporated learning the words under his portrait: "Pravda Vitezi" (Truth Triumphs). This slogan, together with the red, white and blue flowers which were often placed behind the picture frame, representing the colours of the Czech national flag, braced me for the future.

When I was six years of age my parents moved to Plzen (Pilsen), where I was to begin my schooldays. This drastic departure from the gentle village folk and the serene countryside to a heavily industrialised town, perpetually shrouded in billowing black smoke, seemed to choke me and caused my emotions to erupt. The school swallowed me ruthlessly and the transition to life in a large town split my mind and body apart. For a long time I resented school and during lessons my mind would wander to recall the kind people of my native village. One lovely summer's day the whole school went on an excursion to a place called Làny, near Prague, where I underwent a transformation into a boy eager to learn. Làny was the president's summer residence and it was here where he found the time, away from state duties, to embrace his children, millions of them, as he walked among them. My love for my country and my 'father' – Tomas G Masaryk – was wholly re-affirmed. From that time on, I was happy at school as I eagerly wanted to become a worthy citizen of the Czechoslovakia Free Republic.

My parents' home was situated adjacent to the town's abattoir, where my father was employed as an analytical chemist. He was a hard man, at times unkind to my mother and never sparing the rod where I was concerned. My mother, who by now was a qualified maternity nurse, was kind and loving towards me, her only child, but often was not at home when I needed her protection.

Whilst continuing with my education, which ultimately led me to become an engineer, my ever-present yearning was for a life of freedom – like that of a bird. This yearning prompted me to visit the West Czechoslovakia Aero Club. It was situated not far from the western terminal of the town tram, about twenty minutes walk. When interviewed by the club manager, I soon realised that the cost of flying lessons would be prohibitive for my means, but I was not to be deterred.

After I had made it clear that my aim was to become a flyer, I was told that I would have to be willing to offer my services free of charge, carrying out detailed work in exchange for flying lessons. To this suggestion I happily agreed and, thereafter, spent all my spare time inside the hangar. My first task was to 'navigate' a broom and a pan around the aeroplanes. During the following months I worked hard, learning all that I could about servicing aeroplanes. Under expert guidance I was introduced to the ins and outs of all the essential repairs, including the splicing of cables linking the pilot's joystick to the rudder, elevators and ailerons.

Some three months after my initiation with the hangar sweeping broom, came a day of extreme happiness, I was told to fasten myself into the back seat of one of the bi-planes standing in front of the hangar. The aircraft was a First World War antique, and looked like two tea chests stuck together; one for the pilot to sit in and the one behind which I was told to climb into, which I did in double quick time – not stopping to ask any questions. Of course, I made quite sure that the wings, engine and the tail were all very much in evidence. I was sitting quite comfortably when the test pilot came to me and said, "You are being given this free flight as a reward for all your past hard work." He continued, "I want you to keep your eye on that gauge, making sure that the needle remains pointing to the green line. If it should, at any time, start to move towards the red line, you must tap me on the shoulder, whence I shall make for a landing as quickly as possible." He then added, "If the needle starts dropping fast, operate that lever, it will help to maintain the pressure." My reply was quick; "Yes sir, I will do exactly as you wish, you can rely on me." I had no illusions whatsoever; I knew the significance of the gauge needle dropping towards the danger mark.

However, as the pilot climbed into his seat this matter did not concern me unduly, and I was determined that the ensuing flight would be the making of my day. I was about to fly and to experience for the first time in my life what it was to be free as a bird. My pulse began to race when the pilot, after completing his pre-flight checks, shouted to the mechanic standing by the propeller: "switches off, throttle set." The mechanic repeated these commands before beginning to rotate the prop in order to suck fuel into the engine cylinders; all eight of them. When this was done the mechanic replied: "contact" and held up his right thumb. The pilot, having made sure that he had remembered to switch the fuel on, repeated: "contact", whilst at the same time giving a thumbs up sign as well. At this point, the mechanic swung the prop over and to my amazement the engine spluttered into life, coughing through the exhaust pipe a cloud of stinking smoke. I simply prayed that it was 'all systems go'.

At last we were on the move. The man who had been responsible for coaxing life into the engine was now holding on fast to the starboard lower wing, helping the pilot to turn towards the grass airfield. When this was achieved, the engine throttle was eased forward and we began to taxi towards the northern perimeter of the field. The exhaust smoke was no longer enveloping my cockpit and I had a clear view of the instrument that I had been placed in charge of. The needle was remaining close to the green line.

The pilot had completed his pre-take off checks, opened the throttle and the roar of the engine blasted me with a very clear message that we were on our way towards the thrill of my life. As we sped across the field, I became more and more exhilarated. With the bouncing of the plane over the uneven grass and the wind grasping hold of my hair and trying to inflate the cavity of my mouth, I began to feel like a baby being cuddled in the arms of its mother, or in my case, by my beloved grandmother, who proved to be my guardian angel on more than one occasion. All of a sudden we were airborne, no more bouncing along, but a smooth, floating sensation had taken over – I was being caressed.

For me, there was no altimeter to look at, not that I cared about our precise height. It seemed as if I was at the gates of heaven, the ground below was as a moving map, over which we seemed to be flying at the speed of destiny. Hardening my feelings to face up to the reality of the moment I remembered to look at the important dial. Unbelievably, the needle was glowering at me, pointing to just above the red mark. As a matter of priority, I grabbed the lever and began to feverishly move it back and forth. It seemed an eternity before the unfriendly gauge needle began unwillingly to move upwards and towards the green line. When this had been achieved I began to think – if I kept on pumping, the pilot would never know what was going on, thus the flight could go on and on, until he was ready to land. I could risk telling him later and say that being strapped in so tightly in my seat had prevented me from being able to reach forward and tap him on the shoulder. To my absolute delight, we remained airborne for about half an hour. We eventually made an approach towards the airfield and a superb landing, followed by parking what was now, my beloved and most beautiful plane in the world. It had all been well worth disobeying the given orders.

To my relief and surprise my day of glory was not in any way blemished when I informed the pilot, whose name was Venca Slouf, that I had disobeyed his instructions. To my intense pleasure, instead of reprimanding me he placed his arm around my shoulder, squeezed me tight and said: "Frank, I can well remember the day of my very first flight. Like you, I was only fifteen when I too experienced the thrill of my life. Very likely I would have done exactly as you did."

Venca and I became very good friends although he was almost ten years older than me. As time marched on he taught me, not just how to fly, but how to become a vital part of the plane – to fly as if the wings were bonded on to my body. Some years later, Venca and I flew with the same squadron, our wings strengthened by the bond of our beliefs, that a freedom must be defended. Later, as members of the Royal Air Force we were proud to give a good account of ourselves.

A week or so after my inaugural flight, I found that it became somewhat difficult to concentrate on my studies at college. I remained intoxicated by the addictive spirit of the heavens above. Previously I had enjoyed my studies, in particular, producing technical drawings of electric motors, turbines and associated circuits. As a side line, I became interested and attended lessons about the internal combustion engine, both 2-stroke and 4-stroke petrol, and also plumbed the depths of the diesel engine functions which, at that time, were not considered seriously.

When one of the college tutors noted that I had become rather lax in my attention during lectures, and that my hitherto high quality drawings were not up to the required standard, he asked me to visit him in his office. He was perplexed about the sudden downgrading of my work. He asked me if there was a plausible explanation. Encouraged by his benign and caring attitude, I told him of my recent experiences and ambitions to become a pilot. After some contemplation, he looked me straight in the eye and solemnly declared: "You have a natural talent to become good at what you are presently studying, do not place that in jeopardy. By working hard, as you have done until recently, you are set to achieve success." He went on to say: "So far as your dreams to become a pilot are concerned, there is nothing at all wrong with this notion. Indeed I applaud your strong determination." At that moment, once again looking me full in the eyes, but with a few wrinkles appearing on his forehead, he urged me to 'go for it' but at the same time, to get my priorities right. He pointed out that I had only three more years of study, during which time, he could see no reason why, in any spare time that was available, I could not carry on with my ambition to become a pilot as well. We concluded the conversation with me explaining what motivated me to emulate what the birds did naturally.

As a result of that very friendly advice, I began the process of connecting my hitherto crossed wires, to a polarity I knew would energise me towards what I was destined to reach. Indeed I switched myself on, tuned the dial of priorities and thereafter found it easy to recharge my capacitors of knowledge. I graduated from the college, with honours.

Whilst furthering my education, every opportunity was taken to avail myself of time at the aero club, where later, I was fortunate enough to gain a state scholarship to train as a pilot and to realise that freedom and flying are tightly interwoven.

Except when the weather made flying impossible, lessons were given every weekend. I was grateful, that by the grace of the state, these lessons came free of charge. It was a privilege that could never be taken for granted, knowing that it was paid for by those, who like me, were Czech patriots, living in their free democratic beloved country – Czechoslovakia.

Having, in the opinion of my flying instructors, received sufficient dual tuition, the day was appointed for me to take my very first solo flight. I tried my best to control my overwhelming emotions. I was determined to do my best for the instructor who was pretending to be unconcerned, but at the same time standing near enough to see if I was losing my nerve – which was not the case. I felt aware that for every move made or command that was given, there were many pairs of eyes watching me. This was so every time somebody was about to go solo for the first time. It was very important to do everything that was expected of me. It was essential not only to satisfy the instructor and all those watching, but also vital to prove to myself that flying was what I was destined to be good at, from the very first 'flap' of my wings.

I busied myself with all the pre-flight checks; asking the mechanic if the chocks were in front of the wheels, turning on the fuel cock, making sure that no loose articles were about, checking the instruments were all in order, including tapping the altimeter gently and making any necessary adjustment to its setting.

The next procedure was to ascertain that the flying controls moved freely; that the rudder and elevator on the tail responded correctly, that the ailerons also responded, noting that when the right one was deflected down, the left aileron was up. This done, everything looked and felt smooth, all the responses were satisfactory. With the fuel cock turned on, all was ready to initiate the engine starting procedure. In order to breathe life into it, help was needed from somebody suitably trained, to turn the propeller which ensured that fuel was sucked into the cylinders prior to switching on the ignition.

The mechanic, clearly in view, was awaiting my orders. Making sure that the engine ignition switches (yes, there were two, the circuits being duplicated) were in the 'off' position, the throttle was set slightly open and the friction nut tightened. At this stage I shouted "switches off, throttle set." No sooner had this command been given than the propeller began to move clockwise, pausing each time the engine compression was overcome. With this completed, the cylinders were primed, the mechanic stood aside and shouted "contact", which I repeated while switching the ignition to 'on' and holding the joy stick back towards me as far as it would go. The mechanic placed himself with the utmost care at the end of the propeller and, balancing his body on one foot set slightly forward pulled the propeller very smartly downwards. As eagerly hoped, the engine burst into life, its pistons pumping power to the propeller, very like my heart pumped blood through my veins.

The engine was allowed to purr gently at just about the 'tick-over' pace in order to warm it up and prepare itself to be my willing servant. Just like my own blood pressure can be monitored, the engine oil pressure, the temperature and the rpm were transmitted back to a set of dials arranged along the instrument panel.

Making doubly sure that the chocks were in place under the undercarriage wheels and after checking the instrument readings, the throttle was gently opened to its fullest extent. The engine gained in revs and decibels whilst the joy stick was held back and the whole plane strained to leap forward. I turned the ignition switches 'off' and 'on' in turn, noting that the rev counter did not indicate any drop. Throttling the engine back, it and I took a breather. My thoughts were concerned with having performed all the necessary checks whilst the engine, much like a racehorse, seemed impatient to rev-up and 'charge'.

Satisfied that all was in order, I wasted no time in asking to have the chocks removed. With the mechanic holding the starboard wing tip and by application of full right rudder and a gentle opening of the throttle, the plane turned to face the expanse of the grass airfield. By careful nudging of the throttle even further forward, the plane gathered speed, the prop fanning more air back over the fuselage towards the tail. By operating the rudder and elevator, the plane responded by maintaining the direction in which I was aiming to taxi.

In the knowledge that the instructor would not let me go solo unless he was fully satisfied as to my complete proficiency, I felt confident that it was time for take-off. The day chosen for my solo flight had turned out ideal, the sky contained only scattered fluffy clouds, floating patiently at about 3,000 feet and seemed to be welcoming me into their territory. The visibility was crystal clear and the wind was blowing along the length of the airfield at a steady 6 to 8 knots. With this type of gentle breeze it was easy to maintain a course towards the edge of the field from where I was briefed to take off. As with all the planes that I had flown so far, this too, had an open cockpit; the propeller slip stream keeping me fresh and ready to take to the air.

After turning into the wind I looked across the mile long airfield. At the perimeter was the infamous Bory prison and beyond that the tram terminal where I alighted so often for my walk to the field, in order to fulfil my dream of learning to fly. The engine patiently ticked-over whilst I carried out a pre-flight check; all instruments in the normal position; one more quick 'stir' of the flying controls and a good look ahead. My heart felt in unison with the aircraft and at full throttle the engine flexed its power to full potential. As the plane gained speed use of the rudder was necessary in order to maintain a straight line and with the stick pushed gently forward, the elevator at a slightly downward angle, the force of the air lifted the tail up; the skid cleared the grass. As further speed was gathered the plane bounced over the ground until, as if by magic I was airborne, striving to reach the sky.

Almost two years previously I was privileged to fly, as a passenger, for the first time free to enjoy the freedom of the skies. This time I was in sole control of a much updated and streamlined purpose-built bi-plane trainer aircraft. I was very much aware of the reassuring power of the air-cooled radial engine (the cylinders arranged round the crankcase to form a star). With throttle fully open, the engine's surge of power propelled the craft ahead with the ensuing stream of air vitalising the wings, the controls responding to my urging command – or were they? Was there an unseen force behind the controls, and in charge during the vital stages of the take-off? My left hand remained grasping the throttle lever, my right on top of the joy stick by which I was controlling the elevator and the ailerons. With feet firmly placed upon the rudder pedals, I had an uncanny feeling that some unseen power was energising my limbs, making sure that my first solo flight would turn out to be perfect, never ever to be forgotten.

The cool stream of air, trying its very best to flow under my flying helmet, made sure that I maintained a cool head which helped to dispel any doubts as to who was in control of my plane. I was the pilot in charge, making sure that the speed was correct, the aircraft in perfect, gentle climbing trim. The altimeter hand was beginning to indicate that sufficient height was being attained to fly safely over the edge of the town buildings. The airfield now lay a distance behind and below and out of sight. On looking sideways I had a view of the park where people were walking, or sitting on the many benches. Towards the middle of the park some tennis courts were set out. A quick scan of the instrument panel gave me satisfaction and confidence that all systems were functioning properly and, having continued the climb, I was just about to reach 2,000 feet, at which height I had been instructed to level off.

On reaching the prescribed altitude, it was now time to perform some flying exercises, carrying out a few gentle and some steep turns, also flying at a very slow speed at which the aircraft would threaten to stall. At this low speed, the flying controls become unresponsive and any further decrease in speed would bring about a stall – the nose of the aircraft would drop suddenly. This is an exercise, which is of vital importance to all would-be flyers who wish to survive. After diligently carrying out all the allotted tasks the time had arrived to have a gentle cruise around the town of Pilsen. Coaxing my plane into a left-hand turn, I began to fly along the town's perimeter, at the centre of which towered St Bartholomew's church, its high steeple could be seen from a great distance even when on the ground. The bird's-eye view that I was enjoying made me recall my prayers to that solemn looking edifice whose steeple, like me, was reaching for the heavens. Looking northward over the roof tops was a view of the vast factory complex known internationally as 'Skoda'. The river Radbuza glistened and captured my attention. It wound along the southern periphery of the oldest part of Pilsen, almost touching, like the Skoda factory, the famous Pilsen brewery in which the world famous lager was made. The brewery was easily identified by the high tower into which spring water was pumped for use in the manufacture of the beer.

Once again, flying seemed so effortless, as if the plane was taking care of itself, apart from the occasional minor turbulence caused by the warm air (thermals) rising upwards. Fluffy heaps of thinly scattered clouds were just above my present ceiling of 2,000 feet. What a supreme experience of enjoyment it was to fly alone, emulating what comes naturally to the birds that I had watched with envy as a boy. It must have been then that the yearning for freedom was ingrained into my soul. After a descent to 700 feet there was no problem in joining the airfield circuit, carrying out a final turn into the wind, closing the throttle to reduce to a safe speed, and gliding down. The plane was brought closer to the ground and, by levelling off and then pulling the 'stick' back, eventually settled down on the ground. When safely down and with the engine and the propeller gently turning over, a sigh of relief was murmured by man and plane alike.

Once the aircraft had slowed down and at the appropriate moment, right rudder was applied to steer a course towards the hangar. Outside the buildings ahead I could see the club staff eagerly awaiting my return.

The wing of the aircraft was caught by an attendant who guided me to the appointed parking spot where I switched off the engine and the fuel cock. A wave of applause washed over me as I climbed out of the cockpit. Before reaching the ground, I was ruthlessly snatched, my outstretched arms and legs bundled into a heap on the ground. The gang sang an initiation verse, whilst those holding me swung my body like a hammock, deliberately lowering my rump on to the grass. This deed was repeated three times, then finally, once more for good luck. There were no apologies offered, instead one after the other vigorously shook my hand. The congratulations were warm and hearty and bought tears into my weathered eyes.

My instructor stood by, approving of all the goings on, with an amused squint in his eyes. When able to, he placed a strong arm over my shoulder saying: "Well done Frank, I'm proud of you. Never forget – always fly with due care, take nothing for granted and try to develop eyes in the back of your head." Those wise words remained with me forever and years later, flying a Hurricane or Spitfire fighter, they were to prove significant in saving my life.

During the following months, much more flying and many more classroom lessons were to follow. At times the flying was under the tuition of an older instructor named Mr J Rais, who taught me very complex, and at times, punishing manoeuvres such as learning how to initiate and recover from a spin. Frequently, a stalling exercise followed during which the flying controls become sloppy and ineffective and were a warning that losing speed, particularly at low altitude, could be disastrous. Aerobatics also formed part of the instruction, proficiency at which was to stand me in good stead, and proved vital in order to escape being shot down.

If bad weather prevented flying, I reverted to the mundane work in and around the aircraft in the hangar. Lessons about the principles of flight, aerodynamics, meteorology and navigation continued and at college my studies also intensified in the final months ahead of the vital exams and pending graduation. With the encouragement of my tutors, I maintained a good standard of work until the end of the final term, when I passed with honours.

A job was waiting for me at the Skoda factory situated at the southwest end of the town and I was involved with the design and manufacture of various electrical components associated with turbo-generators. With my flying graduation test becoming imminent, I became absent minded at work. When I explained the cause of my inattentiveness to my superiors, it was with great relief that I was given a period of one month unpaid leave. Once more I began to sense that a hand of destiny was behind the evolving events.

My flying finals in 1937 proved that I was proficient to fly. I became the proud owner of a private pilot's licence (PPL) – which bestowed upon me the freedom of the skies. Since 'hatching' from the egg, my feathers had grown and now the rest was up to me to prove that I was worth the faith and support of my kin, my tutors and my employer.

CHAPTER 2

NATIONAL SERVICE AND PLANS TO ESCAPE

With the growing tension between Germany, Great Britain and France, Hitler became more and more threatening. His intention to invade Czechoslovakia was a pretext to protect the Sudetenland, the border region of Czechoslovakia lying along the Sudeten Mountains. Everyone was beginning to worry but at the same time putting their hopes in the hands of the diplomats, whose task it was to pacify Hitler and persuade him to change his planned course.

My mind and body were heavily concentrated on the work at the Skoda factory and my activities at the aero club. However as the belligerent attitude of Hitler continued it began to disturb my peace of mind and, when President Dr Eduard Benes (who succeeded Tomas G Masaryk) ordered the army to strategically place itself along the Czech borders, my optimism began to weaken. Any unease that I did have was temporarily dissipated when the aero club manager decided to hold a small flying display. It was an attempt to raise some badly needed funds for the club coffers and I was selected to take a part in it, albeit a very small one. The manager explained what was expected of me and I realised the insignificance of the task – but what was there to complain of – the flight was free and the task a simple one.

The show was well attended with the promise of an exciting programme. The pilot that I was flying with had an easy job, which was to position the plane along the windward side of the airfield and, at an appropriate height and time, he would instruct me to heave over the side of the cockpit, a bag of sand. This was attached to a parachute and suitably secured by a length of cord to the plane (static line). I had been carefully briefed beforehand, that at a nod from the pilot, the bag of sand was to be dispatched overboard. When the 'nod' came, owing to a very strong slipstream, I was prevented from lifting the sandbag. Without hesitation I pulled the pin from my seat harness, braced my body and heaved the bag over the side.

By leaning over I managed to observe the parachute opening, and the sandbag, taking the place of a parachutist, floated gracefully towards the spectators. The task completed, I settled down into the seat feeling satisfied with my performance. The feeling was to be short lived. At that precise moment the pilot started to dive, my body becoming weightless as I floated around the cockpit without the benefit of the safety harness. An unseen hand once again came to my aid when I felt as if I was being pushed back into the seat. As the pilot began pulling out of his dive I was subjected to the G-force. My body gained about four times in weight from this gravital potency. My hands remained glued to the seat whilst the pilot performed aerobatics and I was dragged out and then compressed back in the seat with my shoulders heaving against the side of the cockpit. This went on for about fifteen minutes until, at last, the aircraft resumed a more normal flying attitude. On the ground, it was the turn of the pilot to feel shocked when he was informed that during the performance of loops, barrel rolls, spins and stall turns, I was very much in the hands of providence.

The pilot had been completely unaware that I had not been strapped into the seat and on being informed of my predicament, was stunned. After regaining his composure, he, quite rightly, told me off for undoing the harness straps. He was right, of course, but at least I was still alive to offer my apologies. The air display was considered a success and the finances of the club received a boost. Unbeknown to the spectators, the air display's most dangerous feat had been performed by me!

In the weeks that followed I gradually increased my solo flying experience and, with a PPL, I was soon considered proficient to fly some paying passengers. My first such flight was with a young man called Mr Benes. He, like me, was only about nineteen years of age. I was to fly him to a small rural town named Klatovy, which was situated about forty miles due west of the airfield. Mr Benes wished to be flown over the town, positioning the plane so that he could drop a message, which was contained in a cardboard tube. The plane being used for this trip was a 'Praga Air Baby', a side-by-side two-seater with a canopy enclosing the cabin. The engine was an air-cooled, two cylinder, which due to the low mounting, left the prop only just clearing the ground. The fuselage was wide and short with a single wing placed on top, just behind the cabin. It was a very nice-looking Czech-made aircraft resembling a duck and was a treat to fly.

As a result of some unforeseen difficulties, the plane's engine was reluctant to start and accordingly, we took off much later than had been originally planned. The weather was very good, a slightly overcast sky with a cloud base of over 3,000 feet and very little wind. Mr Benes was relaxed and talkative and altogether good company to have on board. He proved to be good at navigating us towards Klatovy where, on the outskirts, we were to find the house on which he intended to drop his friendly 'missile'. According to my flight plan, the town should have loomed into view after about thirty-five minutes. I knew the town well, having passed through it many times when cycling to Sumava, where I had spent my early childhood years.

Another ten minutes passed before two church spires came into view. Our goal had been reached and we spent another fifteen minutes in circling and dropping the canister with its message, before returning to base. Having set course for home, we both expressed the thought that it was getting a bit murky. Flying over the outskirts of Klatovy the streetlights were all on and it seemed to be dark unusually early, or so I imagined. At a height of some 2,000 feet there seemed to be few clouds about and what there were happened to be ahead of us. With the horizon no longer distinct, the darkness was deepening and I became concerned. Mr Benes still looked relaxed, and might well have thought that I was used to night flying but he could not have been more wrong, this flight would be the first.

Using the headlights of cars that were moving in our intended direction, it was possible to navigate, as I was familiar with the straight road that lay beneath us. It was the main road between Pilsen and Klatovy. Further confirmation that we were on the right track was, when after descending to 1,500 feet, it was possible to see the glow of the Pilsen town lights reflected by the clouds. The engine that had earlier proved difficult to start was purring sweetly, powering the propeller and, through its halo, we were scanning for a view of our base. Like our take-off, the landing had to be into the wind and this meant that the approach would be made over the Bory prison buildings. The high dome in the centre was something to be avoided at all costs.

As darkness descended, staff at the aero club became anxious and requested that the prison authorities switch on all their available lights in an effort to guide us back to base. The dome was illuminated like the Star of Bethlehem and when it zoomed into sight my eyes remained fixed upon it. It proved to be our saviour. Circling the field at 1,000 feet, I made a long approach, gradually losing height, aiming the nose of the aircraft slightly to the right, before flying over the prison. I had no time to feel concern for my passenger who, fortunately, had remained silent.

Clearing the buildings rather high meant that we made a bumpy touch down almost at the end of the field. With no brakes fitted and our fingers crossed, we fortunately came to a halt only a few yards before the trees at the forest edge. Once again I felt my guardian angel had been present. The reception we received on landing was rather subdued with something of a reprimand handed out. Mr Benes was obviously in a forgiving mood for, when paying for the trip, he had a smile on his face and gave me ten Czech crowns as a tip. Little did he or I realise that we would meet again very soon at a place called Hradec Kralove, where we were destined to start our national service training. Although he did not train as a pilot, we met up again when in the RAF in England.

My flying career continued at the aero club where I flew as often as possible. When not in the air I carried on providing free engineering services and became, as time went on, more skilled and consequently, sought after. I soon began to appreciate that those using college-applied theories were, from time to time, outclassed by the craftsmen that I was working with. These practical men really had the know-how. I learnt to admire them and, at times, envy their skill.

My work at the factory was still proving to be of great interest. I was assigned to a department manufacturing large armatures, which formed part of a turbo-generator for the provision of electricity. When I found the work becoming repetitive, I was able to detach myself and gave a lot of thought to the dark clouds that were spreading over Czechoslovakia. They were threatening to obscure the very innocent fleecy 'balls of wool' I was so happy to be flying amongst. The black smudges of cloud were no longer billowing from the factory chimneys but drifting from Hitler's Germany as a warning to the peace-loving Czechs.

Upon the death of our 'father' – President Tomas G Masaryk – our new president, Dr Eduard Benes did his utmost for our industrious and democratic nation. It was not long before my call-up papers arrived with instructions to attend the Czech Air Force base at Hradec Kralove, where I would be required to fulfil my compulsory national service. I left with the good wishes of my mother but my father was less enthusiastic. Only a month before I had had angry words with him concerning him striking my mother. Warm farewells were offered to me by all those who worked with me at the factory and there was to be an emotional send-off from the members of the aero club. At last, I was off, desperate to do my patriotic best for my beloved country.

Training at the air force base began almost immediately and the emphasis was on instilling discipline into the new recruits, it was essential to do as we were told without question. This was particularly so during the 'square-bashing' period and, to my relief, the drill periods were less frequent once the flying training started.

In order to establish the country's self-respect, the factories worked day and night; farmers reaped large harvests, the intellectuals, the artists and the professionals excelled in all that they did. By doing so, the Czechoslovak nation gained the admiration and respect of the whole world. Here was a peace-loving country stretching out her arms across her frontiers to reach, what she hoped would be, friendly surrounding nations. Across the English Channel an understanding and a pact of friendship was sealed.

Flying lessons at the base were aimed at turning us conscripts into fighter pilots. It was intensive and enjoyable. The methods were more radical than those I had encountered at the aero club but there was no cause for complaint. After all, we were flying and when on solo flights, I, for one, felt free.

To my dismay, the discipline of 'square-bashing' that was adopted at the camp was applied with sadistic vigour by the corporal and sergeant in charge who used 'Prussian-style' methods. The ground training proved very harsh and, at times, apparently stupid. One early morning, after I had made my bed, the corporal decided that my neatly stacked and folded blankets were out of precise alignment. Knocking the pile on the floor, the corporal ordered me to adopt a squatting position and, with a rifle held over my head, waddle like a duck down a flight of stairs to the front of my squad who were assembled on the square. I was next ordered to stand up and quick march to a corner of the cookhouse, which stood on the edge of the parade ground. Here I was forced to bellow into a drainpipe "I am a fool!" several times. This mad order issued by the likewise mad corporal made me see red. Fortunately, just before my fuse burned out, there was a decided change in the arrangements at the camp.

I spent some time debating with myself as to whether I would stay in the Czech Air Force as a regular flyer or, when my national service stint was over, return to my job at the Skoda factory. My mind was made up for me by Hitler's threats. Only during my solo flying, carrying out detailed instructions, was I able to feel free from such worries. Hitler's threats never did seem so serious as when my feet were firmly off the ground.

The Fatherland was only twenty years 'young', so surely, I thought, with the promised help of the British and French, Hitler would never dare to invade Czechoslovakia – a small country of twelve million unaggressive loving souls. I did, however, consider just how any help would or could reach us, should we be invaded. Being at the centre of Europe, we were surrounded by not only Germany but Poland, Russia, Rumania, Hungary and Austria; each of whom had their own problems to consider. Russia in particular was politically non-committal but at times gave the impression of fraternising with Hitler and this gave rise to additional worries about the future. Flying made it possible to avoid the depths of despair.

When not flying or being subjugated by the sadistic corporal, I kept myself and my mind occupied by writing letters. Correspondents included my mother, my friends at Skoda and at the aero club. Most frequently, however, I wrote to my girlfriend Jarka. I had fallen for this girl only a month before my call-up papers arrived and I was drafted.

We had met for the first time at the aero club, where one of her brothers had some business to attend to. She was the prettiest seventeen year old girl that I had seen; was about four inches less than my 5' 10", slim and shapely and had hazel eyes. The dimples in her cheeks and the upward corners of her mouth gave the impression that she carried a permanent smile. When she was not looking at me I was positively jealous. She had a soothingly quiet voice, which was distinctly refined. Our relationship grew closer and closer, my passion for her was like the flames of an inferno. On my departure for Hradec Kralove, that fuse remained intact – our bonds of friendship were very strong and I was sure of her loyalty.

My mother, writing from home, reported that all was well in spite of her very busy schedule as a maternity nurse. Her private circuit of expectant mothers and those needing her professional care for their babies made constant calls upon her. She was a much sought after midwife and dedicated to her profession. My father never added a line to my mother's letters – he too was kept very busy with his job at the laboratory in the town's abattoir.

A well established routine was set up at the base where our national service was being carried out. The time was divided between discipline, brainwashing programmes and our flying training. The classroom sessions revealed how to fly strategically as a member of a squadron, or a flight, or even as an individual. All of us attending these lectures took the lessons very seriously. Later when actually flying in formations it was possible to put the classroom theory into practice. The team spirit grew and we became interdependent. There was no time for us to feel bored or dissatisfied. We were becoming a force to be reckoned with. Mr Hitler, beware!

A special assembly of all camp personnel was organised at which we were addressed by an air force general. It was a morale-raising speech, considered by the politicians to be necessary in view of the ever worsening international situation. Hitler was becoming even more bellicose against Czechoslovakia; peace was standing on very shaky ground. It was during the assembly that I, unbelievably, met up again with the young lad Benes who, not long ago, I had flown to Klatovy. Like everyone else, he was dressed in the air force uniform and carrying out his national service two-year stint.

The surprise meeting was mutually pleasing and thereafter we met as often as the allotted spare time would allow. I discovered that he came from a non-orthodox Jewish family and, although my upbringing was by Roman Catholic parents and a deeply religious grandmother, we became good friends during our time at the camp. Strange as it may seem, we were destined to meet again during and after the war.

Not long after the visit from the general, the order was given to forego the usual first light morning parade The officer in charge directed us to climb aboard some waiting trucks which transported us fourteen miles away, to the edge of a forest. Approaching the area, one could not miss the long line of lorries, camouflaged with paint and containing heaped loads also covered by similarly camouflaged tarpaulins. Our first task was to remove all the tarpaulin coverings, whereupon an awesome sight was revealed as we gazed at stockpiles of bombs. They looked evil, causing shivers to run up and down our spines. Our job was to unload all these bombs and move them to a point under the trees. Here they were re-stacked, a most tiresome task. The bombs were of muscle-straining weight and it took two or three people to carry each one. It was necessary to toil all day with food and refreshment being brought to us from the camp kitchens. For the first time I felt the threat of war was becoming an inevitability and my involvement in it shocked me. Nevertheless, what we were doing was vital to our nation's self-preservation.

The horrendous and depressing task of stacking bombs continued for another two days. We were then allowed a twenty-four hour rest in order to allow the depleted muscle power to recover before we had one more day of energy sapping bomb stacking. By the time these evil devices were under the sadly bowing branches of the pine trees, they resembled tombs of insanity – pyramid in shape – reminding me that history had not taught us how to settle any discord in a peaceful manner. They were simply very sad monuments to greed.

It was in a state of disbelief that an instruction was received from President Benes, ordering the army, who were poised to defend our country, to withdraw from all the well fortified frontier posts and return to their bases. The order was given before a shot had been fired by the Nazi troops who then lost no opportunity to pour through the Czech frontier's open doors. I was stunned.

Was the president acting out of cowardice or was it a wise diplomatic act? I am sure that others at the camp were like me; quite ready to fight for our country if asked to, but confused by the strange tactics employed by those in command.

The Nazi troops advanced, marching through Sumava, where the village of my birth was trampled over by the jack-booted, Satan-driven troops, onwards towards Pilsen and Prague. Those in charge of the Czech Air Force personnel stationed at Hradec Kralove base remained impotent. We seemed to have been abandoned like a flock of sheep without a shepherd. The wolf drew closer and closer to its prey.

What were we to do? As members of the Czech Air Force, running away was unthinkable. Without doubt such action would have labelled us as cowards. But just where were the shepherds? Had they abandoned their 'flock'; having been scared out of their wits?

Who was I to think that my president had lost his nerve? Had the members of his government and the generals given him the wrong advice? I was completely inexperienced in the art of politics, only motivated by my love for the country of my birth and with an absolute determination to live a free life. I wanted to be able to soar over the green pastures of freedom which the invading army was surging over towards their goal, to ruthlessly oppress and dominate.That I was in a dilemma would be an understatement.

My life's blackest day came when the German troops occupied the base; a high-booted Nazi officer ordered me to throw my drill rifle onto a heap in the centre of the parade ground. It felt as if my heart was being gouged out of my deeply humiliated body. My soul was in anguish, and seemed to shout out: "Raise your head and spread your wings. Rise above it, you and your nation's freedom will be redeemed." Just as now when writing these words, I cried and cried.

Upon being officially discharged, the documents were no longer stamped with the Czech twin-tailed lion. The Swastika became the official emblem on all free rail travel passes. I returned to my home at Pilsen where seemingly nothing had happened in my absence. My parents were working as before and I was accepted back to work at the Skoda factory. This time, however, it was under the control of a German director. The entire work force was unhappy and, like me, completely dispirited.

The aero club had been closed down on the orders of the swiftly installed Gestapo commandant so that no more flying was possible. Besides work at the factory, my girlfriend Jarka, whom I met as often as possible, brought me much happiness. At times I joined her and her parents when they went to their small country chalet to enjoy a quiet weekend. Those were happy times which unfortunately did not last very long.

It didn't take long for me to realise that I could not live as a subjugated citizen. To be separated from Jarka was heartbreaking, yet to live with her as a slave under the Nazi dictatorship was not a choice I could live with either. It was time to put into action some carefully worked out plans that had been made by an esteemed past member of the aero club.

I had many meetings with my mentor and finally he instructed me to memorise the name and address of a person living in a town named Moravska Ostrava which was situated about 100 miles east of Prague, very close to the southern borders of Poland. At this address I was to exchange my Czech money for Polish currency. He also told me that during my journey from Pilsen I would be joined by four young lads and together we would cross the frontier. We were to pose as art students, carrying in our briefcases, suitable instruments and papers, so that, if necessary, we could prove who we were.

Not a shred of written information passed between me and all those whom my mentor had dedicated himself to help. Later on he was to be betrayed and we learnt the tragic news that he had been caught by the Gestapo and executed.

Whilst waiting to receive information about the date of my departure, the pace of production at the factory intensified and we were forced to work overtime. Our shift started at 6am with a 6pm finish. The work of producing turbo-generators was phased out and all departments began producing intricate, menacing looking components that would not deceive a trained eye. When assembled, these were to become weapons of war for use by the Germans.

CHAPTER 3

THE LONG JOURNEY BEGINS

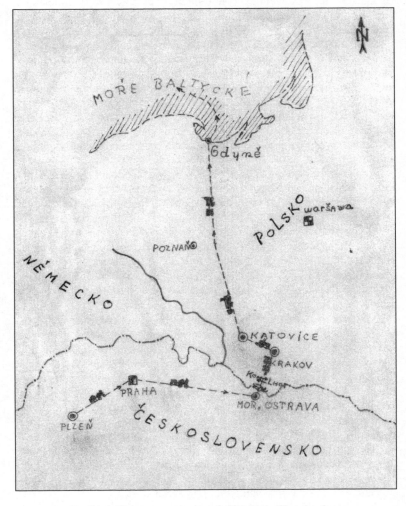

Frank's journey starts as recorded by himself at the time.

On Friday June 16th 1939, I was feeling like a very tired traitor, aiding and abetting the German war machine, as I passed through the factory main gate on my way home. Suddenly, I heard my name called from across the road and it turned out to be my flying tutor Mr Rais. He got straight to the point: "Frank, the departure is tomorrow at 5.30am from the railway station, are you prepared to go?" Although there was no doubt in my mind about my wish to help my country I felt utterly numbed by the suddenness of the ultimatum, my voice became drawn and I found it difficult to reply. I spluttered: "Please sir, can I give you an answer later this evening?" He replied, "Yes, yes, I fully understand how you must be feeling, do come as soon as possible." With that he walked away, his head tucked into his shoulders.

Whilst travelling home I tried to compose myself and by the time I had reached the front door, I was no longer hesitant – I was going. Fortunately both my parents were at home and on breaking the news to them, my mother began to feel shocked while father remained impassive. My mother at first thought that it was a joke. For safety's sake I had not been able to tell her of my plans beforehand. When she finally realised that I was deadly serious, she began to cry and pleaded with me to change my mind. Why couldn't I stay at home and continue with a job which, at the time, seemed so secure?

It was only two stops along the tramway from my house to Mr Rais's. He opened the door and directed me into a little room which I took to be his study. There was no sight or sound of anyone else at home. Before asking me to sit down, Mr Rais looked me straight in the eyes and with a gentle tone in his voice asked – "What is it to be Frank, are you going or not?" With my moist eyes fixed upon his saddened face I replied, "Yes Mr Rais, I am. I will do all I can for this country of ours. What you and Venca Slouf taught me will be used to good advantage I'm sure." We sat down and I was given a final briefing. My mission had begun.

My next visit was to Jarka's home. In the presence of her parents, whom I liked very much, I told them all of my impending departure and the mission that I was undertaking. To my astonishment and for the very first time, her normally soft voice became hard when she said – "If you go, I will not wait for you." Her parents were silent and that was the way we parted. For a long time I could not believe that she meant those harsh words. I was glad that our platonic relationship had not progressed further and my Jarka remained as pure as a white lily in my mind.

Returning home, I borrowed my father's briefcase. The clasps and straps strained under the load of art papers, watercolour paints, brushes, pencils and an eraser rubber. Added to all this were two pairs of underpants, some socks, a few handkerchiefs and a shirt.

At 4.30am after wiping my mother's farewell tears from her eyes and with a brief shake of my father's hand, I caught the bus that stopped outside the railway station. It was here that I met the first of my travelling companions, Tony Kaspar, a twenty-four-year-old school teacher who, like me, had some flying experience. He had a shoulder bag which, no doubt, contained necessities for his survival.

I was not bothered about train tickets, having been briefed that Tony would obtain these before I arrived. Since the occupation by the Germans it was necessary to show some form of identity when entering a platform. Without raising any suspicion we boarded the train for Prague and found all the seats to be taken. Fortunately, in another carriage, we managed to squeeze ourselves onto a bench.

I was aware that Tony was an art teacher at one of the Pilsen comprehensive schools and that he was a liked and respected member of the aero club. He had an outstanding sense of humour and proved to be great company. I also knew that he liked a drink, the rumour being that, sadly, he was an alcoholic. I thought these rumours were slanderous but later I was to be proved wrong. However, in his defence, he was a gentleman even when drunk and I never had cause to dislike him. We sat and talked, weighing each other up, expecting to be joined at some later stage by three other young men who would share the rest of the journey. It took almost three hours to reach Prague.

Upon our arrival, Tony and I alighted from the carriage separately in accordance with our agreed plans. I was the first to head towards the platform exit where my ticket was scrutinised by the ticket inspector. Any feeling of relief was short lived when a uniformed German Army guard, standing a few paces on, sternly demanded to see my identity card. Steadying, not only my nerves but also my jellied legs, I obliged. After looking me and the card over, his face dropped its stern look, and he handed the card back to me carefully folded. With a "Ya", he nodded me on. At this point I noted the revolver strapped just above his right hip.

Tony's and my eyes met at the station foyer, its patterned floor echoing from the high glass-framed roof, with the sound of people walking around. In a leisurely manner we walked into a food bar to obtain a cup of coffee and an open sandwich and settled ourselves in a corner of the room. The station was crowded which probably accounted for the way that Tony walked unhindered through the check points, thus sparing him the trauma that I had encountered.

The next stage of our journey began with a train that was due to leave at 10.40am. It was to be in one of these train carriages that we would meet up with Vladimir Michalek and Jan Chalupa whilst the fifth member of our group, Albin Nasvetter, was destined to join us at an address in Moravska Ostrava. The two of us remained inside the bar quietly going over and memorising the plans. It was essential to adhere to the organised arrangements if success was to be achieved. In Pilsen we had been shown photographs of our compatriots and these too, were stored in our memories. A meeting had been arranged to take place outside the Moravska Ostrava railway station. Once more, we separated and found boarding the train quite uneventful. We had been recognised by Michalek (I always called him by his surname) and Jan and vice versa, so with a nod of confirmation, we occupied separate carriages.

As the train pulled out of the station, Tony and I had deep feelings at being parted from such a beautiful city. The train was speeding us across our much loved country on our way through Bohemia towards Moravia, both of which were part of Czechoslovakia surrounded by the Bohemian massif. Through the carriage windows we saw the densely wooded lands, rich in natural resources with rivers and lakes abounding, that we were so dedicated to saving.

The capital city of Prague was founded by the Czech and Hungarian kings in the 13th century. The Czechs and Slovaks achieved their independence only in 1918 and rapidly established a democratic society. A liberal constitution was adopted, similar to that in the United States and France. The people became a source of supreme power, electing their representatives by a free, direct and secret ballot. The republic made impressive progress in all the fields of education and science under its first president – Tomas Masaryk. All this was to change just because Hitler demanded the return of Sudetenland which was that small area within the western part of Bohemia, not very far from where I was born.

The train journey from the beautiful city of Prague to the Moravian town of Ostrava took four hours, a seemingly interminable time. At one stop four German Army officers boarded the train entering the carriage that we were in. Tony, a skilled artist, began to do a pencil sketch of my face. Fortunately for us the Germans sat at the end of the compartment and took no interest in us. In spite of our very heavy breathing, the other passengers sharing the compartment with us were friendly and brought an air of normality to the scene.

At Ostrava railway station, Tony and I lingered, letting the German officers alight from the carriage first. We took our time in reaching the ticket collector who routinely checked our tickets. I made my way through the gate uneventfully while the German guard was occupied in examining the papers of two loudly protesting boys.

Sticking strictly to the pre-arranged instructions, my friend and I stayed apart until we were both outside the station where we waited for our other two compatriots, Michalek and Jan. When finally they did appear they walked nonchalantly past, quietly bidding us to follow them. Keeping a distance, we shadowed them until, at a dark narrow street, they stopped and leaned against the wall of a house waiting for us to eagerly shake their hands. The grip was painfully and purposefully sincere. We were united in our search for freedom and our desire to fight until liberty was restored in Czechoslovakia.

Michalek was similar in height to Tony and possessed a slim body which supported an intelligent face with bright blue and friendly probing eyes. He was a year younger than Tony's twenty-four years. Jan was stockier in build with an oval face, fleshy cheeks and dark eyes that were deep and could not be read. He was about one or two inches shorter than my 5′10″. He had full lips which were capable of modulating his perfect French; later to become life-saving for us all. He was a student with a voice that was round and cultured. Michalek had left behind in Prague a position as a film editor.

It took us a long time to reach our destination in Ostrava because, for safety reasons we could make no enquiries and the map we followed had no street names, so our memories had to be relied upon to guide us. Thus united in body and spirit, we walked for an hour and a half before reaching the house that we had been briefed to locate. It was here that we expected to obtain vitally important and willing help to guide us on to the next stage of our journey.

The house stood in a tree-lined road, nestling behind an iron railing. Thick stone pillars supported a double, ornamental, cast iron gate. Inset in the right hand pillar was an engraved name plate – 'Ing.Vlasak'. Recognising the house and the name, we opened the gate. Its hinges screeched. An upward sloping gravel path wound its way in a gentle curve, avoiding the trees that stood on either side. The tree branches formed an archway towards the house, which lay beyond. What, we wondered, was in store for us behind the large, carved and somewhat forbidding door?

Mounting several steps to reach a patio, it was left to Michalek to handle the large knocker. The door, in the solid baroque style facade of the house, stood firm. Much more, and louder banging was needed before the door opened and there appeared a rather portly man, his height difficult to assess since he was standing two steps higher than we were. He appeared to be dressed for a funeral. "Who are you, is there anything you require that I can do for you?" These were the words that we had been led to expect and so Michalek replied, "Yes sir, we are on a mission from Prague and Pilsen, seeking your help." With these formalities over, Mr Vlasak's previously stern face transformed into a broad, welcoming smile.

Responding to the friendliest of welcomes and an invitation to enter the house, the engineer guided us along a carpeted corridor. Directing us to a wash room he said: "After you have freshened yourselves up and are ready, please enter through that door where my wife will provide some refreshments." Before we could express our thanks he had left us.

His wife, compared with her portly husband, was slim and of average height. She was perhaps sixty years of age but a shapely lady, dressed in a quietly coloured, patterned dress, which was of calf length. Her auburn hair was streaked with silver which befitted her face. There were a few wrinkles over her forehead and her smiling eyes bade us welcome, the first such feeling we had experienced since leaving our kin.

The room we entered was a nice-sized dining room with a bay window facing west. The furniture, of polished wood, consisted of a large dresser and an extended oval table, both of which were mahogany. There was a door at each end and upon the walls many paintings. The most prominent one was a large picture of President Masaryk which had a red, white and blue ribbon placed across the right-hand corner. A highly starched, white linen cloth covered the table which had been set with cutlery, high quality china side plates and a cut glass cruet. My first impression was that a banquet was to be held there whilst we would probably be fed in the kitchen. However, this was not the case; we were to be the honoured guests.

Before being asked to take our places at the table a young man was ushered in and introduced as the fifth member of our party: Albin Nasvetter. Albin was the son of a doctor and had arrived from a Moravian town named Olomouc, which was some fifty miles south west of where we were at present. When Mrs Vlasak invited us to take our seats at the table, Albin and I were talking to each other so it was natural that we sat beside each other. When it was politely possible, we carried on talking and discovered that our interests and points of view were in harmony. From that moment onwards the bonds of friendship between Albin and me grew stronger and stronger. He proved to be a very precise person who, before making a vital decision, would give it a great deal of thought. I, however, was inclined to be more impetuous and yet we seemed to operate on a similar frequency.

The food was served to us by a middle-aged woman named Marie, who was probably a servant but was never addressed as such – more like one of the family. The meal started with a plate of beef and an onion soup. The main course was traditional Czech roast pork, sauerkraut and dumplings with plenty of gravy. It all tasted just perfect. Finally, there was a cup of coffee with a slice of gateau. Second helpings were offered and accepted. We had arrived hungry but were now completely satisfied. After the feast, our hosts led us through to a large living room, which also had a bay window. Just like the dining room, it was tastefully furnished and decorated. There were two settees and several comfortable chairs on to which we gratefully rested our tired bodies.

Mr Vlasak had been briefed about our arrival and the mission that lay ahead of us. He soon brought up the subject of our need to exchange our Czech money (Koruna) for Polish currency. He informed us that the same person appointed to carry out the transaction would act as our guide to a suitable place along the frontier, where crossing into Poland should not be too difficult. In other words – a place not heavily guarded by Germans. After being offered cigarettes, which only Tony accepted, we chatted easily with our hosts. They expressed an interest in our past, how much flying we had done and what our plans were for the future.

Unable to stifle our yawns, Mrs Vlasak conducted us up three flights of stairs to two double bedrooms, in one of which, an additional single bed had been added. All physically and mentally exhausted, there was no need to count sheep before falling asleep. Roused at 7am on Saturday June 17th 1939, I was relieved, on looking out of the window to see blue sky, almost clear of cloud. The slightest hint of foreboding did, however, cross my anxious mind. I strained my eyes eastwards towards the forested Beskydy Mountains, straddling the Czech-Polish border which we were aiming to cross. Our plans had been made to cover the thirty-five miles that lay between us and the border crossing.

Having washed and shaved and stowed away our few possessions, we made our way downstairs where piping hot coffee with rolls, butter and jam awaited us; a typical Czechoslovak breakfast during which, slices of salami were offered. Mr Vlasak was not present but his wife and Marie were serving and sharing the table whilst awaiting the arrival of Mr Hrubes who was to change our Czech money and guide us to the border. Collectively we had 7,800 Koruna.

To our dismay, we were kept waiting until mid-morning when, without too much ado, he took our money and gave us instructions to wait where we were, promising to return very soon. The waiting continued with Mrs Vlasak becoming very nervous at the apparent delay. She did not appear to be well acquainted with Mr Hrubes. The earlier foreboding of mine was beginning to prove justified and as evening approached we thought we should prepare a 'plan B'. Mr Vlasak had now returned and was as much perturbed as ourselves. He too knew very little about Mr Hrubes. The money transaction arrangements had been made with an intermediary in Prague. We all eventually retired to bed in an extremely worried state. Sleep did not come easily.

The following morning found no need for us to be roused. Mr Vlasak was not present, so we breakfasted in the company of a very nervous Mrs Vlasak. She hinted that if the man did not arrive by 10am something would have to be done. The hour of ten o'clock ticked past. Mrs Vlasak announced that we must get ourselves ready and said: "When you hear the sound of a car horn, come quickly and, providing no one is about, get in as fast as you can. I will then drive you a little way out of town – as far as I dare, towards the border. Here is 100 Koruna which is all that I can lay my hands on whilst my husband is away." Looking as if struck by thunder, she departed. In less than twenty minutes a car horn was being sounded. After a tearful goodbye with Marie, we ran to the waiting car.

We crammed ourselves into an old Skoda car; one beside the driver and four squatted across the back bench seat. On closing the doors, the car driven by Mrs Vlasak, accelerated. The engine pounded under the strain. After half an hour, when well out of the town Mrs Vlasak drove onto the road verge and stopped. With no time to waste she wished us good luck and drove off to become just one of our memories.

Watching the car disappear into the distance we felt utterly forlorn. With insufficient money, no guide and some twenty-five miles from a place called Carbal, which was our next target we realised that reaching the frontier would require, not only our stamina, but also a great deal of luck.

Our biggest fear was running into the German soldiers with trained dogs who closely guarded the borders. Walking close to the border was impossible. Our only hope for success was to remain as inconspicuous as possible, staying clear of the open road and using lanes whenever possible. Without delay, we set off on a quick march, conscious of the need to look for somewhere to hide in case of emergency. We came to a path branching through a field of corn, which offered us some protection. We carried on, slowing down in order to conserve our energy. Visibility remained good and it was not too difficult to weave our way towards a distant mountain that loomed clearly ahead, whilst avoiding a village we thought to be Nydek.

The day and a half spent at Mr Vlasak's had not only given us the chance to rest and refuel but also to check our progress and plan our journey using a proper map. We made good progress towards a place at the foot of the Beskydy Mountains, from where we hoped to cross into Poland. Although we had made it this far we could not afford to be complacent, every decision we made was a matter of life or death. The Gestapo had made it clear that anyone caught trying to escape would be shot, if they had not already been mauled by the frontier patrol dogs.

Close to 6pm we emerged from a copse to find a narrow tarmac road laying across our path, there was thick forest rising upwards behind it. Returning to the relative safety of the forest we stopped to discuss our options. We recalled the map which we had studied with Mr Vlasak and realised that our current position left us with a choice, we could climb up through the forest, hoping that the route would be manageable or, staying under the cover of the trees, follow the road westwards in the hopes that we could reach our intended crossing point.

For the first time, we were not unanimous in our preferences. The extreme fear of being apprehended was very much uppermost in our minds. Tony and Jan were for climbing the mountain while Albin, Michalek and I voted for the second option. The decision having been democratically arrived at, we set off to make our way westwards under the cover of the trees. After travelling for no more than half an hour, we saw through the branches that the road passed by a single-storey building. We waited, watched and listened. I felt a chill as the alarm bells rang in response to a very distant sound of barking dogs.

CHAPTER 4

POLAND

In desperate need of refreshment and confirmation as to exactly where we were, Michalek crept to the side of the building – the rest of us remaining out of sight. We listened intently and made sure no one else was outside or along the road. Michalek half opened a door and entered – we became frozen with apprehension. Very soon he came out and waved us to join him. We obeyed his sign with much relief. The room was sparsely furnished with bare wooden tables and bench-like seats. It was a simple café, fortunately empty of customers, German or otherwise. Michalek was talking to a woman who we assumed was a waitress or even the owner of the place. Thankfully, the money that Mrs Vlasak had given us proved sufficient to pay for a glass of beer, some bread, butter and cheese. While eating we very cautiously asked the woman to tell us exactly where we were and whether she had a map that we could look at. She replied reluctantly, "I do not know how to be of any help," and added, "I have not been here long, I come from the town of Tesin." At this point I took over and asked her to fetch her son, who supposedly was somewhere on the premises. She agreed to this and disappeared through a door. My compatriots looked at me with reproachful and fearful stares, at which, a feeling of dread swept over and depressed me. Eternity passed before a man appeared who, like his mother, had a scared unwelcoming look upon his face. Before he could speak I told him that we were pilots who were aiming to escape in order to fight for our country. At the same time I showed him my identity card. After a quick look at the card and a more measured one over my friends, he introduced himself as Oldrich and extended his hand.

Without saying another word he turned and left through the door by which he had entered. After a short spell of temporary relief, the fear of being betrayed returned to haunt us again. Albin was standing beside me whilst the others were slumped over the tables, their heads supported by their arms. My heart was pumping blood through my body at a great rate. What more could we do? Should we take to our heels or stay, putting our trust in providence?

I was terrified that I may have just inadvertently betrayed my friends by divulging to Oldrich and his mother our intent to flee into

Poland. My fears mounted and my courage failed me as I glanced from one stricken face to the next. How could I have brought about a situation of such despair? Never in my nineteen years had I experienced such trauma. The thoughts raging through my head were asking me – "Is Oldrich phoning the Germans or has he fled to fetch the guards?" We had earlier heard the guard dogs barking. Was Oldrich, like Mr Hrubes, aiming to profit by an act of betrayal? The depressingly drab room was not at all helpful. Was it, I asked myself, about to become a prison cell; had the doors been locked already? Whilst, as if in a dream, I was musing over these thoughts, the door opened. Oldrich had returned. He was waving a map, urging us to hurry as the German guards were not too far away. Pointing in a westerly direction at a distant mound of earth separating the road from the forest, Oldrich told us – "From there upwards is a shallow depression, follow it and keep climbing until you reach the mountain top. That is where the Polish border is to be found." Wasting no time at all and with a brief thank you, we were off.

After ten minutes at a fast pace and with the benefit of the trees, we descended into a wide ditch, which provided a most useful path. No words had been uttered. The climb began in earnest; our courage came back with a belief that luck was again more on our side.

We found ourselves engulfed by the forest. Embraced by the trees, whose fallen needles formed a cushioning carpet, our previously jangled nerves were soothed by the strong scent of pine. The distant barking of the guard dogs did not dampen our absolute determination to achieve our freedom. After travelling for over an hour, and beginning to feel very tired, we emerged from the protection of the trees to find ourselves in a small clearing, at the centre of which stood a small hut. We decided to rest for a while but it was cut short when the barking of dogs became louder. Promptly re-entering the forest, we silently prayed that the dogs would not lead the German guards towards us.

The stunning realisation that we had walked in a circle came when, exhausted, we arrived at the same clearing and the hut that we had departed from some two hours earlier. This was when my 'guardian angel', whose help was readily accepted, directed us to take a different route. Descending over the rough terrain it seemed ages before we emerged onto open land and the safety of Polish soil. It was almost dark and a fog had begun to form. With no blankets or warm clothing and our strength evaporating, it was imperative that some kind of shelter should be found soon.

We had climbed a mountain of 1,300 feet, which was now standing behind us, level pastureland spread out ahead. Owing to the darkness and the quickly forming fog there was no time to waste. On we walked until a dim light appeared in the distance which eventually became a light shining through a small window which was set into a tiny wooden house. As soon as we knocked on the door it was opened by an old man who obviously wondered what five young lads were doing outside at that time, looking so weather beaten and dishevelled. Although none of us spoke Polish, due to the similarity between our two languages and with the help of some hand gesticulation, we managed to get our message across.

The man invited us in, where his much wrinkled but kindly looking wife offered us something hot to drink; a gesture which we found particularly welcome. While the woman was making coffee, the man put on his coat and supported by a stick went outside. The hot drink proved a lifesaver, especially for Tony as it was laced with rum. His face lit up! The old man, and much to our disquiet, soon returned accompanied by a policeman.

The officer, who was in no mood to waste time, sternly looked us over and enquired in Polish: "Where have you come from, do you have any identification papers?" His voice matched his facial expression – a very official start to our unofficial entry. Jan, who was the linguist amongst us, replied with a tense voice and did his best to explain just why we were in Poland. The policeman was not impressed and gave us a tongue-lashing, spewing words that did not require any translation. Whilst spitting the incoherent abuse, he fidgeted with the butt of a pistol that protruded from a holster. He used a handkerchief to wipe the saliva from his venomous lips and then deliberately uttered the words, which to this day I long to ram back into his larynx – "Dlacego jste se nebranily....", in English – "Why have you not defended yourselves, having such a superb army?" According to him, we were cowards.

After his outburst and before we had a chance to have another drink, he ordered us to follow him out into the darkness. He walked towards a door which he opened without so much as knocking first. Inside, we were met by a man dressed in a dark tunic to whom the policeman passed on a staccato of orders. Turning towards us he said, "Here you will stay, have somewhere to sleep and be provided with food." Even more sternly he added: "You are under open arrest while I seek orders from my superiors as to what is to be done with you." With that, he departed.

In contrast, the person left in charge placidly asked us to follow him along a corridor, up a flight of stairs, to a landing, at the end of which he opened a door, waving us in. The room was large, bare floored, with a few chairs scattered about. At the end was a double bed on which was laid a pile of blankets and pillows. There were no sheets or pillowcases. At the other side, bolted to the wall, was a wash basin with a mirror above. A cake of previously used soap was evident. In one corner stood a wardrobe in which were some clean towels. Our host introduced himself to us as Alois. He was a kindly man, quite unlike his 'Gestapo' boss and settled us by announcing: "When you are ready, come downstairs where a hot meal will be waiting for you." Having existed without food since leaving the café on the other side of the border, we were more than ready to eat. After washing our hands we trundled downstairs, lured by the heavenly whiff of goulash. In the room, apart from Alois, was a middle-aged woman wearing a grey scarf on her head, slightly stooping, with a semblance of a gentle smile. She beckoned us to take our places at the large pine table. Her voice was soft and friendly although she did not have a lot to say. The food that was served was simple, wholesome and very tasty.

The meal over, we offered our sincere thanks to our hosts and decided that we should retire. With trembling limbs we climbed the stairs to the bedroom. Placing the pillows under our heads and the blankets around our bodies, we slept soundly until 9am when the rays of sun shining through the windows prodded us to rise to wash and shave. We spruced our clothes and shoes the best we could before taking our aching bodies downstairs to breakfast. This was served by the same two who we took to be 'angels' in disguise. While we were drinking tea with milk, eating slices of wholesome bread and butter which was in plentiful supply, we discussed our present state of affairs and what we might do if the policeman returned with unacceptable orders. It was unanimously decided that, for a short while, we would wait and see what developed. According to Alois, we were allowed out of the house so long as we did not disappear from view.

For the remainder of the morning we rested our bones and souls in a downstairs room whose bare floor supported a sofa, which protested when we sat on it, and several upholstered chairs which were all in need of repair. The sun shone through the dust-smudged windows – there were no curtains in place. Apart from a large crucifix hanging on the wall opposite to the windows, there were no other adornments. The room was reasonably clean and restful.

Lunch was served and consisted of smoked sausages with pickled cabbage and boiled potatoes, all of which we enjoyed. Venturing outside, we surveyed our location and enjoyed the sunshine. The house was standing alongside a road, which had deep ruts in it. The walls were whitewashed and there was a respectable shingle-tiled sloping roof. The ground around the property was fenced and appeared neglected except for an apple orchard and some cherry trees, all of which looked laden with fruit. I was reminded of my 'scrumping' days when growing up.

Apart from the shack that we had entered the night before, there were only five or six other buildings some 200-300 yards down the road. We set off at a leisurely pace towards them. It was difficult for us to conclude if our accommodation belonged to the police or whether it was used as a kind of community hall or possibly a disused school. It was necessary to always be on our guard as we were not able to communicate freely. Serious talking and any planning had to be done whilst outside the house. Our next objective had to be an escape in order to reach the town of Krakow where the Czech Embassy was taking care of escapees and supporting them until arrangements could be made to send them to France.

I was beginning to be concerned about Tony, his normally cheerful self began to take on a morbid look and he was becoming very nervous. His usual good nature was deserting him, especially when his last cigarette had been smoked after breakfast. I was fearful that, without a drink or a cigarette, he might not be able to stand the stress and strain of our situation. Something would have to be done, and soon. If we were to be subjected to any more traumas – would he cope? I was the only one of our party who was aware that Tony was an alcoholic and, whilst I was not about to make his faults known, I needed a second opinion. To this end, I confided in Albin so that together, we came to the decision that, come what may, we should try and get a packet of cigarettes and possibly a drink for him. Albin gave me his assurance that all this would be held in confidence.

By the time we reached the timber-built, shingle-slated roofed houses, we had arrived at the decision that, if within three days no good news came from the police, another escape would be mounted that would take us to the nearest railway station. The intention was to take a train to Krakow and hide on board. If we were discovered on the train or at Krakow, we felt confident that the Embassy would bale us out.

The houses that were now in our view were simple, neat and homely – for the first time since we set out, we felt the pangs of homesickness. There were not too many people about so not much notice was taken of our presence. This may have been due to our close proximity to the Czech frontier where they were used to people like us passing through.

As we returned to the house, we scanned the countryside over which we might have to flee. There was no news awaiting us back at the house where we gladly accepted the kind offer of a cup of coffee and a biscuit. Two more days of impatient waiting were to elapse before we decided to let ourselves out in the early hours of the following morning. That night I crept down the stairs, to check the front door, which I found unlocked. Hopefully, our minders were either asleep or not in.

The following morning we stepped outside the house, making as little noise as possible. We walked northwards to where a railway line connected with the town of Tesin, straddling the Czech-Polish border. Our aim was to reach Krakow and, with luck it was hoped that in five or six hours we would be in the care of the Czech Embassy, where we would feel secure at last.

Maintaining our northerly direction, the ground sloped gently downwards and with not too many fences or ditches to overcome, progress was relatively easy. Fortune smiled upon us, for down in the valley we caught sight of the railway track, which cheered even Tony who had been walking as if he no longer cared. Before long, we saw in the distance along the line, a small town, which grew in size as we approached, spreading itself on both sides of the track.

We decided not to make our way to a road until rested and tidied up so as not to cause any suspicion when arriving in the town. After resting sufficiently on the outskirts, with the town only a mile distant, tension was beginning to mount as the time came for us to cross the track to find a road that would lead us to the nearest buildings. This proved to be more difficult than we had imagined from our resting place, due to the presence of a stream, which was wider than could possibly be jumped. It separated us from the railway line and the road beyond. Almost an hour was spent in following the stream in the direction of the town before we came across a hut squatting alongside the rail embankment. Beside the hut was a thick plank that straddled the stream. Much to our relief, after crossing it proved easy to climb over the railway line and then down to the road.

From then on we were hidden by the houses and on finding the station, made an illegal entry. On boarding the train, which had arrived from the southwest, we employed the same tactic as before. Avoiding the ticket collector was easy but making an exit from Krakow station was more difficult yet, nevertheless, successful. When outside the station, with the remains of our money I was able to buy some cigarettes. Tony accepted these without a word, letting his eyes do the talking. One more escape had been achieved, and we proceeded to find the Czech Embassy.

Presenting ourselves in Krakow, we were expecting to be welcomed with open arms, perhaps even by the ambassador himself. However, news of our 'impudent' escape from being under open arrest had already been communicated to them. The embassy protocol suggested that we should have stayed there until given permission to leave. Our action was considered to have placed those following us, in jeopardy and we were severely reprimanded.

While the rest of us were reeling from the sorry welcome we had received, luckily Michalek took over. He quietly told the rubber-stamping officials about the insults that we had endured. He explained our uncertainty as to whether we would be allowed to stay in Poland, or be forced to go back. As the message sank in the official had a change of heart. We were absolved of our sins and given a proper welcome. After that small hitch we were escorted, by one of the embassy staff, to a large building which was at the disposal of the embassy, providing accommodation and catering facilities for all of us arriving at Krakow.

In a dormitory-type room we were provided with a camp bed, blankets and clean sheets. The room held twenty beds and almost all were in use at the time. An adjacent room revealed a row of wash basins with hot and cold water, plus a couple of shower cubicles standing against the wall. We tossed for the use of these before descending to a restaurant where food was being served free of charge. As we reflected on recent events we were conscious, that in spite of the present comforts and the free food, nothing should be taken for granted.

After several days of being spoilt and with time on our hands we surveyed the beautiful town with the Wavel Castle; its gilded domes shining in the distance. We found ourselves able to mix with the locals, who proved to be very friendly, even extending hospitality in their homes. Unfortunately, reciprocation was not possible as although the embassy had provided us with some Polish currency, it was only enough to purchase the bare necessities.

When the embassy could no longer cope with the ever-growing numbers, the entire contingent was transferred to a disused Polish barracks at Bronovice situated some two miles from the edge of the town. The barracks could not compare with the comfort that we had enjoyed in the embassy. The billets were dirty, draughty and the beds hard. The cleanliness of the bedding was doubtful. There was a large Mess where some food, lacking in any imagination, was being served. In spite of all this we had little right to complain – we were free and felt safe. The only festering sore was the disciplinary attitude of one or two Czech officers who were in charge. Apart from this irritation, the only thing that occupied our minds was when we would be able to continue our journey to France. The decision was not ours to make – we had to await orders from the embassy.

As the days passed into weeks, we became more impatient to move on. One day Albin and I walked into town where we found jobs at the city tramway workshops helping to repair electric motors. We had to obtain a pass in order to be able to leave the camp, as it was necessary to exercise some control over the comings and goings. It did not surprise us that we were given a chance to work because the Polish people, like the Czechs, were very patriotic and our cause was warmly supported by everyone we came into contact with. The foreman at the works had the warmest and softest heart anyone could wish for. He was very helpful and patient whilst we were learning the assigned tasks. At the end of the week the wage packet allowed us to replace some of our badly worn underwear and footwear. We considered ourselves very lucky, not only for being on the payroll but because our work took our minds off fretting, as we still heard nothing from the embassy. Time was passing by agonisingly slowly and, to make matters worse, in early July, rumours began to circulate among us at the Bronovice camp that the embassy was fast running out of money and would not be able to support us for much longer.

Another unsettling rumour was that those with less than 200 hours of logged flying time would not be accepted into the French Air Force.

When I heard this I felt as if I was standing in front of a firing squad – and the order to shoot had been given. It was an effort for me to 'take off the blindfold' and search for the lost horizon of faith in our mission.

The unrest at the camp subsided when, during a morning assembly, a visiting gold-braided Czech officer told us that arrangements were in hand for us to travel by train to the northern port of Gdynia where a ship had been chartered to take us to France. The precise date of departure was not given but, when pressed for more information, the officer impatiently announced that it would be quite soon.

The conditions in the camp were gradually deteriorating, particularly the quantity and quality of the food. Believing that our departure was imminent, Albin and I decided to hand in our notice at the Krakowska M.Kolej Electryczna Wydzial Warsztatowy (the Polish name of our employers). Our foreman was deeply moved by the news, probably more in fear for our safety than anything else. Tears welled up in his saddened eyes as he wished us good luck. We thanked him for his kindness and said our goodbyes to the rest of the workshop staff. Collecting the last of our wages, we were able to do some shopping in the town before returning to camp.

Reunited with Tony, Michalek and Jan, Albin and I handed over almost all of our remaining money to be divided up between us. It was not very much as we had only worked a three-day week so our pay was relatively small. Later that night Tony returned to the dormitory drunk but amiable, reasonably quiet but very sick. In the morning he had shame written all over his face and he withdrew into a shell.

The good news about our impending departure from Bronovice came suddenly and left little time to spare. At a hastily arranged assembly at the camp centre square, we were told that the train departure would be the following morning at 9.30am. The first stop would be Katovice. No one was complaining, although with our preparations complete, the night proved to be very long, as sleep was very nearly impossible.

During the night I prayed that our efforts to reach France would be successful and, if a war were to erupt, I would be given the chance, as a pilot, to fight for freedom. I just hoped my flying skills would make a contribution to democracy. I prayed that my parents would be spared the wrath of the Gestapo if they were ever to realise that I had joined the forces against them. I also included Jarka and her parents in my prayers.

Much to our distress, we did not leave the following day, instead we attended various patriotic assemblies, following which we were asked to confirm our allegiance to President Benes. We did so gladly. The last words to us by a Polish priest were – "Do Widzenia" and in Czech – "Na Schledanou" – both of which translate into English as 'Hope to see you again'. There followed Czech and Slovak hymns.

At the end of the service a messenger arrived with the news that our departure had now been set for the following morning – Tuesday July 25th 1939. Our march to the station was carried out in dry weather and the train left precisely on time. We were boarding a train legally, with no German guards to fear but I began to have that tight feeling in the chest as the distance between myself and home was lengthening.

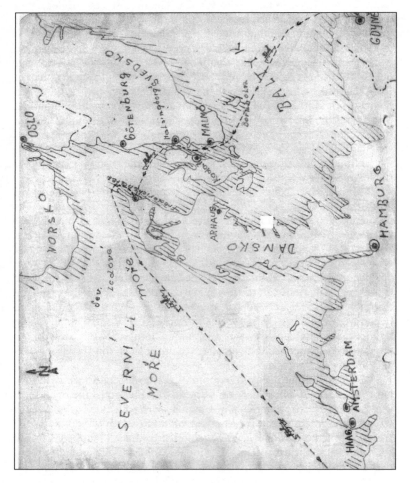

Frank's journey continues.

It was a slow train bound for Katovice where the carriages that we occupied were due to be hitched to an express train which would convey us to the northern Polish port of Gdynia. Five hours later we arrived at Katovice. The morning's breakfast having been long digested, our thoughts were now food oriented.

Before leaving Bronovice camp we were all given four slices of bread, a piece of cheese, one bun and an apple, all wrapped up in a newspaper. We had been reminded that the ration had to last us until we reached Gdynia, some twelve-fourteen hours after leaving Krakow.

The Gdynia-bound express set off from the station at 7.30pm and sleep came easily soon after leaving. Our small party of five occupied the same very comfortable compartment. Throughout the night we ate our provisions and availed ourselves of the hot drinks which could be bought with coupons. While we were comfortable however, each of us were apprehensive about what might be in store for us when we reached our next destination.

A howling gale greeted us at Gdynia as we assembled on the platform. Heavy rain pounded upon the station roof. When the rain had eased a little we were guided towards a tourist restaurant where breakfast was served. There was no limit as to what we were allowed to eat. The station was at the edge of the waterfront and it was possible to watch the sea breaking over the pier. This was the first time I had ever seen the sea.

With our hunger and thirst assuaged, our guide introduced us to a representative of the Polish Government. He had been sitting alone in the restaurant and appeared interested in our presence. Upon being politely welcomed by one of the Czech officers in our party he was offered a chair. He was apparently empowered to offer places in the Polish Air Force to us provided we were sufficiently trained as pilots, navigators, observers or gunners. Mechanics would also be considered. The offer came as a bolt from the blue, leaving some of our party in complete amazement. I never did find out whether anyone accepted the offer. The five of us did not consider ourselves to be qualified. We did not volunteer as we thought that any stay in Poland could not last long in view of the threats Hitler was making against Poland and since the German Army had already overrun Czechoslovakia.

We followed our guide down a long pier to where a smart looking liner was berthed and which we boarded without hesitation. The liner was named *SS Kastelholm*. On deck everything looked 'ship-shape' with a very smartly dressed crew. Arranging us in groups of four, we were led, one by one, down the steps to the cabins.

In spite of the ship being moored in a sheltered bay, it heaved, making walking very difficult and, to some extent, nauseating. The cabin, B24, was assigned to us and contained a pair of stacked up berths on each side, looking remarkably like children's cots. In the centre were back-to-back sofa-like seats. In one corner, a small door hid the toilet, with a wash basin and a stack of towels. The young looking steward pointed towards the end of the corridor and said "jildo" – meaning 'food' in English.

This message was easily understood and after freshening ourselves up, we found the restaurant. It was not a large room but luxuriously appointed. With the wallowing of the ship, the plates laid on the table began to slide about. The steward showed us how to raise the table rim above the surface and to lock it into place. This helped with the plates but our stomachs were still wondering just what was going on. The food was tempting and very tasty – but as it was not long since we had eaten in the tourist restaurant most of it was left on the plates. The heaving of the ship increased as the anchor had been weighed and the ship was navigating its way out of the harbour towards the open sea. What welcome could be expected at the next port, which would be Calais, was written in the stars – mine being Leo.

Another stage of our mission had begun.

CHAPTER 5

FRANCE – WHAT ARE WE WAITING FOR?

Before the ship had nosed its way out of the harbour we climbed the stairs in order to get some fresh air on the heaving deck. Once on deck I grabbed the nearest railing, whereupon I was promptly sick; wishing and praying for the storm to calm. My sickness prevailed until only the urges remained – my stomach having nothing more it could part with. At this time I truly wished that I was back home.

This embarrassing acclimatisation continued with frequent bouts of indisposition, either whilst holding on to the deck rails or even in our cabin down below. I was concerned for Michalek who had been separated from us during the berth allocation. The ship danced its way out of the harbour to be greeted by mountainous seas, the crest of each wave trying to break over the deck. The trough between each wave lured the bow of the ship down as if to fathom the depths of the ocean. Never having crossed any sea before I found the ship's motion very scary. As I got used to the power the sea had over the vessel, I became awestruck.

The sea, driven by a gale force wind, made the boat's progress towards the Kattegat so hazardous that the captain decided he would have to seek calmer waters somewhere along the German coast. Before he made any change of course he was visited by a high ranking Czech officer who persuaded him to change his mind, convincing the captain that we would all rather drown than fall into German hands. The *Kastelholm* continued heading northwards and eventually put into Frederikshavn, a port on the east coast of Denmark. On the arrival of calmer seas the journey continued round the northern tip of Denmark, then sailed a southerly course towards Calais.

The change of course took place on Saturday July 29th which just happened to be my birthday. In response to the prayers of us all on board, the weather was now calm and we sailed under a clear sky. The ship's crew worked hard to restore the liner to its usual smart looking self. The five of us, now at the same table, thoroughly enjoyed all the steward brought us in the way of food or drink. It was not only Tony that got up from the table with unsteady legs. The sea, remaining balmy, was not to blame.

The good weather continued and the sea reflected its innocence with a blue-green hue. The surface was parted by the ship's bow as if eager to make up for lost time and reach the destination on schedule. We began to feel as if we were on a cruise – sunning ourselves on the deck or enjoying a walk around the ship. I was fortunate enough to gain access to the engine room, which was evident by the hissing steam power, while the outer casing of the boiler hid the inferno within its bowels. I could not understand the engineers but they were eager to show me round the spotlessly clean room with its highly polished brass and copper fittings.

Returning to the open deck, I was thinking about what may lie ahead of us. Was it going to be a smooth and easy passage towards our goal or would we have to face a force more powerful than the engine down below which was driving the ship forward? We had plenty of time to think, not only about our homes and loved ones but also about how the people of our country were faring under the German Army who were now ruling Czechoslovakia. Had Dr Benes made it too easy for Hitler's army to invade? Was Poland going to be the next to suffer? What lay in the future for me? I retired to bed early that night and was woken from my dreams by the sound of the anchor dropping, the chain rattling against the aperture through which it was moving. The time was 2.30am on Monday July 31st. Wondering just where we were, I put my trousers and coat over my pyjamas before climbing onto the deck. It was pitch-black save for a glow of light a mile distant, which indicated that we had made a landfall. Seeing one of the crew, I pointed out the distant glow, to which he simply said, "Calais". Back in my bed but, unable to get back to sleep, I quickly dressed again and hurried off to get a view of the harbour through the haze of the early dawn.

An earlier than usual breakfast followed, during which the anchor was raised to allow the ship to move slowly towards the harbour entrance, sailing through majestically with its horn sounding. We were all on deck, complete with our luggage.

Finally docking and with the ramps lowered onto the pier, the captain, his officers and crew formed a line to give us a cheerful farewell. It was the first chance I had had to see the captain at close quarters. He was a smart looking man, sporting a stern expression, probably a result of the heavy responsibilities he carried. Judging by his mature age, he had been shouldering these for some time. The manner of his crew gave ample indication that he was not only liked but also well respected. I am sorry that I missed the opportunity of asking him for his autograph. The memory of events aboard the *Kastelholm* remains deeply etched in my mind. It was a good ship under excellent command. Our senior Czech officer shook hands with the captain, proving that our good name and respect was intact. I turned my head to the ship and said, "God bless and farewell *Kastelholm*."

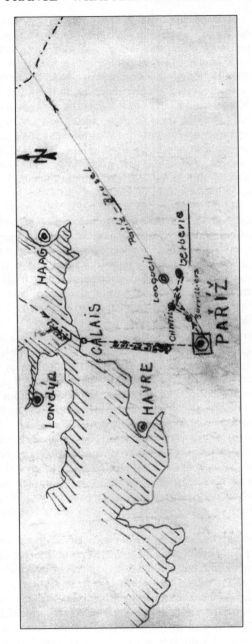

Frank finally makes it to Paris.

The walk down the ship's gangway was with very unsteady legs as if still afloat on the rolling decks. I thought something might have been wrong with me but I soon noticed that everyone ahead was similarly affected. Still unsteady, while being led off by several French Army soldiers to a nearby café, we were introduced to a Mr Pernikar – a Czech vice consul who was to accompany us all the way to Paris.

It was just about 9am and the train departure was not until 12.15pm which allowed plenty of time to pose lots of questions to the vice consul. Our main concern was the rumours that had circulated at Bronovice camp: that we would have to sign for five year's service with the French Foreign Legion and that pilots with less than 200 hours flying experience would not be accepted into the French Air Force. Mr Penikar did not deny these rumours!

From the café we walked to a single-track railway siding where a locomotive, hitched to a few well-worn wagons, was standing. This train took us to the main railway station at Calais where we would occupy three very comfortable carriages specially reserved for us – a batch of rather despondent Czech patriots. The five of us settled down in the same compartment, feeling the impact of the disillusioning news given us by the Czech vice consul earlier. It was not easy to estimate the height of the forthcoming hurdles that would have to be overcome in order to achieve our original aim.

At an almost unbelievable speed, sometimes approaching eighty miles per hour, the train arrived at a very large station in Paris at 5.40pm. Now in France we worried that our inability to speak the language would become a handicap. We were fortunate in this respect that Jan spoke perfect French and so long as we stayed together, communicating our aims and desires to those in charge of our welfare, we might possibly divert their intention of having us join the foreign legion.

The railway station was packed with people rushing to and from the trains – the hiss of venting steam from the locomotives added to the state of neurosis we experienced during the march towards some military vehicles, which did nothing to raise our morale, as we wondered if we were on our way to be disposed of. With only the back canvas rolled up we had a restricted view of Paris but the vista was inspiring.

The lorries arrived at a large camp into which an army sentry allowed us to pass, telling us that we were beside an air ministry complex. We then entered a typical service mess in which the tables were covered with stained table-cloths and the cutlery lacked lustre. However, we found there was nothing to complain about when the food was served; it was good and plentiful. There was no water on the tables but the wine – gallons of it – was very refreshing. It was a rather dry red, which the French called 'Pinard'. I got used to the flavour and liked it very much – at times, too much. After a meal and a general tidy up of ourselves, we were led to the air ministry building where we were introduced to a French Air Force officer. Our vice consul had to translate the speech that was given, from which we learnt that it would be necessary for us to sign the foreign legion enlistment document, should we wish to remain in France. There was no choice for us but to accept the five year's enlistment and upon signing on the dotted line, we were informed that any necessary vaccination would take place at a time and place to be confirmed.

After having signed our lives away we were re-united with what little kit we had and driven off a short distance across the River Seine, to a disused factory which bore the name 'Zig-Zag' over its portals. This was to be our accommodation. The first floor was tiled and we were provided with bales of straw and a pile of blankets. The cold water ablutions were situated on the ground floor – stark, but clean. Our meals were to be served in the camp, which was a twenty-minute walk away. No payment was required for the accommodation or the food. We simply had to await the outcome of negotiations about our future.

Sleep was difficult on the thickly piled straw beds, not because of any discomfort, merely due to the worries of what might be in store for us. This sleeplessness was apparent until I could feel my grand-mother's arms about me, whereupon, I slept soundly. At the instant 'Reveille' was sounded there was a stirring in the straw beds – an emergence from some of them as if from burrows. It was 7am, the first day of August, the year 1939. We had woken to a very questionable prospect.

In the large washroom down below, was a line of basins, so we set about washing and shaving as best we could with the meagre facilities. There was a line of flush toilets, which offered us some privacy, and the supply of paper was remarkably soft. What more could we have wished for? Well, we could have wished for interior sprung mattresses together with sheets and a duvet; a bathroom where hot water was in abundance, with towels aplenty. Yet, in spite of all the disadvantages, no one seemed to be complaining.

Our 'exclusive' disused factory quarters were situated in that part of Paris known as Exelmans. It was almost 9am and feeling invigorated, we set off to the mile-distant barracks. The adjacent air ministry building standing as a navigation marker, guided us towards our breakfast. When we arrived at the camp, feeling hungry, we made a bee-line for the mess. The breakfast was plentiful and enjoyable – our only criticism was the evident waste of food by the French servicemen.

The daily routine soon became rather tiresome, crossing the river three or four times a day in order to be fed, or simply resting at our residence. The lack of news on our situation was the hardest to bear. Our little group increased to six when Jarda Kucera decided that he would like to join us. Jarda, like Tony and me, had arrived from Pilsen, was an ex-member of the aero club and had first made our acquaintance in the Bronovice camp. He was easy to get on with, although his sense of humour was an acquired taste. Now, as a party of six, we split ourselves up into two batches of three. Tony, Michalek and Jan made one group whilst Albin, Jarda and I formed the other. We remained the closest of friends and were quickly united if there was a matter of importance to be decided upon. The small sized group made for ease in travelling about Paris and, with the money we had been given, we could afford to ride on the metro.

Early one morning, one of our friends complained of not feeling too well and we realised that we were very vulnerable. At the Bronovice camp, access to a sick bay had been available but here, in our primitive residence, there was no such facility. Not even a telephone. The officers of our contingent had been accommodated elsewhere and could not be reached. It was decided that two people should remain with the patient whilst the rest of us would head off to the barracks and make our plight known. The response, by the French, was quick and the sick lad was removed to the camp sick bay where he recovered in a few days. One bright outcome of this little incident was that a telephone was installed in our residence without delay.

One morning, Jarda's satirical sense of humour backfired when a comrade misunderstood his sarcastic jibes. Threats were hurled around that the misunderstood comments would be rammed back into Jarda's mouth. The deed was very nearly carried out in the washroom and might have been but for my intervention. Jarda was brave with words but not physically so and it was me that almost took an intended blow. The assailant did not make any further attempts. After this Jarda, nursing his shame, steered clear of us.

With no news about our future prospects forthcoming, we decided that we should enter the inner sanctum of the French Air Ministry. We went the following morning after breakfast. The lobby was very spacious and elegantly forbidding. There was an enquiry desk, manned by a uniformed person. Near the stairway stood an armed guard. It was left to our linguist Jan to plead with the clerk to arrange for us to see someone in authority. After a lengthy phone call, which left us apprehensive, another uniformed person guided us to a lift from which we emerged several floors higher. We were led along a corridor to a door on which our escort knocked, opened and bade us enter.

Apart from a filing cabinet and a few charts on the walls, the only furniture in the room was a large desk, from behind which rose an officer who was wearing pilot's wings on his tunic. His ensuing conversation with Jan was lengthy and mutually emphatic. The French officer made a long telephone call and after further discussions with our negotiator, we were ushered out and escorted back to the hall by the guard.

We sat down on one of the long benches at the edge of the ministry lawn where Jan was impatiently prodded to 'get on with it' and reveal the official response to our pleas. Jan had explained to the officer that we were driven by patriotism and determined to fight for our country's freedom by joining the air force rather than enlisting in the foreign legion, which would just crush our spirits. As a result of his pleading and the officer's talk with his superiors, arrangements were made for us to work in the air ministry kitchens. We were to help with the washing up and the general cleaning, and be available to be contacted very quickly. Finally he promised that all would be done to try and get us enlisted in their air force. With this, our morale was boosted; the clouded sky disappeared into the heavens above.

Next morning we found that the kitchen staff had been expecting us and they welcomed us in a most friendly fashion. We set about washing the dishes and even volunteered to help clean various offices. On one occasion, the French orderlies delegated to spring-clean a very large storeroom, asked for our help. They were most anxious to get through the job quickly as they wanted to keep a date with their girlfriends. We readily agreed and they provided us with the necessary buckets, hot water, clothes, sponges, dustpans and brushes. Most importantly, they brought a pail full to the brim of wine, which came supplied with a mug tied to the handle! When the work was finished, not being used to heavy drinking, I could not recall how or when we returned to our sleeping quarters at the Zig-Zag. The following morning's dishwashing was somewhat delayed.

Our money was by now running low. Tony was out of cigarettes and had resorted to collecting fag ends to roll into full-sized cigarettes. It was obvious that something had to be done. A plan was hatched. We approached a very athletic member of our contingent, by the name of Stetka ('brush' – in English) with details of our scheme. With Stetka duly prepared, the six of us set out to assemble on the middle of the iron bridge which spanned the River Seine; the same bridge that we used to cross on our various excursions between the air ministry and our billets.

Choosing a time when there were many pedestrians about, Jan addressed the passers-by very loudly in French. His speech began – "Ladies and Gentlemen, there will now be performed a most heroic feat, before your very eyes." He pointed to Stetka, who by this time was disrobing very theatrically, "This man will climb up to the summit of the arch and dive into the river." With hat in hand, Jan walked among the staring crowd and coins began to fill the begging bowl, while our hero, Stetka, wearing only shorts, showed off his rippling muscles. With outstretched arms to maintain his balance he started to climb. At one point he pretended to lose his balance, to heighten the tension, of course. Reaching the top of the arch, Jan uttered another volley of words before Stetka, with arms at full stretch, commenced to dive. The onlookers craned their heads over the parapet, holding their breath, waiting for our friend to surface. The five of us were, with fingers crossed, praying for Stetka's safe return. In no time at all he appeared on the surface and briskly swam to the bank. Returning, via the embankment, to the centre of the bridge, Stetka took a bow – the ensuing applause drowning the noise of the traffic. The hat, glistening with coins, temporarily solved our financial troubles even though we considered it only fair that Stetka should receive the largest share.

We now had some money in our pocket and an excursion of Paris was long overdue. With the beautiful sunny morning that followed, we considered the time for such an excursion had come. We split ourselves into two groups of three, which included Stetka, setting off to walk along the river embankment until arriving at the bridge which had the famous Trocadero on one side and the Eiffel Tower on the other. We made our way to the tower, a climb of which would mean spending money which had been earmarked for clothes. A glance at the prices brought home to us that we could not afford very much. A raincoat was a high priority but with insufficient funds I decided that the only possible solution would be to sell my Longines wristwatch. Naturally I was reluctant to do this because it had been a birthday present from my mother. However, with autumn just around the corner, common sense prevailed; the watch just had to go. By pooling resources with Albin we were both able to purchase a suitable raincoat. Following an exhausting day of sight seeing, we returned to our residence. The remaining funds enabled us to travel on the metro.

We arose the following morning, August 5th, and whilst walking to our breakfast, swapped stories about our experiences in Paris, the night before. It was unanimously agreed that Paris, much like our beloved Prague, was a very beautiful city. Stetka had apparently lost his way and quite by 'accident', strayed into the red-light district. It was completely 'unintentionally' that he found himself in a very posh salon where one of the many scantily clad girls fell for him. Stetka was taught more than a thing or two about the art of love. His words were: "It was worth every franc I had on me. I had prudently kept just enough back to be able to return by metro." He was a very good raconteur and from the way he told the tale, Albin and I wondered if spending our money on raincoats had been a mistake!

On returning to our residence, we found an army truck standing outside. It was very similar to that which had transported us some time before and, much to our surprise, there were ten more of our country-men arriving. Among them, Tony and I recognised Venca Slouf, our one-time instructor at the Pilsen Aero Club. We could hardly believe our eyes. The sheer delight of seeing one another was mutual and to me, extra special, as it was with Venca that I had flown for the very first time. Since that flight my love of flying and my patriotic enthusiasm had never wavered for a moment.

He explained to us just how bad things were under the Nazis in Czechoslovakia. We learnt that the German occupation of our land surpassed in brutality all that the citizens had ever experienced in the long history of the country. The Nazi terror was directed primarily against the Underground Movement, the students and the Jews. The Gestapo leader installed in Prague proved to be merciless. In spite of all this, the brutal terror did not quench the fighting spirit, resistance was gradually building up and a Czechoslovak Government was being formed in London. War against Germany seemed inevitable.

Venca had been able to escape some time after we had, but by a different route to ours. He had first made his way to Krakow and had been let down in some arrangements, so his party made their way to France via Turkey. He had also been required to sign up for a five-year stint in the foreign legion which distressed him very much. We also learnt from him that a Captain Novak, the Czech Air Force aerobatic ace who held the world championship, had also been able to come across. Unfortunately, Captain Novak was in a Paris hospital, suffering from stomach ulcers. Sadly he died.

Venca Slouf was not a regular Czech Air Force pilot but had been offered accommodation together with our officers. When he discovered that we were at a different location, he chose to join our party. He and I remained good friends until long after the war. When his health problems prevented any further flying, he became so distressed that he committed suicide. Flying had been his entire life – without that he had nothing to live for. He left behind a daughter who is married and has a grown-up family and now resides in Canada. Although we have never met, we regularly correspond.

CHAPTER 6

ESCAPING ENLISTMENT IN
THE FRENCH FOREIGN LEGION

The days passed by and we continued to carry out the daily chores at the air ministry. The time was put to good use as we were able to practise our French on the kitchen staff and Jan coached us in our studies of the language. He found it somewhat hard going but did his best to achieve some satisfactory progress. Michalek had produced a Czech-French and a French-Czech dictionary which proved invaluable so that with practice, we were able to communicate with our French friends.

One of the staff at the air ministry, who held the rank of sergeant, was aware that we had been forcibly destined for the foreign legion, and he regaled us with stories of his experiences during a six-month period of service at Algiers. What he had to say about life in the legion did not appeal to us. Our idealist patriotism was not in any way compatible with the sort of regime he described. He encouraged us to be patient – pinning our faith on the words of the air ministry officer. With these hopes, our morale was boosted.

However, we were later disturbed by a rumour that a small contingent of Czech officers and men had already been sent to Sidi-Bel-Abbes to start their five-year term of service. In order to compose ourselves, Tony and I walked along the bank of the River Seine to where one of the barges was moored and, having taken along all the necessary equipment, we painted the waterside scene that lay ahead of us. While Tony was concentrating upon his art, I was more interested with what lay beyond the horizon of our uncertain future. The result of Tony's effort was a masterpiece, mine just a painting, but with our souls rested and soothed, we returned to our base.

Whenever out walking, either to or from the air ministry or merely sightseeing, military activities attracted our attention, we wondered whether all this training was an indication that Hitler's war-mongering was intensifying and, if so, whether the French were at last, taking it all seriously. We relied upon our tutor Jan to confirm any information from the newspapers. The African-based foreign legion loomed large in our minds and we felt threatened by its presence.

The following day, Albin declared that he was a bit 'off colour' after our session of dishwashing so Tony and I took ourselves off again to do some painting. This time our subject was a statue of a nude woman standing on a pedestal in the precinct of the Trocadero. I had never mastered the art of drawing the human body in proportion so when I had finished I did my level best to hide my work from Tony. I failed to do this and he burst out laughing. On the other hand, I loudly praised his work, which as usual, was superb. It should have been of course, after all, he was an art teacher.

On returning to our quarters I was pleasantly surprised to find that a small parcel was waiting for me. It had been sent by my mother but I was greatly disappointed that there was no letter inside. The content was a Czech-French lesson book, which I had requested in a letter I sent to her soon after arriving in Paris. I had explained what a handicap it was not being able to speak the language. The lack of a letter was partly explained when I later learnt that the close relatives of all the escapees had been interned in a prison somewhere in Slovakia. With Jan's tutoring and the new book, our learning progressed a lot faster.

With our money once again running low we conspired together before mentioning to Stetka, our brave athlete, the idea that he should repeat his diving feat once more. Stetka's reply was a very disappointing look with: "You must be crazy to think that I would risk breaking my neck again." Not surprised at his response, we had to come up with other fund raising projects. During our washing-up sessions next morning, we mentioned our plight to our French friends, who told us of work available at the Paris vegetable market. "If you are prepared to work at night when the produce arrives – help is always welcome and would be paid for." That same night we earned ourselves twenty-five francs each and a sore back to prove it.

Thursday August 17th had arrived and proved to be one of the blackest days since our arrival in Paris. An order had arrived for a large group of highly experienced former Czech Air Force pilots to be transported to the foreign legion base at Sidi-Bel-Abbes – with immediate affect. Among those ordered to go were some well known to us and included officers Hrubacek, Perina and Puda; all top grade pilots. How could those of us with less than 200 hours of logged flying time hope to fare? Surely there could be no reprieve but to follow in their footsteps. When these valuable pilots refused to go, I thought that their rebellious act would prevent us from becoming members of the French Air Force. Just what was going on? Had the French, like Hitler, gone mad or was I being naive in matters political, failing to understand the significance of these orders? It was simply beyond my understanding.

The arrival of this latest 'thunderbolt' caused us to believe that the end of the world had arrived. It took some time to sink in that we would have to submit to the same order and there were no appeals permitted – not even direct to the ministry. Our brains began to work overtime while we packed in readiness for our deportation the next day. Our contingency plans were agreed. The army trucks arrived on August 18th, a day that was engraved on our hearts. Our departure from Zig-Zag was at 8.45am – the destination was the Gare du Nord railway station. The train, which was to contain a carriage of miserable souls, acting under merciless orders, departed the station at 9.30am precisely.

One of the options that had been considered earlier was to visit the American Embassy in Paris and declare ourselves to be political refugees. This idea was quickly dismissed when we realised that this would undermine our main purpose – to make ourselves immediately available to the French Air Force as soon as the impending war broke out. The decision having been made, we prepared ourselves to be ready to strike the action button. The plan was to bale out of the train at the first opportunity and this occurred some thirty-five miles out of Paris when the train was brought to a halt by a red signal. To the surprise of our fellow compatriots in our compartment, we dropped safely onto the track and ran until out of sight. As soon as the train moved off we walked peacefully towards a village at the edge of which, was a small farm. The main section looked exactly as if it had previously been a church.

The train that we had escaped from was now long out of sight but it was not out of our minds. On board still were our friends who the previous day had sworn not to comply with the deplorable orders. Their change of heart was brought about when they were given an assurance that when a state of war was declared against Germany, they would be brought back to the French mainland. They would then be immediately integrated into the French Air Force in ranks comparable to those they held in the Czech Air Force. As our party of five had not been given any similar assurances there was no alternative but to implement our escape plan.

With the train now long gone, it was imperative that we found ourselves somewhere to hide until the war was actually declared. When the French mobilised their forces, that would be the time for us to return to Paris and surrender to the air ministry. Technically, of course, having signed up for five years in the foreign legion, we could be considered as deserters and, if apprehended by the army authorities, would face a firing squad. In spite of the possible consequences we were prepared, on our knees if necessary, to plead with the air ministry to let us enlist in their air force. That was our plan and we considered the risks worth taking.

The farm complex looked unusually orderly, very well maintained except for a small heap of manure which a number of chickens were busily taking apart. Wild flowers were growing between the cobblestones and along the walls of the buildings. Never before had the aroma of manure, aided by that of the flowers, appeared so welcoming.

According to the only watch we had between us, which Jan was wearing, it was 5.45pm when we knocked on the pine door of the farmhouse. It was opened by a middle-aged lady who stood with her arms firmly wedged on top of her nicely proportioned hips. Her enquiring words were – "What is it that you want, is there anything that I can do to help?" In a very clear voice she made it abundantly clear to us that it was right to accept her invitation to enter and follow her into a large room which had a ceiling of no more than six feet in height. At the far end stood a black cooking range, at the side of which was a neatly stacked log pile. There was a wide pine dresser on the other side of the room. We were most grateful to lower ourselves on to a long settee and chairs – our legs, in particular, appreciated the rest. Before introducing herself she offered us some very welcome hot refreshment.

Her name was Madame Gene Mureau and the steady gaze of her blue eyes concentrated upon Jan who was doing his best to answer all the questions that she had put to him. Madame Mureau wore a plain black skirt, the hem trimmed with a red ribbon. A short-sleeved grey blouse complimented her elegant self. Her dark straight hair was combed back to reveal dainty ears, which had been pierced to permit the wearing of diamond-topped gold studs. When speaking, her thin lips framed a nice set of white teeth, giving the appearance of a friendly smile with every word.

In a very gentle manner she enquired: "What is to be done with you? Our son Pierre is serving in the army and with our daughter married, we could, with a bit of a squeeze, put you up." Such an offer would have to await a final decision by her husband but, she added: "Don't worry, he is a kindly person." She then offered the suggestion that as the harvest was in full swing, the two farm workers would welcome some additional muscle.

Monsieur Mureau arrived – a broad-shouldered and muscular man with a suntanned sinewy face, which sprouted fresh dark bristles. He let his eyes do the talking, moving from the bemused face of his wife to each of us in turn. Before actually uttering any word, he sat down, took off his boots, and then asked his wife for an explanation. The keenness of her response prompted him to rise from his chair and shake hands with each one of us. Any tension there might have been quickly subsided when, without hesitation, he said, – "Of course you can stay, you are indeed welcome." It was obvious that he clearly understood our plight, being a patriot himself. After absorbing the situation, he warned us that it was necessary to have a permit in order to work. Our particular situation made this a virtual impossibility and he made it clear that our stay would have to be kept secret.

With that decision having been made, Madame Mureau escorted us up the stairs to two bedrooms. It was more than we could have hoped for. The bathroom, across the landing, had hot water taps which was something we had almost forgotten about; the morning shave would be painless! Down the stairs once more, where a hearty meal had been prepared by Gene, we were encouraged to talk about the determination that drove us to leave behind our comfortable homes and the events that we had encountered since setting out.

We were full of apologies the next morning for oversleeping and these were quickly accepted. After breakfast we were supplied with a pair of overalls and taken to a field where the harvest was in progress. The two farm workers were very pleased to see us and welcomed our help. With the introductions out of the way we set about helping to load the sheaves of grain onto the large ladder-sided carts. The grain was unloaded at the farm, for the threshing to be done in one of the barns. The all-important weather remained dry permitting the harvesting to continue at a feverish pace. One of the staff had a feeling 'in his bones' that the weather was about to change, bringing rain with it.

Albin, who before all the drama of our escape was due to take up an appointment at the university, was definitely not used to sustained physical effort and began to look drained but he would not hear of easing off when asked to do so. The thought went through my mind, that apart from myself, none of the other four were accustomed to using their muscles, all their strength was in their brain power. In my later years I realised that while physically strong, I did not take advantage of the skills that they possessed.

From the five of us, the first casualty was Tony who suffered a swollen and painful left cheek. A further two days passed without any improvement so Gene made arrangements for him to visit a doctor. On being told of the appointment, Tony refused to go and in reasonably understood French said: "I am not going to betray our presence here – I shall be alright." Given salt mouthwashes and hot poultices, the swelling gradually subsided and with that, the pain went too. Tony was able to take over the job of feeding the threshing machine as it was now the turn of Madame Mureau to feel off-colour.

The weather forecast, originating in the bones of the farm workers, proved to be correct and it began to rain. The cereal gathering had almost been completed but there was still plenty of threshing to be done. I had previously noticed a broken down stationary gas engine in a small barn. With Albin's help I took off the cylinder head, cleaned out a large deposit of carbon and lapped the four valves in their seats. Putting everything back together I then serviced the magneto ignition and the primitive carburettor. Albin cranked the monster into life and, with another threshing machine coupled to it, the farmer was unable to believe his eyes or ears. He was well pleased with our work. With a further two days of warm sunshine, which dried the fields, the last load of grain was stored in the barn and the pace of the work eased.

The speed of the approaching world disaster increased when Britain gave Hitler a final warning that unless he withdrew from invading Poland, a war would be declared against Germany. The French prime minister meanwhile announced general mobilisation and with that came the time for us to make haste and return to Paris according to our pre-conceived plan. That evening our hosts gave permission for us to tune their radio to a broadcast in the Czech language. This started 'Vola Londyn' which, in English, means 'London calling'. The news in our language confirmed all that we had heard – everything looked set for war to be declared against Germany very soon.

We broke the news to Monsieur and Madame Mureau that the time had come for us to return to Paris where we were determined to be accepted into the French Air Force. They expressed their understanding and wished us and our cause, good luck. Monsieur Mureau handed us the wages that we had earned and, most generously, nothing had been deducted for our keep. The five of us were individually able to thank them in French.

On Saturday September 2nd 1939 we were driven to the small town of Verberie to catch a train where it was possible to legitimately board the carriage with tickets. Having a compartment to ourselves, we talked about the procedure to adopt once back at the air ministry. There were no apologies to be offered for disobeying orders; our demand would be to speak to anyone of rank in order to plead our case, with hopefully, a positive result!

Before reaching Paris I searched for the words to write up in my diary. I eventually settled for:

Must not despair, the mission is patriotic and not in vain,
hold onto faith, despite the hardship and the pain.

Be strong, time has come to strengthen your resolution,
worry not, go forth in faith, not too far awaits your absolution.

CHAPTER 7

WAR IS DECLARED

Our arrival in Paris was a little after 1pm and, sustained by the substantial breakfast which Madame Mureau had provided before we left, we decided to go by the metro to Exelmans and, from the station, make our way to the Zig-Zag 'hotel'. It was a pleasant surprise to find a few Czechs who had just returned from lunch at the camp. We were even more astounded when we discovered that among those returning were some of those who had travelled by the same train as us when setting out for Marseille. The ultimate surprise was to be re-united with Venca Slouf, who like us, had jumped the train a little further along the line.

That evening Venca joined our group and we traded stories. Unlike us, Venca had had money in his pocket and was able to walk to the nearest railway station and return to Paris. Having brought ourselves up-to-date we settled into the straw nests which did not in any way compare with the beds that we had left behind at the farm only seventeen hours previously. Before falling off into a deep sleep I was sorely troubled about our questionable future. Our pending visit to the air ministry began to weigh heavily upon our troubled minds. We tried to console ourselves with the recent news that as the Germans were waging war against Poland, our value as pilots would be noted with more appreciation by the French.

During our return to the Zig-Zag after breakfast, I bought a newspaper whose headline highlighted the awful tragedy that had befallen Poland. The Luftwaffe had bombed four cities. One of them was Krakow which had been badly hit and many people killed. The previous day's address by the French prime minister, Edouard Daladier, also commanded prominent front page space as it suggested that a war was no longer an option but a certainty. After conferring with Venca and a few other people we respected, we decided to make our way to the air ministry, we could no longer bear the uncertainty. We walked into the large entrance hall whereupon the French uniformed personnel seemed to be agitated by our presence. As one, they shouted that Britain had also declared war on Germany half an hour ago. The clock hanging on

the wall over the reception desk indicated that it was 11.30am on
Sunday September 3rd.

Our request to see someone of importance was followed by a short
phone call. Our access to an officer upstairs proved easy, even
welcoming. After enquiring how we were, instead of the expected
reprimand, he gave us an assurance that our acceptance into the French
Air Force was imminent. Once our cheers had subsided and he could
make himself heard, he advised us to await further information, which
he firmly assured us would come within the next few days. With our
promises to comply and with thanks profoundly given, we returned to
Zig-Zag. That night, while celebrating at a bistro, Tony's liking for
Pernod proved too much for his legs. Getting him back to our billet was
amusingly difficult.

During the following few days our nerves eased, our faith had been
restored and our patriotic verve was revitalised. To pass the time we did
some sightseeing and shopping. Tony bought himself a Zenith
wristwatch and the rest of us invested in items of underwear to replace
the worn out articles. From the state of our clothes it was easy to understand our lack of success with the girls. Our French lessons continued,
Jan was not only teaching our group but the whole contingent.

After prior notice, on Thursday September 7th, a truck arrived to
take us to the military hospital for a medical examination and an X-ray.
Having never considered our state of health as an impediment to
enlisting, it was an added bonus when all of us came through with
'flying colours'. We were fully convinced of our acceptance into the
French Air Force when the uniforms arrived. Each of us was provided
with a blue tunic, matching trousers, a blue shirt, black tie, black socks
and boots. Having previously been measured, the clothing was a good
fit. Fully dressed, our conceit was something to be ashamed of. As
French servicemen use of the metro was free, compliments of the
French Government.

On return to our billets we gathered around a radio which had been
tuned to the Czech 'London calling' programme. It was announced that
President Benes and his government, exiled in London, had now
declared war on Germany. The president's proclamation on September
8th reminded us that until we officially became members of the French
Air Force, our patriotic allegiance was to our exiled president.
However, with no orders to the contrary, it was logical that as we were
on French soil, wearing French uniforms, our prime loyalty was now to
the French authorities. Despite this 'limbo', the prevailing circumstances dictated that we stood fast – as patiently as possible.

With the knowledge that savage hostilities were raging on Polish
soil, and our own country was under the Gestapo jack-boot, I was
beginning to feel the pangs of cowardice by running away and not
facing the enemy. On the other hand, the 'London calling' broadcasts

revealed that the young people of Czechoslovakia were being compelled to slave in German factories thus helping the Nazi war machine. If the 'limbo' we were in would end and our flying skill be recognised, we could contribute to the ultimate downfall of this evil regime.

We were feeling somewhat desperate, our patience wearing a little thin, when some eagerly awaited news came through to us on September 10th. We were instructed to be at our billet by 8pm, when some very important news would be announced. Needless to say, this order was obeyed with willing anticipation and all ears were strained to receive the announcement that tomorrow morning, twenty-five named, experienced pilots and mechanics would depart for an undisclosed air base on the French mainland. There were loud cheers which drowned out the Czech ambassador who, when order was at last restored, gave notice of even better news that on the following morning, another batch, yet to be named, would depart for another base. The joyful uproar that followed seemed to suggest that there was insanity amongst us. There was dancing, back-thumping even some cheek kissing. In the second batch, my friend Venca Slouf was included and I shook his hand, squeezing very hard and shaking for a long time.

Our party of five, now part of a bigger group of twenty-three similarly inexperienced pilots, were desperately disappointed not to be chosen to start any flying training. We could only offer all those who had been selected, our very best wishes. We were very happy for them and their departure made us all the more determined to pursue our aim and to eventually join them. In our utterly dismayed state we thought that we could have just as well been somewhere in Africa, where, as foreign legionaires, we would have at least been kept busy. The cleaning of our officers' boots would be better than sitting around, feeling forlorn with tension at breaking point, rumours abounding. Our status was now that of 'forgotten legionaires'.

Despite carrying out our chores at the air ministry kitchen with diligence, our patience with the ministry was frayed and with our sour behaviour being noted, an assembly was called to take place at the camp. A Czech officer who we had not seen before, stood on a podium, and decreed that as from the next day, starting at 10am, we would be obliged to undergo some French drill. In addition, classroom lessons would be given to teach us how to handle ourselves when outside the camp, wearing French uniforms.

We were drilled by a French sergeant who took it for granted that we could understand him. Anyone watching would have been well entertained. After a period of three days the task was considered complete and we all thought the sergeant a very good sport for his tolerance.

On September 16th I received a postcard from Venca Slouf, which I read aloud to all those gathered round: "Dear Frank, I hope that you and those from Pilsen are well, including those who remain at Zig-Zag with you. Our base is near the lovely small town of Chartres. All of us are well – the food is top class. The accommodation, if compared with yours, is a luxury. Have started flying Dewoitine and Morane fighters. Wishing you all the best, Venca." That same evening I sent him my thanks and wished him the best of luck when flying. The rest of my letter was full of bitter complaints about being forgotten. One small improvement in our conditions was brought about by an increase of our weekly pay from ten to fifteen francs. We also enjoyed free postage and public transport and with food and accommodation supplied, no one was seriously complaining.

Mastery of the French language remained a priority but our own tutor, Jan, became more and more reluctant to devote his time to giving us lessons. His command of the language provided him with an opportunity for unlimited socialising and he was frequently absent during evenings and weekends. We realised that we should not rely on him but would have to make do with some simple book learning.

Providence granted us a helping hand in the form of a message delivered to Michalek, whilst we were at our dish washing chores. It was an instruction and an invitation to attend some French lessons, free of charge, given by Madame Fournier or Mademoiselle Watson at La Terrasse de l'Entresol, Boulevard St Michel, where we would be taught and refreshments provided.

Madame Fournier was tall, slim and plainly dressed in a dark three-quarter-length skirt and a white cardigan. Her face could not be described as beautiful; distinguished would be more appropriate. She had dark, slightly wavy hair, which was combed back. Her matching eyebrows were dark and thick above penetrating eyes. Around her floated an aura of authority. Her age was difficult to assess but I put it at about thirty-eight. She spoke excellent English with a very soft voice that defied one to disobey. Miss Watson, as she liked to be called, was an American with an immediately recognisable accent. At about 5'9" she was an inch or two shorter than Madame Fournier and carried a little surplus weight though it would not be fair to describe her as fat. Her face was round and very kind, lips nicely curved and smiling, blond hair was swept back and held in a clasp. When speaking she reminded me of a nurse talking gently to a patient under her care.

As time passed, the numbers attending gradually dropped to twelve including ourselves. Attending one Saturday we were invited to stay overnight and on the Sunday, were given a guided tour of Paris. We soon discovered that the establishment was a finishing school for young ladies – correction – beautiful young ladies! At the first sign of our interest, Madame Fournier made it quite clear that these ladies attended to be taught the very best of manners and behaviour. Our influence, should it be deemed bad, would not be tolerated. Following that warning, a special effort was made to be 'good boys', but it proved difficult.

It was on Tuesday September 26th that our patience with the military bureaucrats ran out. It was decided that Albin and I should go to the air ministry and once again, ask the receptionist for an appointment to see someone of authority. It took quite a while for us to persuade the receptionist to do as we asked – just to pick up the phone and pass on our request. His response was reluctant, dialling slowly and then talking nervously. On replacing the phone his unfriendly voice said: "pas possible". With our determination showing we walked towards the stairway. As anticipated it was barred by a sentry so we stubbornly sat ourselves down on the second step and awaited a reaction. After a wait of ten minutes the lift doors opened and a civilian and a uniformed official appeared with a view to ending our 'sit-in'.

The civilian spoke perfect French and emphasised that they were appalled at our unorthodox manner. We remained seated, calmly trying to explain our dilemma, saying that our aim was to be like our other countrymen who were now engaged in flying. We wanted the same treatment, so that when the time came we would be ready to fight for freedom and democracy.

Our show of 'nerve' undiminished, the civilian stood flabbergasted whilst the officer, after having a word with the guard, asked us to follow him up the stairs – this we promptly did. After a hurried climb to the fourth floor the officer ushered us into a medium-size room dominated by a large desk. There was a smaller desk in one corner behind which sat another uniformed person. Filing cabinets made up the inventory. Whatever happened to the civilian could only be guessed at, probably suffered a heart attack – we and the stairs proving too much for him.

Asked to sit down, we were subjected to an interrogation as to why we invaded the air ministry. When he finally ordered us to leave, he offered no promise of help. Albin and I conveyed our experience to Tony, Jan and Michalek who were quite passive – probably recalling the uphill struggles we had faced before and worrying about the future.

When ten members of our remaining group, rather like the sediment in a barrel, received orders to be ready for departure, an awful thought crossed my mind – might we not, when our turn came, be destined for a firing squad? There was little relief from this dreaded notion when we discovered that those leaving were not, in fact, flyers. The state of anticipation remained for almost another week before the ten of us were taken by a truck to a railway station for a journey to an air force base somewhere in France. On that day I received another letter from Venca at Chartres, enquiring whether we were still in Paris and letting us know that he was very busy training to become a skilled fighter pilot.

We remained dissatisfied and utterly confused. We could not understand how the French could ignore our pleas to help fight our common enemy. After all, we were offering our services to, and in the defence of, France! It did not seem right to us that instead of sharing the mortal dangers and hardships with our brothers in Poland, we were being pampered with plenty of food to eat, and warm and dry accommodation.

When we told Madame Fournier how desperate and infuriating our situation had become, she suggested that perhaps the Czech Embassy could do something. The very next day when our grievances were conveyed to them, we were told that we had been classed as 'sport pilots' and as such, our value to the French Air Force was negligible. Perhaps it would take the spreading of hostilities into France and Britain before any change in our status could be brought about. They also reminded us not to complain and be thankful for being looked after at Exelmans. Leaving the embassy, I wished that I possessed a stick of dynamite!

On October 6th, a few more of our recently arrived friends were driven off to serve as ground staff, apparently at Chartres, where Venca Slouf and some other Czech pilots were under training. Only seven of us now made up the remnant of our party and in order to maintain our sanity we tried to keep ourselves busy. After clearing and cleaning the large factory space, which had, for a long time, been our dormitory, we set about investigating a small room in our building that could be seen through a window. The answer was to pick the lock and, once inside, we saw it was about the right size to accommodate the seven of us comfortably. We bought a small electric heater-cum-cooker, which we used for washing and making tea. Later, a small cooker was obtained on which some delicacies were prepared.

By now the weather was turning colder and any money that remained was spent on extra thick underwear although this was a little premature as we were issued a kit of winter clothes consisting of an overcoat, gloves and another pair of boots. Wearing these made us feel a lot better – maybe there was someone behind the scenes who was thinking of us. Could it have been the clothes store man using his initiative or had the order originated from somebody in the air ministry?

On our next visit to the young ladies finishing school we reported to Madame Fournier and Miss Watson, telling them about the fiasco at the Czech Embassy – they could hardly believe their ears. Just lately, only five of us had regularly attended the French lessons. They told us that no matter what happened, even after leaving Paris, their school was to be regarded as a place where we could stay and be offered food for as long as any leave would allow. This most generous offer bolstered our courage and was an aid to help us face up to anything that might confront us.

Monday October 9th saw the arrival of the fourth letter from

Venca which I was thrilled to receive, indicating that he and the other pilots were well and being kept busy flying. There was some sad news contained in his letter, which was that Sergeant Barton had been killed during an exercise. He had flown into a turbulent cloud formation, lost control of his Morane fighter, and went into a spin from which he did not recover. Apart from Captain Novak, who had died in hospital, this was the first fatality of a Czech pilot since our arrival in France. I wondered how many of us would return to a liberated Czechoslovakia when the war was over.

Michalek received a letter, this time from one of the group who were based at St Etienne. Just like those with Venca Slouf, they were all training very hard although the type of plane was not mentioned. Over the course of time one or two of these pilots wished to pay us a visit during a leave period. Unfortunately, the only reply possible was our depressing news that we had no accommodation to spare and had still not, as yet, been accepted for flying training.

Time passed uneventfully whilst we impatiently waited for news of a posting. The boring routine was only interrupted if any one of us should be unwell or, if Tony had over indulged the night before and returned in a drunken state. Sunday October 15th was one such occasion and required a lot of clearing and cleaning up.

On the morning of October 16th, Tony remained in his bed whilst the four of us walked across the River Seine to have our breakfast. His embarrassment was as prominent as his underpants which were hanging over the electric fire that had been left switched on. It was a shame, for when sober, Tony was a person of talent and great personality. Despite his addiction, I had a great affection for him.

Breakfast over, we departed for the air ministry kitchens to carry out our usual duties. Albin was subdued as he dried the china beside me, "Frank, I am beginning to think that if an order does come from the officers above it will be for our arrest for absconding from the foreign legion or even for our rebellious behaviour." My only response was to nod my head in agreement. Just then the plate that I has been washing slipped through my fingers and shattered on the tiled floor.

This was perhaps just a simple accident but I am more inclined to think of it as a 'message' – a premonition maybe. I recall feeling my gran's presence very strongly. At this juncture of writing this true story, I have to implore you, dear reader, to believe me when I tell you that after my grandmother had died, I was completely heart broken. I had bonded with her very soon after my birth, and always felt her closeness to me when I needed her most.

Upon returning to our quarters, we were surprised to be met by a very excited Tony, with eyes shining like two bright stars. With no vestige of shame now showing on his face we could not begin to understand just what had got him so excited. I thought he might still be drunk but he was undoubtedly sober as he passed a document to Michalek and implored him to read it.

We couldn't believe our eyes. Was it a sick joke? A forgery, drawn up by Tony who was certainly capable of such artistic deception? Being used to disappointment, the impact of this order took time to register with us. After two solid months of being kept in the dark – a bolt of lightning had struck from the sky.

The document was an order to take us by car to the railway station early next morning. We were to board a coach, on which seats had been reserved, to transfer us to the city of Bourges where transport would be waiting to take us to a nearby French Air Force base. Our flying training was about to begin. The bolt of lightning had penetrated to the very core of our patriotic hearts, swelled by our belated gratitude to the French authorities. At last, the reasons for our being in Paris were fully understood and it was now up to us to prove that we deserved this chance and, in some small way, to repay our debt.

CHAPTER 8

FINALLY FLYING

Tuesday October 17th dawned and we got up for the last time from our straw nests. It was 5am – time to prepare ourselves for the final departure from what had been our billets over the past two memorable months. Tidying our room, leaving behind the electric fire and the small cooker, we were ready long before any transport arrived. Our departure was not before time; the winter was almost upon us and we felt very pleased.

A large blue station wagon arrived driven by a sergeant from the air ministry. His job was to take us to the station and to ensure the train carriage seats had been reserved. Being chauffeured thus, it was as if we had been high ranking officers. The sergeant made sure that everyone was comfortably installed on the train and at 7.10am, our journey to Bourges began with him waving us off.

We were not bothered about the kind of reception that might await us at Bourges railway station but just what sort of welcome awaited us at 'Ecole Auxiliare Pilotage de Bourges' was a matter for our concern. Now on our way were student pilots Kaspar, Michalek, Mares, Nasvetter and Chalupa; all bearing an air of determination that our mission would be successful by our valuable contribution as future fighter pilots – helping to destroy Hitler's mania for ever.

The only stop made by the train was at the small town of Etampes, we then passed through the historic town of Orléans to Vierzon and by 11am reached Bourges, 120 miles south of Paris. A small truck, driven by a blue uniformed airman, covered the distance to the air force base in less than fifteen minutes. We passed through an imposing entrance gate without stopping. Outside an office block building we were met by two French Air Force officers who extended a very warm and cordial welcome before taking us to the sergeants' mess. After freshening up, a meal was served while the officers waited in a rest room. The food was very enjoyable with wine aplenty, thereafter, we were conducted over a short distance to a squat building in which we were allocated a room containing five iron beds, fully made up with mattresses, sheets, pillows and blankets. Everything was spotlessly clean, the billet centrally heated, and the adjoining wash facilities had clean basins, hot and cold water and a line of toilet cubicles.

After allocating ourselves beds, we placed our belongings in separate lockers and were able to relax in comfortable chairs which were in a line at the far end of the billet. After a suitable rest, and being in need of necessities, Albin and I walked into the city centre to admire the inspiring twin-towered cathedral. It appeared to us so very high that by comparison, the surrounding buildings looked like a group of dolls-houses. We were drawn to enter the cathedral, kneel down and thank God for not abandoning us. Albin and I sat there as one, with peace on our mind and in our souls.

From the cathedral, we walked along a street to a row of shops. We found one with just about everything that was needed, such as razor blades, soap and some hair dressing. The city itself was clean and tidy. There were trams, all driven by women, and a park with benches to rest on and with fresh air to breathe. It was with great pleasure that we were now in Bourges.

The return walk back to camp took twenty-five minutes which gave us time for a quick wash and then to attend the airmen's mess for dinner provided at 7pm. We joined our three friends who were in a hand waving conversation with the French servicemen. As with our friendly relationship with those at the air ministry, we felt completely at ease in our new surroundings. The one difference being that on this air force base the meals were not served up to us at the table. From hereon, like everyone else, our food had to be fetched from a serving hatch. It was in plentiful portions and bottles of Pinard, with tumblers, complemented our meal.

The long tables were able to accommodate ten people with five chairs placed either side. Opposite us on our table were five French servicemen with whom we had made an acquaintance upon our arrival at the camp. They were friendly company to have a meal with. Having got used to the way food was consumed in the French servicemen's mess in Paris, we were not at all critical of those sharing our table. There was however, a notable difference – as well as using the cutlery provided, they managed to lift morsels off the plate by using pieces of bread held in their fingers. The way they scooped up gravy was, in my opinion, a work of art to say the least. It did occur to me, that as guests in their country, we should not be too hasty with our criticism of their table manners – after all, they might not approve of ours.

After eating, a feeling of contentment began to spread and I wondered how on earth the prevailing goodwill amongst ordinary people that existed on each side of the table, could manifest itself in such a heartfelt manner. Such harmony was so often perverted by misguided politicians and incompetent bureaucrats. I could not understand why Hitler's orders were being so obediently carried out. I felt it was possible that the ordinary citizens of Germany were no keener on a war than we were.

At 6am the following morning, I was feeling particularly fresh as the tap marked hot had responded so readily to my fondling. Breakfast that followed consisted of coffee, croissants with butter and jam spread on with a knife. Our French friends preferred to dip their buttered croissants in their coffee; a method which we quickly adopted. After returning to our billets, some of the French servicemen visited us for a chat, which I thought was one of the best ways to learn the language. Of course, the ideal teachers were the French girls who we were hoping to meet on visits to the city.

Over the weekend, our priority was to spend as much time as possible on the airfield and around the hangars. The field was much like that at Pilsen where I had taken my flying lessons. It had very green grass, cropped short and was absolutely level. Along side the main access road was a hangar with an adjoining workshop. The administrative building incorporated a sick bay. The rest of the accommodation consisted of stunted buildings, grouped some distance away in the corner of the field. The surrounding countryside was very flat; the only visible obstruction of any note was Bourges Cathedral with its twin towers.

Access to the twin-domed hangar was by a pair of sliding doors. Inside were parked the aircraft, Hanriot 175s and the 182s; high wing monoplane trainer aircraft with which I fell in love at first sight. The only difference between the 175 and the 182 was the engines; the 175 with the Salmson 6TES 170 CV; and the 182 with the Renault 140 CV. In the other half of the hangar stood some neatly parked trucks, crash and fire fighting vehicles and a military ambulance. The adjoining workshops displayed tidy benches with vices and tool cabinets. We had not been invited into the administrative block, the back of which faced the airfield with a three-sided window projection which we took to be the flying control tower. The French national flag could be seen flying from a short mast at the side of the admin building.

Whether I was wandering around the base, resting in our quarters or even out in the town exploring its quaint lay out and peaceful atmosphere, I could close my eyes and the past traumatic experiences would disappear. The peace that I was now enjoying and clinging to, was worth fighting for – to the death if necessary. The dreams of Albin and me remained in our private domain and before going back to our base we entered the cathedral once again.

Back in camp while updating my diary entries, an officer, whom we had met on our first arrival, came into our room and pleasantly asked us to follow him. He made sure that we were properly dressed in clean and tidy uniforms and hats on straight, before leading us out. Inside the administrative building we were told that our flying training was to begin forthwith, after attending the store rooms to be issued with a flying suit and a hard top leather helmet which, incidentally, I treasure to this very day. Signing for the kit, we were led onto the airfield and handed over to the chief flying instructor.

The instructor had a comparable rank of warrant officer in the RAF and was wearing the standard French Air Force uniform. A peak cap rested on his head. His face was thin and sported a short clipped beard. His voice, like his eyes, was keen and friendly. His very slim figure fitted the uniform perfectly and his general appearance was dashing. His age, somewhat hard to assess, was probably between thirty-five and forty years old.

Inside the hangar, he lectured us on all the aspects of the plane. Its design and characteristics when flying; speed at take-off, climbing, cruising and most important of all, the speed at which it would stall. All these oral instructions were, if necessary, translated by Jan. Before dismissing us, each was handed a notebook with a recommendation that we study it carefully that night. Being written in French, I concentrated on the salient points to commit them to memory.

That evening our excitement was at a peak, the five of us prayed that we would be able to prove ourselves worthy of the decision to accept us into the French Air Force, above all, to be recognised as potential fighter pilots. On the dot of 7am next morning we reported, as instructed, outside the hangar wearing our flying suits, and with our helmets under our arms. Not only were the planes standing outside but our destiny was too.

Waiting my turn on the ground, watching the others take to the air, I grew impatient, thinking that the others were airborne much too long and that the perfect weather would turn bad or lunch time would arrive before it was my turn to fly. However I was soon approached by another instructor who asked me to get on board and strap myself into the cockpit. I hardly had time to discover what he looked like but his words were music to my ears when he said: "Let's get on with it, start up the engine."

Remembering my drill, I gave the appropriate commands in a loud steady voice, turned on the petrol, set the throttle mixture lever slightly on and pressed the starter button. The whine of the motor was short lived and the engine fired whilst I held the stick tightly back. When all was set, I asked for the wheel chocks to be removed. With my feet firmly on the rudder bar, the right toe touching the brake pedal, there was no need for any assistance. The plane turned and the taxi run to the take-off point began. I memorised where those before me were taking off, and made certain that no one was approaching to land. After the final pre-flight checks, I turned into wind, opened the throttle to its fullest extent and with my adrenalin at full flow we became airborne sooner than I was expecting. All the past dangers, deprivation and despair were forgotten as I was once again flying – towards restoration of peace on earth and, in particular, liberty in Czechoslovakia and Poland.

After three circuits consisting of take-offs and landings, I was reasonably pleased with my performance and the instructor likewise. I assessed that perhaps a few more take-offs and landings would see me going solo. But it was not to be. We had to contend with the autumn weather and of course, classroom lectures had to be attended. When flying resumed, the all-important exercise of carrying out a simulated engine failure, which would demand a forced landing, was practised. This meant flying with the engine throttled right back but not actually switched off. The stall procedure was practised, whereby the speed of the plane is reduced until the flow of air over and under the wings is insufficient to support the plane; whereupon the nose of the aircraft would drop like a stone towards the ground. Recovery from such an attitude is an associated lesson. Recovery from a spin is a very precise procedure that must be carried out correctly. The flying lessons continued until I had logged ten more flights during which I learnt to respect the instructor.

The instructor had to be satisfied that I was capable of carrying out the recovery procedures from a spin, a stall or an engine failure and I would not be allowed to go solo until then. When the time did come, I was very confident and my reward was a flight of sublime enjoyment. This time, I was not circling Pilsen but the very beautiful city of Bourges, the majesty of its cathedral a sobering sight. The flight lasted under half an hour and ended with a perfect landing at which my instructor expressed his pleasure. Flying exercises continued whenever the weather permitted and our proficiency as aviators was boosted by the lectures. To our surprise the subject of compulsory drill was added to the curriculum and before we even had a chance to question the necessity, we were lined up on the parade ground where the station commander announced that we were to be upgraded to the rank of corporal pilots in the French Air Force. No sooner had we assimilated that honour, we were then told that training would resume and, on passing-out, promotion to the rank of sergeant would follow.

Comparing the Hanriot with the planes that I had learnt to fly with was quite enlightening. This monoplane responded instantly to the elevator, rudder and aileron movements. Its sensitivity made the plane a joy to handle in calm weather conditions. However, in a strong wind or in unstable air due to the prevailing thermals, flying became quite an effort. I was enjoying myself to the full, especially when allowed to fly solo. One of the lessons that I did not look forward to was practising entry into, and recovery from, a spin. It was essential that this had been well and truly practised for use in turbulent conditions and, moreover, in combat.

Whilst some planes would spin leisurely, making recovery easy, the

Hanriot wound itself up very quickly and took its time to come out. The first time I performed this it scared the pants off me. In order to be master of the aircraft, I found it necessary to treat it with a great deal of respect, never taking anything for granted and listening to the experienced pilots from whom a great deal could be learnt.

It was now November and the weather conditions were getting more unsettled. Rain, gusty winds and poor visibility kept us grounded. On these occasions we were kept busy in the classroom with lectures on meteorology, navigation by visual observation, map reading and compass use, which was especially important as there were no radios fitted in the planes.

Our spare time outings to the city became more and more interesting. At a particular bistro one could be sure of catching the eye of some young ladies and, perhaps, receive a welcoming smile. Dressed in our drab, worn out civilian clothes, our luck with the girls had been zero but, when wearing our uniforms, it was a different story.

On one occasion, just for a change, we visited a small wine bar and sat ourselves at a round table. We were joined by two men, one of whom sat next to me. I guessed his age to be about forty-five, of a very pleasant disposition and kind enough to order some drinks. It was enjoyable to be in his company, that is, until he placed his hand on top of my thigh. Never having encountered a man with gay tendencies, I was naive and baffled as to the implications. My perplexity began to mount when his hand gradually moved upwards to my fly buttons. Naive or not, that was where I drew the line and I firmly removed his hand. He showed no sign of being upset and ordered me another drink saying that if our preference was for girls, he knew just where to find them.

While all this was going on, the man sitting next to Albin and Tony was equally hospitable but I could not tell whether they were receiving the same treatment. As the time came for our departure, the two French men decided to accompany us. Having had a little too much to drink we were all walking a little unsteadily. I noticed Albin, Tony and Michel (as we now called Vladimir Michalek), were all looking a little uneasy. Leaving the street lighting behind – 'My man' put his arms around me and began to kiss me. In that instant, I saw the light and shoved him away. He chose not to heed my warning and started to drag me towards a grassy bank. I hit him, a message which he finally understood and I caught up with my three friends. It was a salutary lesson learned; we never visited that wine bar again.

For the following six days the weather turned out to be beautiful, the flying became intensive with a great deal of navigation theory being put into practice. During one cross country flight my instructor tested my navigational skills with a series of exercises, the first proving unforgettable!

The first leg of the flight from base was to find a village forty miles south-west of Bourges, then turn north-east, heading for the small town of Vierzon and finally flying south-east back to base. When unable to find the airfield, I had an attack of hot flushes. There, to my right was Bourges, the cathedral towers reaching up to me, but where, oh where, was my base? The thoughts of being lost went through my mind together with the disgrace that would result. Even worse was if I was to run out of petrol and have to make a forced landing with a possible 'prang'. The solution to letting my imagination and panic run riot was, of course, the sun. It was morning, the sun, low on the horizon glared through the scratched perspex hood of the cockpit and the refraction made visibility very poor. By calming down and using sound reasoning I turned onto a westerly course and there, hey presto, was the base. The good landing that followed was an added bonus.

Flying, ground lessons and intensified 'square bashing' were shared according to the weather. As our flying and theoretical exams were pending, visits to the city became more infrequent. We were obliged to delay our interest in meeting the girls; hard work resulted in early nights. Before going to sleep we would review the latest information about the German occupation of our country and the atrocities occurring in Poland. Added to all this was the news that Stalin and Hitler were conniving over the spoils of war. The massing of Russian troops along the borders of Finland was yet another worry.

During the correspondence with Venca and other friends stationed at various bases, we received the tragic news from Toulouse that a Czech pilot, carrying out an exercise of a simulated attack on a bomber – a French Potez 630 – collided with it and both planes crashed. All seven aircrew, including the Czech, were killed. Venca also had news from his younger brother, Karl, who had escaped from his home, travelled through the Balkans and was now serving as a soldier at Agde in France. The letter disclosed the news that 2,000 Czech students had been sent to a forced labour camp in Germany. The Gestapo closed all the high schools as a punishment for the students rebelling against their evil presence. The news in the *Paris Soir* newspaper suggested that Hitler was not having it all his own way with Stalin – we were not surprised and a cartoon in the paper, illustrating the situation, was so imaginative that I copied it onto a page of my diary (see opposite).

The Hanriot served us well in the beginning, however, the plane was not designed to withstand aerobatics or any violent combat manoeuvres such as would be necessary to shoot down enemy aircraft. Whether it was our thoughts or sheer determination to fly in defence of what we believed in, we shall never know but it was not long before our French superiors at Bourges realised that it would be better for us to be flying purpose-designed, fighter planes.

The only way that we could accelerate our posting was by showing

our instructors that we were proficient. Hard work was the only weapon we had. The blissful life at the base continued, seemingly unaware of the fact that France was at war. This attitude infuriated me as I was determined to get into action before it was too late. A re-read of my diary finds the following entry. 'At an appropriate time the United States of America will not stand idly by, if the Germans are not withdrawn from Poland or if they become even more ambitious, the United States will then intervene.' The date was November 30th 1939. To me, this meant that if the war became a real shooting match, it would not last longer than one year before Germany would be defeated. If I survived I would be home soon after, although I predicted my chances of survival as less than ten percent.

The number of pupils at the flying school steadily increased; most were French students, making it necessary to split the flying programme into two groups. We became members of 'B' Flight and the flying was between mornings and afternoons. On one occasion, when our flight was in the morning and with no classroom or 'square bashing' scheduled for later, we paid a visit to the city. Leaving before dinner and with money to spare we decided to have something out of the ordinary at a restaurant that we had previously dismissed as being too expensive. We had a superb meal and the wine was not to be compared with the Pinard served up in our mess. After the meal, rather foolishly, we went to a bistro instead of first going for a walk in the park. One drink followed another, Tony particularly heavy on the Pernod. This harmless looking drink is sweet, turning milky when water is added, and for me to have a couple was sufficient, to my friends' displeasure, to start me singing. When the time came for us to return to camp, Tony was legless. It took Michel, Albin and me all our strength to drag him back. We managed to pass through the camp gate unnoticed or more likely with the acquiescence of the guards. Tony was, by now, in a revolting state. Normally, when drunk, he would remain friendly but for the first time he became violent and took a swipe at Albin. With his bed now unfit to sleep in he was made to lie on the floor, and that was where we found him in the morning. Leaving him there, we ran to the mess, dodging the rain, to have our breakfast. There was no time to waste and the next hour was spent in not only cleaning Tony, but his bed also. My previously held respect for him was at a low ebb.

When flying, I had been taught to keep a very keen lookout for other aircraft, particularly those at the same height. Apart from other Hanriots I would often see a Morane advance trainer, especially if I ventured towards the south-east. I enjoyed these encounters and made imaginary attacks upon them. If my approach was noted, the Morane would out perform me, much to my displeasure. I would simply be left standing as if my tail was tied to the Eiffel Tower.

A circulating rumour had it that the exams were scheduled to start on December 14th, passing which would result in a posting to Avord. This was the same base that the Moranes I had tried to 'shoot' down were flying from. I made a point when I next flew to make a special recce of that airfield. What I saw was very encouraging. The base, although larger than Bourges, had no runways. It possessed more hangars and there appeared to be another base adjoining. This was confirmed as a military cavalry unit but why planes and horses should be so closely integrated puzzled me, even more so when I was stationed there.

Letter writing to Venca Slouf became a routine which I enjoyed as much as Michel did in keeping Madame Fournier up to date with our activities. We were allowed to append our signatures to his letters but reading them was out of the question. Albin and I stayed very close, almost like brothers and, when possible, we would go to town especially to spend a short while in the cathedral. There we were able to ease our anxiety about the families we prayed for; that they be spared the hardships we knew now existed in Czechoslovakia. The park was another place to relax in. We were good for one another; his slower approach to a task compared to my prompt responses began to blend.

That one day he would make an ideal doctor or surgeon was, to me, unquestionable. In our party of five, the only one that I despaired of was my friend from Pilsen, Tony. He too, was a highly talented person with the world at his feet – if only he could be persuaded to moderate or even stop his drinking, as we pleaded with him to do. Each time an oath was obtained that he would not touch another drop. The longest period that I can remember him staying sober was two weeks. While I respected Michel, it was not possible to probe his inner thoughts. He was friendly with one and all but with no one in particular except at a later stage when we were stationed at Avord. Jan was as deep as Loch Ness and to assess his personality it would need the services of a psychoanalyst. He was friendly with everyone but nobody's special friend, except perhaps himself. His linguistic abilities were a great asset to us and, at times, life saving.

Much to our surprise, on December 10th a Czech officer named Pernikar, who we had met soon after arriving in France, visited us. When he enquired about our welfare at the camp we told him we had only one complaint – it was about time that we flew a more advanced type of plane. He told us that the other inexperienced Czech pilots, still being kept at the army base, would start their flying in about two week's time. He also had news that Venca Slouf and others had been posted to an operational fighter squadron, flying American Curtiss (Hawk 75A) fighters.

Whether it was due to his visit or merely in answer to our prayers, on December 22nd, we began to fly the Morane Saulnier 230, a two-seater plane. Like the Hanriot it was a high wing monoplane but capable of full aerobatics. The instructor told us that we had to record a total of five hours dual flying and five hours solo on the Morane before being posted to a more advanced training school. Whilst the good weather held, we wasted no time in becoming acquainted with the Morane. The 220hp engine bonded with my vigour to obtain the very best out of it. Soon the plane and I became compatible, especially when the aerobatic training began.

My first solo flight in the Morane proved to be the most enjoyable since flying the fully aerobatic trainer at the Hradec Kralove Czech Air Force base. At a height of 3,000 feet, and well clear of the airfield, I tried the easiest of manoeuvres – the loop. Although not authorised to do this I encountered no problem. After the second attempt at the loop I went into a stall turn, which I fell out of, performing much better at the next attempt. I found the barrel roll a joy to do. Whether good or bad, my experiments were a secret – or were they? Was someone taking good care of me?

The early morning of December 24th was bright, the sky greenish blue with not a cloud to be seen. The air was cool and crisp as Albin and I walked towards the camp mess, aiming to have an early breakfast. As we made our way back to the billet the sun climbed over the distant horizon, its golden rays gradually driving shadows out of its path before embracing us. As if to remind us, the two beautifully sculptured towers hugging Bourges Cathedral, lit up. What a majestic reminder of the peaceful sanctity that lay under its roof. Our plan had been to visit the cathedral at least once over the Christmas period. After a spruce-up we set off, leaving our friends, who were not in so much of a hurry, to follow our example a little later.

Once inside the cathedral, we were deeply moved by the solemnity and found ourselves overcome by a bout of homesickness. We could hear a children's choir, softly accompanied by the organ. The two of us sat quietly listening to the practising of hymns in readiness for a later service. Unknown to Albin or me, our three compatriots came in and sat themselves on a pew some way behind us. We were at peace with ourselves and wished that it would be so with the whole world.

Instead of the peace and freedom we all hoped for, the bombs I had helped stack as a national serviceman in Czechoslovakia were probably being dropped by the German bombers in towns or along the battlefields, tearing the earth upward to fall upon the broken bodies of men, women and children who simply longed to live in peace. Our offering of prayers at Bourges Cathedral confirmed the purpose of our being in France, which was that our contribution as fighter pilots would lead to the defeat of the enemy. Our resolution was as determined and potent as ever.

Christmas Day, or in Czech 'Vanoce', saw the five of us spending the day quietly on the base. We put up a small Christmas tree and dressed it in tinsel, then celebrated with our French friends with the help of a bottle or two of the Pinard wine. That day, Monday, the weather was not as lovely as we had enjoyed on Sunday but it was still possible to go into the town and enjoy a walk in the park. The benches were filled mainly with women with their prams, some being gently rocked. The thought went through my mind – just what future lay ahead of the babes, would there be peace on earth? How many lives would be lost while fighting went on to preserve freedom for them?

The next two days saw some rain and we were hard pressed to prepare for the forthcoming theoretical exams. The flying checks had been carried out before Christmas and as far as we were aware, we had passed. When the exam papers came I was pleased to be able to answer the questions easily. The results were announced in the evening. We had all passed; we were pilots in the French Air Force, entitled to have 'wings' pinned on our uniform, which we were proud to wear over our Czech Air Force badges.

It was 10am when I returned to my billet to find a letter addressed to the five of us. The postmark was Paris and the sender's address given as Internat, Boulevard St Michel. It was, of course, from Madame Fournier and Miss Watson informing us that they intended to pay us a visit and were due to arrive at Bourges during the afternoon. They had arranged to stay overnight at the Hotel Anglais where they would like to see us the following evening. Over lunch, I told my friends who were beside themselves with pleasure. When we told our instructors of this invitation, we were all given the next morning off. That evening it was decided that Michel alone would go to see the ladies at the hotel, letting them know that we had been given some time off and intended arriving at 10am. A grateful look appeared in Michel's eyes.

On the evening of the last day of the year I made the following entry in my diary:

> 'I am closing this part of my diary feeling confident – if not convinced – that by the end of the following year, the enemy will be defeated. Freedom, peace and happiness will be restored for all those that are now enslaved by the Nazis, whom I have no doubt will be defeated by the French and the British – with a little help from ourselves.

> 'I pray that by the end of 1940 I will be back in Czechoslovakia with my family and all those that I long to be united with.'
>
> (written 31.XII.1939 at 6pm)

I then set about writing to my parents and Jarka via the Red Cross in Switzerland.

CHAPTER 9

ADVANCED FLYING TRAINING AND THE KNIFE TRICK

The meeting with our two lady friends was more emotional than I had expected. They too, were overwhelmed by the reunion. The reminiscing began in the hotel lounge, spilling over into the dining room where a superb meal of roast beef and all the trimmings was served. The two bottles of wine that were drunk made the meal complete. We were congratulated by the ladies on our flying achievements and received their praise for being able to converse in French. They reminded us, that just as soon as we are given leave, we had to go to Paris and stay with them at the Internat. They departed by train at 3.30pm, waved off by all of us on the platform. We made our return to the base with Michel trailing behind, deep in his private thoughts.

The weather for the time of year was beautiful and flying started early on Tuesday January 2nd 1940 – the intensive training continuing with no let up. It was rumoured that we would be leaving soon for Avord so our instructors were determined that when we started flying there, their skill as instructors would show through our ability. It was when my instructor told me that I had the makings of a good fighter pilot that I began to feel really confident. I was curious why I was not being taught a 'slow-roll' as a manoeuvre and after enquiring of my friends, learnt that they were not being taught this either. So one day, when well clear of the base, I tried to execute the roll. The result was that I fell out of the sky. I later asked my instructor why such a manoeuvre was not being taught, he told me that in France it was not included in the flying syllabus but that the 'flick-roll' was. In order to satisfy my curiosity he took me up to demonstrate and the first time that he performed the roll I became disorientated. After a few more flicks I began to get the hang of it. When I eventually learned the slow-roll, I thought the French flick was a more useful tactic in a dog-fight (aerial combat) and some proof of my theory is borne out by being able to write this story. It was interesting that the slow-roll was not taught (perhaps not even permitted) in France whereas the flick-roll was taboo in Britain. From this point of view I considered the French were one up on the RAF so far as flying a fighter plane was concerned.

The first period of leave we were granted at Bourges started on January 7th and was for one week. With a free travel pass we took the first available train to Paris. It left Bourges at 3.14pm for the one hour trip. Sitting comfortably, we contemplated our visit and the stay at the Internat. A metro ride to a stop named Odeon brought us not too far from the Boulevard St Michel and, walking the rest of the way, we were greeted by Madame Fournier at the Internat. She embraced us as if we were her sons returning home.

We were allocated a nice room and, as it was a Sunday, went off to a restaurant for a meal, thereafter returning to the Internat to spend the rest of the evening with Madame Fournier and Miss Watson in their lounge where our 'French tongues' worked overtime. During the remainder of our leave we were shown the highlights of Paris including a visit to L'Opera and at the Casino we saw Maurice Chevalier. In spite of it all being very entertaining and enjoyable I could not really reconcile this with my thoughts of my own country suffering a brutal occupation by the Nazis. Poland and Finland were in a similar position yet, here in Paris, there was no apparent evidence that anyone, apart from our friends at the Internat, cared two hoots about these atrocities or that the same fate may spill over into France. We enjoyed the generously arranged classical and light entertainment, which was provided at their expense. We took nothing for granted. With our leave nearly over we made a last visit to the Louvre where the Mona Lisa 'winked' at me. A sad farewell followed next morning, and then we were in a taxi to reach the station in good time to catch the 11.20am train.

Back at the camp we assembled on the parade ground along with the other pupils, the instructors and ground staff. When the station commander arrived a sergeant brought us to attention. As he climbed upon a small rostrum, an order was given to stand at ease. He then gave his congratulations to the course at having achieved a good standard in flying, in discipline and in passing the exams. We were now deemed to be French pilots and promoted to the rank of sergeant. He also announced that, as yet, there would be no posting for us to Avord – to our amazement there was no room for us there. With this depressing news we spent the rest of the day in low spirits. With no duties pending, I passed the day in my room, painting and writing letters.

As there was no more flying available on the programme, once again we felt surplus to requirements and the days began to drag. One day we were invited to visit Avord and the news injected us with a serum of renewed faith. The atmosphere at Bourges had become 'polluted' by the indifference towards us, so the invitation allowed some fresh air into our lungs. At Avord we received a very warm welcome from the commander of the flight that we were due to join.

After he showed us the planes and general lay out of the camp it was time for us to catch a bus back to Bourges. With confirmation that we had not been forgotten, our patience was restored and finally rewarded on January 29th. The five of us were determined to arrive at Avord looking trim and above all – when flying started – prove ourselves to be potentially the very best fighter pilots that they had ever trained.

When we reached the station nobody was waiting for us. To reach Avord base it was necessary to take a narrow road up a steep hill – the camp was situated on the plateau above. Leaving most of our kit at the station and carrying only our valuables we started walking. Evening had arrived when, out of breath, we reported at the camp gate. A corporal of the French Air Force escorted us to a large billet which was just for us, as if we were infectious. It was a negative welcome indeed, the room provided was dusty, had primitive beds, and the blankets, pillows and sheets were piled up on one of the rusty frames. Before the corporal left us he gave instructions that immediately after breakfast it was necessary to report to the medical officer at sick quarters.

Our belongings were collected whilst we were being led through one formality after another. To our relief we all passed the medical inspection. We were then transferred to another room in a block reserved for flying personnel. This turned out to be a favourable comparison with our quarters at Bourges. Meeting up with another three compatriots lifted our morale one step higher. After making ourselves thoroughly acquainted with the lay out of the camp, we came to the conclusion that Bourges was an exceptional French air base. At Avord there prevailed a kind of chaos that we were obliged to accept as normal.

On Wednesday January 31st the five of us were marched into the station commander's office where he very officially, with no hint of compassion on his hard face, welcomed us to Avord, saying that he expected us to comply with the rigid camp discipline, whether flying or on the ground.

For the first three days of February, the weather, like the station commander, was not welcoming. We made ourselves comfortable in our quarters, which we were pleased to be sharing with some French airmen with whom we quickly became friends. Unlike the set-up at Bourges where the airfield was a little distance from the administrative buildings, the grass expanse and a large hangar at Avord abutted a complex of low buildings. Another group of buildings, with its own perimeter fence and a paddock where horses were grazing, adjoined the camp on the south side and these were the barracks for the military cavalry unit I mentioned earlier. Our main interest brought us wandering towards a large pitched roof hangar – and we were very curious as to what lay behind those closed, triple-sliding doors. Entering through a small gate set in one of the main doors, we found the interior was illuminated by large windows in the roof and side wall.

There were eight planes plus some ancillary equipment stacked on the vast concrete floor. I easily identified four Morane 230s, which I had seen from time to time in the air and had actually flown at Bourges. The other four low wing monoplanes (called Nords), shining like silver, were different altogether. They were North American-built trainers that I knew as Harvards, sporting a 450hp radial engine under well moulded cowlings, driving a metal, constant velocity (CV) propeller.

The following morning, the rain had stopped and the clouds were gradually distancing themselves from the green lush of the airfield. It was announced during our breakfast that flying was definitely on, all pupils being required to report to a briefing room which was a low, long hut, on the east side of the hangar. Breakfast over, we snatched our flying kit from the locker room and made our breathless arrival at the briefing room as if at the end of a 100 metre dash.

When everyone had arrived, the numbers consisted of, apart from we five, seventeen French pupils and three more Czechs who we were meeting for the first time as they had been away on leave. With a rapid improvement in the weather the briefing was short and the five of us were divided into two groups. Tony and Jan were to start flying in the Morane and it was to be a Nord for Albin, Michel and me.

The Nord cockpit was roomy and comfortable and the visibility was very good. The instrument lay out, the controls and the appropriate flying speeds were explained. For the first time since my beginning to fly, the instructor was able to communicate using headphones. After all the necessary checks had been carried out, I gave the usual order to start the engine. After a short warm up, the chocks were removed and I started to taxi the plane, which I found to be easier than ever before. Our take-off point reached, I carried out a pre-flight check and was ready for the all clear to take-off.

We accelerated with the nose of the aircraft pointing towards the distant roof of a building – a few gentle bounces and we were off the ground, climbing gently. The wing below me made the downward visibility rather poor but after climbing to 500 feet, when I began a gentle turn to the left, the side view downwards improved greatly. We flew for one hour during which time the instructor kept me very busy, so much so, that I began to sweat under my flying helmet – now incorporating ear phones. The one mistake I made was that at an appropriate height I failed to feather the prop to a coarse pitch. When asked to do so, the high rasping noise of the prop stopped when the engine was throttled back to a cruising speed. It became a sound as soothing as the instructor sitting behind me. In all, we carried out three take-offs and landings before it was Michel's turn to fly. The de-briefing by my instructor contained no stern reprimands and gave me reason to feel satisfied that I could, at last, fly a plane which resembled a fighter.

With my flying stint done for the day I was obliged to remain outside the hangar and assist the instructor and pupils with seat straps, and when signalled, remove the chocks from under the wheels. I took this opportunity to have a word with Jelinek, one of the three Czechs who had been at Avord for the past three months.

During the next two weeks the weather was very changeable and flying was on an on and off basis and there was a definite tightening of discipline. The French lads who were not used to a hard service routine, similar to what I had experienced as a national serviceman in the Czech Air Force, found it rather hard going.

When it was not raining but poor visibility prevented flying, the parade ground commands echoed loudly from the back of the hangar. When it rained, the classroom blackboard was covered with diagrams of isobars or profiles of wings, whether of high or low aspect ratio or perhaps a drawing of the engine complexities – chalk was becoming a scarce commodity. The result of the intensified activities meant that no one was bored – there wasn't time!

As a reward for observing the discipline, being studious and proving ourselves men worthy of becoming fighter pilots, we were given a leave period of two days. There was no time wasted in setting off on the first train to Paris to stay, as invited, at the Internat. After another warm welcome from our two ladies who, as promised, had kept rooms ready, they had to return to busying themselves with the school curriculum. The main reason for our visit was to attend the Czech Embassy and try and wring out of them a sum of 900 francs that had been promised to us many times. On telling the embassy officials that our promotion to the rank of sergeant was imminent, they agreed to hand over the money. With promotion came the expectation that we should wear a No.1 uniform, the cost of which had been estimated at 1,300 francs. With the money in our pockets we went straight to a tailor who had been recommended by Madame Fournier. Our measurements taken, we returned to the Internat in the evening where there was much to talk about.

During the evening we were given the opportunity of meeting a few of the Internat students. I sat next to a delightful young lady by the name of Gene. Before she left to go to her room she said to me – in French – "Hope to see you again Frank." The door closed as my face turned lustfully red.

Back in camp, the theoretical and practical promotion exams started the next morning. Passing the exams would mean our promotion to Sergent Pilote Compagnie Ecole de Chasse Numero 3. I felt confident in passing the oral and written exams and had no doubts about my flying ability. No, it was the drill that I had made a mess of. When it was my turn to command a squad of airmen, taking them through various turns, standing them to attention or at ease, quick or slow marching, all went well. That is until I gave them an order to 'left turn', which should have been followed by another 'left turn'. I hesitated before the second command and while remaining transfixed, the squad was face to face with a wall. I had to explain; those facing the wall were not in any danger of being executed, rather I had shot myself in the foot. The officer in charge remained quiet, although I thought I heard him mumble: "sacrebleu".

March 16th 1940 arrived and there was yet another parade. A high ranking officer was making a visit to announce the names of all those who had passed the exams and from that moment on, had become sergeants in the French Air Force. I held my breath until I heard him say my name. Our uniforms were worn with a great deal of pride and the silver braid sergeant's rank insignia sewn onto the sleeves meant that, at last, we were non-commissioned officers. My thoughts were of my mother and how proud she would be of me. Not long afterwards some of our confidence was shaken when one of the instructors and his pupil were killed. Whether by accident or design, their Morane 230 went into a spin at only 1,000 feet from which they did not recover. A sad reminder to take no chances when flying and to always try and have that little extra in hand.

Whenever the weather allowed, our flying training progressed. The five of us mainly flew in the Nord aircraft and this made formation practices interesting and enjoyable. Although we did not have radio communication between each aircraft, pre-arranged hand signals and wing waggling helped to change the shape of the flying formations or to indicate who should take up the leading position.

The news from the battle fronts in Norway and Denmark grew more and more alarming. The German forces were bombing or occupying the Norwegian ports of Oslo, Bergen, Trondheim and Narvik; whilst the Danes, in a desperate situation, were about to capitulate. The French, the British and the American president discussed how best to be of help. The British Navy fought battles with German warships and submarines with mounting losses on both sides. At Avord there was no evidence of any preparation for a defence of the base. Talking of the dangers of war to anyone brought the reply – "What war?"

It was beyond our understanding to learn that our Motherland had been sacrificed for the sake of peace. When that mad beast Hitler began to savage Poland – its brave army standing alone, their cities bombed – there was still no help from the mighty British, and the French rested snugly behind their 'Maginot Line' – I was left dumbfounded. The evil of Hitler was fuelled by greed – just how long would that madness be allowed to continue?

The war was obviously expanding towards the French borders but still no sense of urgency could be detected at the camp. The bistros, bars, cafés and restaurants continued to serve their customers, some of whom may not even have heard of the plight of Czechoslovakia, or knew where Poland was. That Hitler was allowed to rampage through parts of Europe did not seem to affect them – the word subjugation was not in their vocabulary.

The feelings of anger were a spur to me and justified my being at Avord. I was determined to fight vigorously against the oppressors of my country, Poland, Norway and Denmark. I dared the maniac to come closer and beware! To lose, give up or surrender was definitely not in my nature.

Offers of help from the British came in the form of the Royal Navy inflicting deep wounds on the German Navy. While America continued to utter prospects of aid the French still seemed oblivious to the real dangers lurking beyond their frontiers. In order to preserve their freedom they needed to wake up and prepare. Like me, they would have to express their anger and be willing to take part in preventing the madness overtaking their borders.

With the weather in April 1940 quite dependable, aerobatic exercises in the Morane were a daily routine. These consisted of 'reversement à gauche' or 'reversement à droit' – flick-rolls to the left or right – practised until they could be performed with our eyes closed, the 'retablissement' – a roll off the top, which had been invented by a famous German pilot, Immelmann, which proved useful in shaking an enemy approaching from behind, the 'retournement' – also an exercise in spin recovery; and finally a loop, done just for the fun of it. When I combined all these manoeuvres into a sequence I would allow my imagination to take me back to the air displays at Pilsen back in 1936 and 1937. It was then that I admired Captain Novak performing such stunts in a Czech-built bi-plane fighter.

Early in May, whilst practising 'V' formation flying in the Nords at 1,700 feet, with myself in the lead, Albin at number two (starboard) and Michel at number three (port), I spotted a large bomber flying across our path some 500 feet below us. Thinking that it would be good practice to make a dummy attack, I began a gentle dive. Before we realised that it was a Dornier with one of its engines out of action, three parachutes billowed out from the plane. As our aircraft were not fitted with guns, we promptly peeled off, returned to base and reported the incident but no explanation or reaction was offered. Our reward was the knowledge that at least we had an enemy plane in our imaginary gun sights and that it was destroyed. Later that same afternoon, still on a 'high' from our encounter with the Dornier, we made a simulated dive bombing attack over our base camp.

The prescribed course period of training was for fifteen hours, which meant that I had four more hours of flying to do. Suddenly training in the Morane took on some urgency as if the French had sensed the need. By the end of each day of tossing my plane about the sky I had very little energy left – only strained nerves!

I received a letter from Venca Slouf, which contained the very sad news that Captain Novak had died after a very long illness. He had succumbed to cancer. He was to be laid to rest on May 3rd. When we informed our instructors, we were given two days off and thankfully were able to catch an early morning train for Paris arriving at 9am. After a short walk from the Odeon metro stop, Madame Fournier once again, warmly greeted us at the Internat. She had prepared a large room for us, which had been decorated and refurbished in a very homely Czech style. There was even a portrait of our President Benes hanging on the wall with a red, white and blue bow on top of the frame.

The funeral service had been timed to take place at 5.40pm at a Paris church, not far away from the Arc de Triumph Memorial, where Captain Novak's coffin stood before the main altar covered with the Czech national flag. A wreath, placed on top, was in the form of the Czech Air Force roundel. The church was full, with many high ranking French and Czech officers occupying the front pews, the service being conducted jointly by French and Czech priests. It was simple but very moving especially to our patriotic hearts. To our utter amazement it was apparently against the rules for the coffin to be borne to the grave by airmen or officers who had served with Captain Novak in the Czech Air Force, instead the coffin was carried out by six men from the funeral establishment.

Feeling very sombre after the ceremony, we called at the Czech Embassy to enquire whether the order for our five-year contract as foreign legionaires had been annulled. Unable to answer, they pointed out that all future matters relating to our present service in France were now being handled by the Czech Consulate in Bordeaux. Leaving us none the wiser, we took the metro, alighting at the Odeon stop and then strolled up the Boulevard St Michel to the Internat. After a comfortable night in our room, we had an English breakfast and then took a taxi, insisted upon by Madame Fournier, to the station for our return to Avord.

After passing the final test in aerobatic training in the Morane, we returned to the more comfortable Nords which had hoods that slid over the cockpit, making flying much more relaxed. Formation flying exercises became a daily routine and our flying hours mounted. The vital practice of 'feathering' the propeller and correct use of the wing flaps was taught often enough for it to become an automatic procedure – this allowed the aircraft to become airborne sooner and permit landing at a slower speed.

We all took the formation flying very seriously and having mastered the 'art', the next practice was that of dog-fighting. Because there is always a certain amount of danger when planes dive at each other simulating shooting, great care had to be exercised in order to avoid a collision. In these manoeuvres the adrenaline flows in abundance and can convert a normally cautious pilot into a dare-devil – the practice turning into 'real combat'.

On one occasion Michel and I got ourselves into a spot of very serious trouble, not whilst fighting it out, but on landing. Our over-excitement in carrying out these combat tactics spilt over and prior to landing, we 'buzzed' the airfield. The result of this was that we were hauled before the station commander (probably a member of the Gestapo), who handed out a fifteen-day sentence of confinement to barracks.

We were unceremoniously ushered into a cell that was large enough to accommodate two comfortable beds, a table and chairs. At one end was a basin with hot and cold taps and a door, which led to a flush toilet. The room was clean and two barred windows allowed sufficient light in and provided a view of the outside. We were allowed the use of books, paper and writing equipment. On the outside of the door, about ten paces away was a mountain of a man, a Senegalese, standing on guard like a statue with a rifle over his broad shoulder. He was in fact the soldier who had opened the cell door when we arrived and had greeted us with a friendly smile, which showed a set of teeth that would surely have been capable of biting through the bars on the window. After settling down, Michel and I gave loud thoughts to the possibility that either the station commander hated Czechs or he was just a decent chap who thought that we were in need of a holiday. On the other hand, perhaps he was a German spy, who having received such good reports from our instructors, set out to delay our progress to the battlefront!

We began to hatch a plan for an escape because, for the first time at Avord, the air-raid sirens had sounded, followed by some distant explosions. Part one of the plot was carried out immediately after our evening meal was brought. It began by befriending the Senegalese guard for a while before he departed. As he closed the door behind him and turned the key in the lock, I placed a knife in the door-jamb, just where the lock tongue would enter the opposite aperture. We waited until Michel, looking through the window, could see the guard return to his post, before quietly opening the door, tip-toeing behind him and tapping him on his shoulder. He turned with a jerk and on seeing us his eyes began to roll as if screwing themselves out of their sockets. Before he could utter a word Michel spoke in a very friendly voice; one word, "magic". The poor guard stood mesmerised as we returned to our room and shut the door behind us. As we expected, he came to the door, tried the lock, and then walked back to his post, his head spinning.

It was as if providence was aiding and abetting our cause, for that same evening the air-raid siren sounded again. Thoughts that it might just be a practice were quickly dispelled when we heard distant bomb explosions. The raid was for real. We decided to put stage two of our plan into effect as soon as the opportunity arose. This came sooner than expected when the guard arrived to remove the empty food dishes. I informed the somewhat bewildered guard that I possessed magic powers. I took a knife, laid it across the palm of my hand, theatrically massaged my arm just above the wrist and made plain that by squeezing blood into my hand it became magnetic. Then, while squeezing my wrist, I closed my fingers over the knife, holding it in a vertical position. I opened my fingers and hey presto, the knife remained as if glued to my palm. Our guard was impressed.

Stage three of the plan now followed and this was to extract a promise from the guard not to let anyone know if we were not in our room, which might occur the very next day. It had to be a secret between us. It was agreed that when breakfast was brought, he would report that we did not feel like eating. He acquiesced to this subterfuge and when the dishes were collected (minus one knife) the guard turned the key in the lock, the knife being wedged in the door-jamb. One more 'sleight of hand' move on our part was for Michel and I to lean against the door as the guard made sure it was 'locked'.

Later that same morning we very quietly walked out, the click of the lock alarming us as we crept around the back of the building and walked to our billet where we changed our clothes and updated our plan. As we could not stay in the camp, I had packed my briefcase packed with a few necessities, fake travel passes and all our available cash and Michel and I walked to Bourges and caught the Paris train. Madame Fournier and Miss Watson could not believe their eyes when they saw us. That evening, after we told them the story of how we came to be in Paris, they issued a gentle reprimand.

During the evening, we had an attack of conscience (aided by the tactful reproaches of our hostesses) and decided to return to Bourges. Madame Fournier accompanied us to the station in a taxi she had ordered, just in time to catch the train leaving at 1.15pm. As the train moved out of the station Madame Fournier waved us off, tears clearly visible in her worried eyes.

During the train journey Michel and I kept our eyes cast upon our boots – our mood a very sombre one. The updated news about the war received at the Internat was very bad indeed. The German Wehrmacht advance continued relentlessly; one surrender following another. Cities, towns and even villages were being bombed unsparingly and there seemed no apparent ability to stop the advance.

It was probably the intensity of our feelings that brought about the sensation of guilt that I was harbouring. I had deceived a decent but superstitious Senegalese soldier by making use of his belief that Michel and I could walk through locked doors. This thought was uppermost in my mind and I felt ashamed of myself. The depth of that feeling increased when Michel confided in me that his reason to proceed with the misconceived plan was that he desperately wanted to be with Madame Fournier. I was aware that he had become very close to her but did not think that he would have considered the misdeed simply for that one reason.

As the train sped back to our base we were both deep in thought. I was in a particularly sombre mood. The continued advance of the German Army, the merciless bombing by the Luftwaffe and now Mussolini was on the point of making a pact with Hitler. The insanity was spreading, leaving us only worry and concern. In spite of the depressing news on all fronts our belief in ultimate victory remained as strong as ever.

CHAPTER 10

IMPOTENT IN THE FACE OF ATTACK

It was 3.50am when the train arrived at Bourges on Friday May 10th 1940. A slow train was waiting to depart for Avord, Nevers and onward south-eastwards. We just managed to get on board and arrived at Avord at 4.50am. There was a slight delay in making our exit when the station guard became suspicious of our free passes. The walk back to the base along the road was a steep one so we opted for the shorter cross-country route. At about the half way mark, the air-raid sirens sounded but thinking it to be some sort of practice we were not unduly worried. However, high up in the clear sky, came the droning sound of aircraft engines. We scrambled up towards a disused quarry when the first bomb exploded – our war had begun.

Michel and I tumbled into the quarry as the bombs rained down. Huddling tightly into a corner of our shelter we felt scared, not just for ourselves but for those at the camp upon which the destruction was being unleashed. Uppermost in our tormented minds was the safety of Albin, Tony and Jan. The other three Czechs were spared the trauma as they had been posted away a month ago. The fate of the Senegalese soldier also lay heavily on our consciences.

The raid seemed to be lasting for hours but actually the last bomb we heard exploding was only ten minutes after the first. When Michel and I began to make our way from the quarry the first evidence of the destruction that had taken place were the trees embedded with shrapnel. As we made our way back to the camp an unreal and deadly silence was broken by the heart-rending cry of a horse. Over the last embankment hurdle we saw the dead and maimed horses and the carnage made our senses reel. By the time we reached the base soldiers had begun, mercifully, to shoot the badly injured animals.

There were no dead or injured humans to be seen lying about as we ran towards the prison building that we had absconded from the previous morning. As only parts of it were recognisable, the two of us thanked our guardian angels for protecting us in spite of our much-regretted sins. The immediate search among the rubble around and inside the ruin brought a sigh of relief, there being no sign of the

Senegalese guard who had probably run for his life to seek safety in a shelter. Later the casualty list revealed that five people had been killed and twenty-five injured, some seriously. There was no mention of the dying horses.

While Michel and I were sheltering in the hollow of the quarry during the raid, Albin, Tony and Jan had been standing outside the billet, listening for the bombers, searching the sky and wondering if the air-raid sirens were a false alarm. They broke the 200-metre record running for the shelter when the first bomb fell.

We were reunited in our, surprisingly intact, quarters to which they returned after searching for us among the rubble of the prison building. Before explaining our lucky survival, the five of us decided to search amongst the rubble for any casualties that might be buried under the debris. The nearest remains of a building was the sergeants' mess, only half of which was left standing, its roof supported by a remaining wall. The part that was previously the kitchen lay in ruins and from the desolation, we heard a faint cry. Following the sound, it was not difficult to trace the source. The moans came from a kitchen staff airman, still wearing a white coat, which was stained with traces of blood and dirt. His bleeding head and one shoulder was visible, the rest of his body under a pile of bricks and timber. Unsure just how serious his injuries were, Albin ran to find, if possible, a first aid orderly, while we did our best to keep the man alive. First of all we placed what must have been a window curtain under his head and neck. He was conscious but obviously in great pain. While Jan kept him talking, three of us began to carefully remove the rubble from his body, gradually reaching his left side and legs. Exercising great patience in removing the remainder of the debris, we then covered him, to keep him warm. We knew the man, though not by name, and eventually learnt that apart from a severely painful leg, his right rib was hurting. We decided not to move him and the bleeding head wounds were stemmed by use of a handkerchief. Almost an hour went by before any first aid personnel arrived and then, as we could do nothing more, we left the cook in the hands of the experts. Our later enquiries confirmed that his leg had been broken, his other injuries were less serious.

The officers' quarters were in ruins but there was no sign of any dead or injured. We continued to look around the camp, giving help wherever necessary. Later, feeling very tired, we returned to our draughty billet – still with the roof on. Our beds were covered in dust and pieces of plaster and, before they could be remade, had to be stripped and the blankets shaken outside. The rest that followed turned out to be short-lived.

We abandoned our beds in double quick time when awakened by the sound of an aircraft engine and the firing of a machine gun. When outside, preparing to run for our lives, we saw a sleek looking fighter plane with undercarriage lowered and flaps down, trying to land as quickly as possible. It was easy to identify the machine from the roundels on the fuselage and wings – it was obviously a British plane. Those who were firing at it were idiots, to say the least. Fortunately for the pilot, not only were they stupid but, luckily, poor shots as well. The pilot had lost his way and, being short of fuel, was landing at the first airfield he could find. He refuelled, took off again and headed west – it was the first time that I had seen a Hurricane fighter and little did I realise that, before long, I would be flying one, and getting my revenge!

Tony, Albin and Jan told us that chaos had prevailed during the raid, even inside the shelter. The base was, apparently, undefended and no fighters had intercepted the bombers. There was much damage to the camp's infrastructure. Luckily the hangar sustained only slight damage and to our great relief, none of the planes were touched. To make matters worse, the news on the radio was that German troops were in the process of occupying Holland, Belgium and Hungary. Swedish towns were being bombed and close to hand, the French towns of Lyon, Lille, Toulouse and Bordeaux were also being pounded. Britain's capital, London, was also being heavily bombed in spite of the German Air Force sustaining heavy losses at the hands of the RAF. It made me wonder, where was the French Air Force, why were they not, like the British, shooting the enemy out of the sky?

Later one afternoon, when the air-raid siren had sounded, panic stations were quickly activated, but no bombs fell. To our amazement and great satisfaction, a squadron of Curtiss Hawk 75A fighter planes flew over. At last we thought, someone had woken up to the fact that it was time to deny the German Luftwaffe the freedom of the skies. The Hawk aircraft that had just flown over would have been better engaged at a height of 10,000 feet where they could have intercepted the German bombers before reaching such targets as the Avord air base. We wondered just why were they not chasing the Huns.

It was unfortunate that we were crouching cowardly in a hole in the ground instead of flying against the enemy. Besides being scared, we were impotent to do what we should have been doing – chasing and shooting down the evil driven German bombers. Michel and I had been imprisoned for having the nerve to fly over the camp when, as fully qualified fighter pilots, we could have been fighting the enemy up in the skies above. Our non-action was simply helping the Germans. After the bombing raid, the weather was perfect but still no flying was arranged. At Pilsen Aero Club, a pupil who 'pranged' his aircraft was immediately given another plane to fly again and given no time to feel sorry for himself. Had we been allowed to fly immediately after the raid it would have raised our morale.

Realising that we were not under any specific orders, we decided to try and find out what had happened to the Senegalese soldier. We came across a first aid orderly who remembered applying a bandage to an arm lacerated by shrapnel that belonged to a soldier resembling his description. Apparently, apart from a deep cut, he was alright – and had been taken to a hospital to have the wound stitched up.

The following night, the billet was deserted, with the exception of the five of us. Due to the perfect flying conditions those sharing our quarters had decided to find somewhere to spend the night. Our decision to stay was not through bravery – the shelter was only a short running distance away and could be reached before the first bombs could fall. We remained dressed, lying on top of our beds. However, we began to lose our nerve, especially when at 11.20pm, the sirens screamed for the third time. We could hear the murmur of approaching aircraft so lost no time in taking to our heels – heading in the direction of the quarry, down the hill. The bombs nearly caught us out as we started to tumble down the slope – I was hit on the head by some debris, and warm blood ran down my temple. Feeling stunned, I was lucky that Albin came to my aid.

We reached the hollow just in time to feel the blast of a bomb. We lay with our faces pressed into the ground, gradually being covered by the soil up-heaved from the explosion. We looked round to find ourselves in the company of many others taking refuge. They too were scared. One or two, like me, were nursing cuts and bruises. The trees around us had taken most of the punishment. My personal injury was no more than an inch long and, thanks to the handkerchief which Albin had applied, blood was no longer oozing. With some of my gore on Albin's fingers we had become more than just close friends – we were now blood brothers!

It was now May 11th; the bombing was more intensive than on the previous day and lasted just as long. After the sound of the bombers faded, our return to base began. We dreaded what we would find. As everyone rose from the shelter, we noticed, not too far away, an airman who did not move. A gentle prod brought no response and, as we turned him over, we could seen that his neck had almost been severed by a large piece of shrapnel. Nothing could be done for him except the offering of a silent prayer. Like Albin and me, he was no more that twenty years old but his suffering was over – only those at home, waiting upon his return, would be left to grieve.

His friends carried him and when we had climbed to the top of the quarry, where once a French Air Force base had stood, only piles of rubble were now visible. Fires were burning, leaving a huge pall of black smoke spiralling up to block the sun. With strained nerves and an aching head, despair began to take hold. What was going to happen, where could we go from here? What of the future, were the Germans going to succeed in having their way at destroying the world? Were the forces of evil proving stronger than those of good or as I was taught, would good triumph in the end? These were the questions I was putting to myself as I pondered our mission.

As during all the previous day's raids, not one shot had been fired in defence of the base. When eventually we managed to clamber over or crawl under the debris in the direction of our billet, we could hardly believe our eyes. The billet was still standing but with many more broken windows and a hole in the roof at the far end. In this state it was just about habitable and our kit and possessions had survived in the lockers. While getting rid of the broken glass and debris an officer appeared and he expressed satisfaction that we had survived the raid. He ordered us onto the airfield immediately. We tried to reach the hangar by various routes, avoiding the fires and rubble. It was some relief to find the hangar still standing apart from the damage to the sliding doors, which three officers were attempting to open. The gap was barely enough to manhandle the planes out. Instead of being asked to fly, we were ordered to get ourselves to a village called Vilabon and then onto a nearby temporary airfield camp known as St Igny.

We came across a van covered with rubble, there was no ignition key but this posed no difficulty for me. I joined the wires together and then pulled the starting toggle. As if by magic the engine sprang into life. With the remainder of the rubble removed, we drove or manhandled the vehicle for the best part of three hours before arriving at the camp exit gate. Our next objective was for Michel, Jan, Tony and Albin to go off to collect our belongings whilst I stayed with the vehicle. Two more hours passed before they were able to drag themselves over the last hurdle and with everything on board, we set off. The fuel gauge was registering zero so we had no way of telling how far we could go.

Before setting off, Albin produced a preserve containing some kind of fish which had been found in our abandoned billet. A fork to scoop out the contents was also found and this, together with a packet of biscuits and a bottle of life saving Pinard, worked miracles.

On reaching a down gradient in the road, I switched off the engine and allowed the vehicle to coast for at least a mile and a half before it was necessary to restart it. The village of Vilabon was only five miles south-east of Avord railway station so it took no longer than half an hour before we entered the very small settlement consisting of four farm houses which were grouped around a village green. There were barns scattered behind the homely, single-storey buildings. Lazily scratching or nibbling at the grass were some geese and chickens. We left it to Jan to make enquiries as to the whereabouts of St Igny – while details were signalled to us by his gesticulations, I turned the van towards a narrow road that led to a farm named St Igny, from which the airfield camp derived its name.

Reaching the farm, beyond which was a very large grass field, had only taken us ten minutes along a well maintained road. The large barn situated alongside the farmhouse was to be our new billet and we were astounded on entering the building to find that there were camp beds, each one piled with blankets, sheets and pillows. We had fully expected to be met with piles of straw. There was a line of primitive washing facilities at one end and behind a wall; a latrine-type toilet completed the system. In spite of the poor toilet arrangements we thought the facilities better than those we had had at Zig-Zag. It was fortunate to have those misappropriated tins kept in reserve for there had been no mention of food.

I was ordered, with other French airmen, to stand on sentry duty between the hours of 2am and 3am – rifles and ammunition being provided. I felt that it would not be right to complain after so severely criticising the lack of any defence at Avord. Neither could I feel justified in using my wound as an excuse to get out of the duty since there were many with bandaged heads, arms and legs arriving at St Igny. So, obediently, I took my turn of duty shared with a French lad whose company I enjoyed – he was as distraught as I was to begin with.

To be precise, the name of the airfield was Nachent and the so-called base was known as St Igny. The airfield was, in every respect, as good as the one at Avord except for the forest bordering on two sides. The planes and a fuel tanker were hidden at the far end of the field – just what was stopping us from flying? Our opinion was that the Avord station commander was an accomplice of Hitler! A standing guard, with only a rifle or Bren gun and a few rounds of ammunition, was not going to save the base if it was attacked. We urgently needed a few RAF pilots flying Hurricane fighters, or even better, some Hurricanes for us to fly.

But there was no flying on the agenda, instead, if the sirens sounded we were thrown into a state of panic, discord and apathy. Our tools consisted of shovels to dig a hole to cowardly hide in. I thought the whole thing rather a sham – why couldn't somebody wake up to the fact that we had to stop the Germans. It was necessary to fight with all that we had got in order to defend the precious freedom we so desperately sought.

Poor Avord was being bombed again on the morning of May 13th and this time it was the field that was being 'ploughed-up'. The hangar, although the biggest target, was proving to be indestructible – possibly because Albin and I were guarding it from inside one of the holes that we had dug. Our Bren gun and rifles were staying cool, although we were not.

Until May 19th there were frequent soundings of the air-raid sirens but no effective effort was made to raise the morale of the servicemen. The officers were rarely seen except to roster the sentry duties. Some of us were sent to guard the Morane and Nord planes which were hidden under the trees at the far end of the airfield. The planes had been re-fuelled but still we were ordered to defend ourselves from the ground.

I was taken by surprise when Albin suggested that one of us should take the van, still unclaimed and standing behind the barn and drive it to Bordeaux for a visit to the Czech Embassy, to enquire whether there were any plans being made in the event of an invasion. It was a good idea and we decided that Michel, our diplomat, should be the one to undertake the mission after we had had a chance to refuel and check over the van.

The next day a rumour began to circulate that the school was to be moved again, this time to somewhere near La Rochelle. Also it was announced that flying would restart the following afternoon. I flew with an instructor, performing a series of aerobatics in the Morane. Not every manoeuvre I was asked to perform came up to my satisfaction so it was a surprise, on landing, that the instructor did not reprimand me in any way.

The rumours of a move soon became fact when, in typically French style, it was announced that the school would depart for La Rochelle that very next afternoon. Chaos was rife during the hasty preparations as we spent the last evening at St Igny packing our belongings. Saying our farewells to the farmer and his wife, we set off to see if our van was still parked behind the barn – to our utter dismay it was not.

The following day the whole of the school contingent was transported to Avord railway station where a goods train stood at a siding. The wagons reserved for our transportation were cattle trucks, containing plenty of clean straw to snuggle into. Being used to such comforts, there was no reason to complain, unlike the French who did so loudly. "La Vache" was the mildest of their expletives – the rest of them were unprintable.

All of us were provided with tins of meat preserve and plenty of bread. There were several bottles of the never-to-be-forgotten Pinard, which made our feast just about perfect. The train was shunted out of the siding onto a single-line track and moved off at 4.15pm in the direction of Bourges. We waved goodbye to the lovely city and the cathedral, which Albin and I had visited many times. We sat behind the sliding door of the wagon, which was kept partially open as the weather was nice and warm.

As no toilet arrangements had been made inside the wagon, personal needs had to be snatched at various stops. It didn't bear thinking about should any real urgency arise. Passing 'water' through the sliding door gap was possible but anything else became embarrassingly inconvenient. Watching the countryside go by, time seemed to pass reasonably well and it was interesting to note the neatly cultivated and patchwork landscape. I rather liked the French style of small houses standing about as if not much thought had been given to any planning rules. It seemed to be a community which needed plenty of air with space between each dwelling. I wondered if, or how much, the occupants of the houses bothered to concern themselves about Hitler's evil actions which were now threatening the very borders of their country. In all, there were fifteen of us inside the wagon and in order to help the time pass we sang some patriotic Czech songs. Our French companions responded to this by singing too. From the lessons that I had been given on the violin, I concluded that the French singing was far superior to ours – mine in particular. Our approximate calculation of the distance to La Rochelle was about 340 miles and that it would take us the best part of twenty-four hours since there were frequent stops being made. Sleep came easily in our tired state, none of us waking until 6am the next morning.

The worry and strain of what lay ahead left us feeling anxious but we were slightly cheered, when in the morning, the train rolled into the goods yard at La Rochelle. There was a clear view of the delightful town whose western end seemed to jut into the sea, much like a finger pointing at a not too distant island which I later learnt was called Ile-de-Ré. The sea welcomed us with its surface gently vibrating and the sun reflecting on the surface, as if it was studded with diamonds. I was spellbound by this beautiful vista, wanting to believe that such heaven on earth could last. The rainbow-coloured fishing boats danced a jig on the sea, as if to welcome our arrival. Had the boats not been tied up like pets on a leash they surely would have spun round to share our pleasure. There were some fishermen on the quay, unhurriedly working on their upturned dinghies, over which some fishing nets were spread. A gentle tang of fish drifted about to complete the authentic scene. Sadly, in sharp contrast further along the bay, the openly hostile Atlantic Ocean supported several warships. I awoke from my ever so enjoyable trance.

The magic spell ended with the arrival of a large bus into which all of us were packed with our kit. The bus took us a distance of five miles to a camp – La Jarne par la Rochelle. On arriving at the gates we were greeted by the sight of long huts, situated along two sides of the wire fence. These were of the wooden barrack type, the insides of which seemed suitable only for a herd of sheep or pigs. The only consolation was when it was announced that the French Army had repossessed the town of Arras but the significance of this was not at all clear and without any radio or press, it was not possible to confirm any of the news.

The next two days were spent in getting the camp into some kind of order. The weather was perfect and very hot so the inseparable five decided to go for a swim. The nearest cove proved to be just less than three miles from La Jarne. For me it was the first time I had ever been in the sea. The water was quite warm, salty and refreshing. Michel, Jan and Tony entered the water in their underpants whilst Albin and I went in 'au naturel'. Later, on our way back to base, we were subjected to some playful ribaldry.

On the morning of May 24th, we were woken early and to our surprise, told to be aboard the camp bus within an hour, the destination was ten miles east, where flying would take place. It was not difficult to get us out of the uncomfortable beds, and with a quick cold water wash and shave and a makeshift continental breakfast in the kitchen-cum-dining room, we were ready. The airfield at Virson was a large grass expanse with a small hangar, the Moranes and Nords were outside being serviced and fuelled.

Back at La Jarne that evening, we listened to a newly acquired radio. With Holland and Belgium having been conquered, the Germans were now making intrusions into France and a big battle was still taking place around the town of Arras. News of any British involvement was unclear, except that RAF fighter planes were making their presence felt – the Luftwaffe was being challenged. Another piece of late news was that the French General Weygand had taken over as Commander-in-Chief of the General Staff on 17th May; his predecessor General Gamelin was sacked.

Whilst pondering over the news and the war situation as a whole, I still felt that it was out of the question to contemplate defeat. The British were a powerful nation, obliged to help with all their might. Surely the Americans would not let the side down either. The German propaganda, its chief exponent, Dr Goebbels, had announced that, in Hitler's opinion Paris would be occupied by German troops by the 15th of September 1940 – in my opinion that was absolute rubbish!

From May 25th and for the next three days the weather was ideal, so each of us flew at least two hours daily. We would soon reach the required fifteen hours flying time and be transferred to single-seat fighters. We were given to understand that after a short familiarisation with the fighter and some quick gunnery practice, the unit would become operational.

On May 29th, for what reason we could not immediately fathom, our contingent was moved to the village of Virson where a large stable became our accommodation. We returned to the primitive style of living, stuffing straw into some sacking to make a mattress. The pillows and blankets had to be fetched from La Jarne. One obvious advantage of this move was that the village was much closer to Virson airfield. Beside the hangar was a building which became the new dining hall, where the food was only good enough to fatten the nearby farmers' pigs.

In the last two days of May, the weather was perfect and flying was possible from dawn to dusk, almost all in the Nord aircraft. The practice consisted of tight formations and combat exercises; it was very strenuous but just what we had prayed for. The sooner that I got inside the cockpit of a fighter plane equipped with guns, the better! Becoming members of an operational squadron would mean we were closer to achieving our prime objective which was to fight and fight until freedom reigned and we were back home. As the Germans were now well into France, it seemed the message had at last reached our superiors, hence the intensified flying programme.

Once more, we felt let down. The required number of flying hours in the Nord and the Morane had long been surpassed but there was still no sign of the fighter planes. There was no explanation given by the instructors or the officers who were supposed to be in charge. The war news suggested that the situation was getting so bad that the five of us began to lay plans for what we should do if the German Army got too close for our safety. I had not received a letter from Venca for several weeks. News was filtering through that the experienced Czech pilots, stationed at Agde, accounted for themselves well by shooting down as many German bombers and fighter planes as possible. One such pilot, by the name of Frantisek Perina, had been credited with twelve enemy aircraft shot down already.

Bad news seemed to flow in steadily, the latest being that Paris had been bombed in June and the casualties amounted to forty-five dead and 150 injured. Some news did cheer us – the RAF bombers had retaliated by bombing six German cities and the RAF fighters were holding off the Luftwaffe whose bombers and escorting fighters were at last, paying the price for aiding and abetting the Hitler mania. One other piece of significant news was that each of us received 300 francs from the Czech Consulate in Bordeaux, where our promotion to sergeant pilots had been confirmed.

It was not until June 9th that single-seater Morane 225s, with a 450hp engine, were flown in. These were in place of the Morane 220s, on which we had flown many hours and, apart from the dual seating of the 220, were almost identical in design. No guns had been fitted so we could not practise firing at targets. Although fun to fly, they were no match for the German Messerschmitt Me109 fighter with, or without, guns. The following day brought the arrival of Dewoitine 500 fighters with guns supposedly fitted, and we were told that we would be flying these planes from now on. I had obviously been too rash with my recent accusations of apathy!

These planes, which looked as if they had been drawn out of retirement in a hurry, were only available for a quick look before they were pushed under the trees out of sight. They were similar to the Hurricane that had landed at Avord, a low wing monoplane with a liquid-cooled, in-line engine under the cowling. The cockpit, if compared with the Nord, was slightly smaller. The controls appeared easy to understand, including the gun firing button incorporated into the joy-stick and a simple gun sight on top of the instrument panel. The reader will know that I had been impatient to get my hands on a fighter plane but when actually sitting in the cockpit of one I was about to fly, the feeling of apprehension was almost overwhelming.

With no flying on the programme for the remainder of the day, before returning to our stable, we popped in at the dining room and listened to the latest news from 'London calling'. The news was distressing. The Germans continued to hammer the French and British forces on all fronts and the allies were retreating. We viewed this as only a temporary setback as there was also news that the United States had promised to intensify the delivery of war hardware and the supply of food for the British. Much was being said about the 'Liberty' ships being mass-produced in the USA for use by the British under a lease-lend agreement, the terms of which we could not fully understand.

The following morning, June 11th, flying began in the Dewoitines and Moranes and when it was my turn to take up the Dewoitine, a Lieutenant Haget briefed me. He was a bit forceful and I had the feeling that he was tense at the prospect of me flying a single seater, with no dual control. I knew that as he had not previously flown with me, he could not be sure of how good I might be or how steady my nerves were. He shut the cockpit hood over my head, descended from the wing and waved me off, my nerves were as can be expected. To taxi the plane was as easy as with the Nord and, with the pre-flight check completed, and everything all clear on the approach side, I lined up the plane in the take-off direction and gave the engine a chance to demonstrate to me how good it was. It responded willingly and, with the take-off accomplished, I flew for half an hour, in accordance with my brief. In comparison with the Nord it was much faster and about equal in control sensitivity. In order to obtain the very best performance, from man and machine, it would be necessary to fly it for several hours. Nevertheless, I got the feel of the plane and managed to land it in one piece.

Listening to the latest news that evening, we began to wonder just how much longer our flying at La Jarne would go on. The German forces were advancing at an unbelievable speed and were only fifty miles from Paris along the River Seine. Adding to the gloom was news that Italy had not only declared war on France but was attacking Tunis and the Mediterranean island of Malta, both being bombed and shelled by the Italian Air Force or Navy. Their ships were being intercepted by British warships that had inflicted heavy punishment.

During the next two days we flew from time to time, the Morane or the Dewoitine planes which, contrary to assurances, were not fitted with guns. It was therefore not possible to learn how to shoot so should, heaven forbid, the German planes intrude into our airspace, we would still be defenceless. Words failed me and the feeling of anger was, once again, spilling over. At the end of two days flying I had accumulated five solo flights, which were basically just flying as I pleased as no special instruction had been given. It appeared that so long as no one bent any of the planes during take-off or landing, those in charge were happy with things as they were.

Believe it or not, and I definitely did not, on June 14th we were given a day off, regardless of the fact that the weather was ideal for flying. No programme had been made and we were left to our own devices. The Germans were now at the gates of Paris, which was in the process of capitulating, yet there was no outward sign of urgency or concern among those in command. No wonder the Germans were having an easy time in reaching Paris, if things did not change they would soon crush the French forces. The prospect of being captured filled us with alarm since all we could look forward to was a firing squad. The British Expeditionary Force was in the process of being pulled out of France so all in all, things were far too serious for us to be having a day of leisure. Another contingency plan had to be worked out – and fast!

June 16th was the first anniversary of my leaving home. Back then I had thought that one year later the five of us, had we survived, would be back in our Motherland. My reasoning was based upon the lessons that ought to have been learnt from the causes of the First World War. However, according to a statistician's opinion, the allies would ultimately defeat the Germans but the war would drag on until 1944. The latest prediction for the war to end in 1944 was nearly correct – whereas my personal forecast from my diary was wrong by three bloody years and a mountain of tragedies. France, I thought, was strong and capable of stopping any aggressor! The experience we gained since landing at Calais led us to believe that in fact France seemed to lack the patriotic will, leaving apathy to fill the void on an unbelievable scale.

CHAPTER 11

VOYAGE TO ENGLAND

As if to underline my naive prophecy, a year after having left home to fight for my country's liberation from the tyranny of the Nazis, their abhorrent regime had since imposed itself upon five more peace-loving countries and now France too was in the process of being subjugated, its capital city, Paris, already trampled over. Instead of us being able to return to a liberated Czechoslovakia, our survival depended on having to retreat and pray that it was not the end of the world. It was vital for us to search for another platform from which we could launch ourselves into the air with all guns blazing. Our morale was kept afloat by regularly listening to the London radio news broadcasts behind which, at times, was an unbending patriotic voice speaking on behalf of, not just Great Britain, but all who like us had lost the freedom to live peacefully in their own country. That voice belonged to Winston Churchill. It was his voice that beckoned us to escape to England. One way or another we decided that we would get there.

Our highest priority was to ask the commanding officer to let us have five planes, fully fuelled, which, with his approval, could be flown to England. We carefully explained our plan to the CO including our appreciation of the risks involved which were nothing compared to the possibility of being captured by the Germans. Our fate, if caught, would be to face a firing squad. The CO listened with a hard look in his eyes and clenched teeth, it therefore came as little surprise when he angrily refused and ordered our arrest.

He had us locked up in a makeshift cell, originally used as a pigsty. It was a mere hole in the wall; it was filthy and impossible to stand upright. While the door was being locked, one of the ground staff managed to whisper: "Don't worry, we'll get you out soon." Before this could be done, the CO gave orders that the planes were to be de-rigged and loaded onto trailers. It would not have surprised us if later he had made a present of the load to the Germans. When it turned dark, five of the ground staff came to the scene and ripped off the lock, releasing us with their good wishes. It was a very emotional time and I have to confess, without any shame, that I was in tears. Before leaving we received kisses on our cheeks, a custom which we were still not used to.

While we had been incarcerated in the 'hole', there had been an assembly, in which the CO announced that the camp would be evacuated on June 19th and all personnel transported southwards. This meant that we would be heading for Bordeaux which suited us very nicely. In view of the latest news that the French Government had fallen and Marshal Pétain and General Weygand were negotiating an armistice set to be signed on June 25th 1940, there was an extreme urgency for us to reach the British Consulate in Bordeaux. Not wishing to waste time, we decided to by-pass the Czech Embassy. With the help of the kind-hearted French servicemen, it proved relatively easy to hide on the bus, our possessions having already been loaded. We clambered aboard in the nick of time, as the coach was about to move off. I felt that the unseen hand of destiny was guiding us towards our only chance for survival. Our friends in the bus, realising that it would not be stopping at Bordeaux, asked the driver to slow down so that we could bale out.

Once more we had to depend on our wits, stamina and determination to complete our mission successfully. It was somewhat unnerving to see our bus slowly moving away leaving us, to put it mildly, stranded. The south-moving traffic was so dense that crossing the road was positively dangerous. An attempt to do so was tantamount to committing suicide, but I had noticed a couple of abandoned cars on the grass verge on the other side of the road, which set me thinking. There was nothing for it, placing our lives in our hands we plunged in and began to weave through the snarling traffic. Deafened by the blaring of the horns, we forced our way through and the fact that we achieved crossing the road unscathed, justified a prayer. I had a distinct feeling that my companions were doing likewise.

It was early in the afternoon of June 19th when, crossing the bridge into Bordeaux, we noticed two officers in Czech Army uniform. They too, were seeking a speedy exit out of France but were of the opinion that the best way to safety was via Spain. We, on the other hand, were determined to stick to our original plan and found our way into the British Consulate building. Here we found the staff inundated but they were kind enough to offer us tea and biscuits, which was like nectar and helped to steady our overstretched nerves. After explaining in much detail, our plight to them, a long telephone call was made by the interviewer, to someone of influence. As a result, we were told to make haste in getting ourselves to a small harbour named Le Verdon sur Mer, situated some sixty miles north-east of Bordeaux, where the *Ville de Liège* was at anchor. This vessel, due to sail to the Northern Ireland port of Belfast, had been radioed, asking the captain to accept us aboard. After wishing us 'Good Luck', they told us to be on board the ship by midday the next day when it was due to raise anchor and sail. Before hastily departing, we thanked the clerk and asked him to convey our gratitude to the consul.

It was essential to have some food for the journey so we bought two sticks of bread, some butter, a jar of jam, a cheap knife and a bottle of wine. We were also in need of some means of transport. I told my friends what had gone through my mind earlier when I saw the abandoned cars and it was judged to be a good idea as there was no time to waste. Tony was left sitting in a café minding our kit, whilst the four of us hastened back over the bridge to where I had seen the two vehicles parked at the side of the road. As luck would have it, the two cars were still there – the one of most interest to me was a Peugeot which had the driver's door ajar.

On gaining access to the engine and luggage compartments, I found some tools or at least a screwdriver and a pair of pincers, which were to prove very handy. Even more useful was a piece of bare wire wrapped round the tool sachet with which I was able to connect one end to the positive lug of the battery, scratching at the negative terminal with the other. This simple test produced a bright blue spark proving that the battery was charged and had not been the cause of the breakdown. As there was no ignition key in the switch, I wrenched the two connecting wires from under the dashboard and joined the two bare wires together. With a quick pull on the starter lever the engine turned over. I removed the distributor cap to inspect the ignition contacts, scraped both of them with the screwdriver and adjusted the gap. Finally, removing the carburettor float chamber, I found it to be full of petrol, which proved that the petrol pump had not failed. Before re-assembling the carburettor I took the main jet out and blew it clean. Finally, after cleaning the ignition cables, distributor cap, plugs and ignition coil, I decided it was time to find out if all I had done was sufficient to get the engine going. One further check on the radiator water level and all was set. After a couple of presses on the accelerator, I pulled the starter cable. The motor whined, I gritted my teeth; the engine fired, spluttered for a moment and then revved up and, with the off-side wheels of the car being on a grassy slope, it was necessary to turn the car round to face the bridge. With a lot of heaving by Albin, Michel and me – at last a firm grip for the tyres was gained. Wasting no more time, Michel, the most experienced driver, got behind the steering wheel and we drove off to collect Tony.

He was very relieved to see us! Albin was sent off to obtain some water to top up the radiator and after a final look over the car we all climbed aboard, setting off westward looking for a road sign that indicated either 'Lesparre-Médoc' or 'Verdon sur Mer'. On the outskirts of the town we stopped and sent Jan to make some direction enquiries to set us on the right track. In spite of these directions it took some time before we found the correct road.

Against all odds, we reached the village of Verdon at 2.30am and were surprised that at such an early hour in the morning there were crowds of people milling about and a little café doing a roaring business. After finding a suitable spot to park the car, whose loyal performance was never to be forgotten, we finished off the food, washed down with the remaining half bottle of wine.

Refreshed after a short rest we walked to the end of the pier where, in the clear air we hoped to make out the silhouette of our ship. There were many people, like us, straining their eyes over the water and having enquired as to the name of a vessel that was at anchor – the answer was *Ville de Liège*. Much relieved, we went to the car to collect our few possessions, then returned to the pier where we were greeted by chaos and abusive arguments among the crowd. Jan understood that most of the discord centred on who should be the first to be taken to the ship by the liberty boat which was apparently due soon. There were women and children being hustled about and, wishing to be spared the anguish, we walked off the pier to one of the harbour slipways to look for an alternative means of getting to the ship.

Having become accustomed to the darkness and able to discern a large block of wood looking rather like a raft floating at the end of a rope, we pulled it towards us and on closer inspection, became confident that it would serve our purpose. A square of tarpaulin hanging on a hook and two pieces of wood that could be used as paddles completed our immediate requirements. Our kit was carefully wrapped and tied to the raft by the mooring rope and after removing our boots and socks our 'boat' was ready to be launched.

Initial progress was made from under the pier with the help of the outgoing tide. We paddled very quietly at first but as soon as we thought ourselves to be out of earshot, the pieces of wood plus our hands were agitated to a state of frenzy. Our paddling towards the shadow of the ship accelerated when the air-raid sirens turned our fury to utter fear and dread as bombs began to fall close behind us. The flashes from the explosions illuminated the ship, which proved to be further out than we had thought. The bombs turned the bay into a mass of froth but there was no time to loiter and we paddled so fast that when the ship's plate rivets came into view we hit the ship's side so hard, that everyone aboard must have thought that a bomb had struck. Rope ladders were dropped down and before any of us could say a word, sailors were down the ladders to heave us and our kit aboard. Had there been an atheist amongst us this was surely the time for searching to the depth of his soul. I knew that my grandmother was right beside me!

By the time we had recovered our wits, many of the ship's crew had surrounded us and some people in civilian clothes arrived to enquire just how we had reached the ship and where we had come from, these people having arrived on board before nightfall. Whilst we were trying to give explanations, the circle around us suddenly parted at the arrival of an officer with gold stripes on his tunic sleeves. The ship's captain introduced himself to us five 'scruffs' in French Air Force uniforms. He expressed his pleasure on meeting us and later autographed my diary – giving his name as Rolf Isachsen of Harshbad, Norway. He gave a New York address as 33 First Place, Brooklyn.

The *Ville de Liège* was not a passenger liner but a cargo ship designed to carry livestock, such as horses or ponies from Ireland to France. Our accommodation was in one of the bays that would normally have been occupied by a horse but was spotlessly clean and straw and blankets had been provided. Having put our boots and socks back on, one of the ship's crew escorted us to the galley where some food was placed before us. There wasn't time to see what we were eating but whatever it was, it tasted delicious. After the meal we returned to our 'horse-box'.

The dawn of Thursday June 20th was accompanied by the arrival of dark clouds and a steadily increasing wind, the noise of which was being overpowered by loud crying and very uncivilised shouting from on board an approaching liberty boat. A second boat was not far behind, both of them packed so tight that the water line lay very close to the gunnels of the boat. As the first one arrived at the ship's side, rope ladders were dropped over, each one supporting a crewman whose outstretched arms assisted a cargo of misery on board.

The ship's crew manhandled the women and their children amidst growing hysteria – some women tearing handfuls of hair from their scalps, having somehow lost their children at Verdon and some their husbands. Their grief was understandable but when one or two tried to throw themselves overboard they had to be restrained. At a later stage, some women were reunited with loved ones whilst others were not, their screaming incessant. These unfortunate mothers would not, or could not, accept the possibility that their kin may have been victims of the night bombing raids.

We remained available to help where or whenever it was needed – comforting the stricken was one of our tasks, at which, by sheer patience, Albin excelled. The depth of suffering endured by those women has remained with me to this day and will certainly do so until I die. One of the liberty boats was hurriedly hoisted whilst the other returned to the harbour quay to look for any lost or late arrivals. That boat did not return.

The air-raid sirens wailed once more and while the bombs rained down the ship sailed out of the harbour where it was attacked, not only by the bombs but by the cruel sea as well. The almost clear sky and light breeze that had assisted us to the ship, changed to a strong wind that drove us mercilessly towards the next port of destiny.

Apart from the ship's officers and crew, the cargo consisted of seventy-five soldiers of various nationalities, twenty-five civilians who were aboard when we were hoisted up, and those arriving in the morning boats added another fifty-eight souls. The total number of persons aboard was almost double that which the captain had originally agreed to take. Just how the ship's cook, in his small galley, managed to keep us alive was a miraculous feat. The captain and his crew deserved medals. The food, whilst strictly rationed, was very good and served with tea or water to drink.

The captain, in his wisdom, directed the helmsman to alter the ship's course every half an hour in order to avoid detection by German submarines. When the ship was beam-on to the huge waves, it rolled so badly that almost everyone aboard felt like dying. The force of the storm did not abate and there was no indication that we could expect a break. In more normal conditions with average weather it would have taken no more than two days to reach Belfast but owing to our 'zig-zag' routine, it was estimated that it would take twice as long. The situation on board was of some concern to the captain when some of the passengers became ill. However, the first-aid-trained crew and a Jewish doctor passenger managed to contain the spread of influenza and the doctor found some tranquillisers, which helped to soothe those who were in so much distress.

The five of us, feeling the physical and mental strain, were more concerned as to what lay ahead of us in England. Would we be seen as traitors or cowards for running away from France? Would we be accepted into the Royal Air Force as pilots? Apart from the lack of firing practice, we thought of ourselves as good fighter pilots and were ready to fight. Was our inability to speak English another mountainous obstacle? What did the British know about the Czechs? It was only a year ago that Prime Minister Neville Chamberlain had handed Czechoslovakia over to Hitler as an appeasement.

Near Arras in France is situated a Czechoslovak military cemetery, containing graves of Czech nationals who laid down their lives during the First World War. Amongst the graves stands a time worn stone into which is carved "Crécy 1346". This simple memorial commemorates the war fought between soldiers of the English King Edward III, against the army of King Philip of France who fought alongside his cousin, a Czech king, Jan of Luxemburg. He was known in the West as Jan the Blind. King Jan was killed during the ensuing battle in which the English beat the French.

History reveals that the English prince, known as the Black Prince (Edward lll's son), when walking among the slain and wounded after the battle, found King Jan's body alongside which lay King Jan's helmet, bearing the crest made up of three Ostrich feathers, together with the motto – 'ICH DIEN' (I SERVE). Out of respect and admiration for King Jan, the Black Prince adopted the crest and motto, incorporating them into his Coat of Arms such as is still worn today by HRH Prince Charles.

It is also on record that the Czech Crown Prince Charles, whose father Jan was slain at Crécy, fought in the same battle and was wounded. In accordance with his status he was rescued from the battlefield and became the Bohemian King Charles IV. On learning that an English prince had adopted his father's crest, friendly links were forged between Bohemia and the English. Fourteen years later, in 1382, his daughter Ann sat on the throne with the King of England, France and Ireland – Richard II. His wife became much respected and well known as Ann of Bohemia. At the time of the wedding, in order to strengthen the bonds of friendship between England and Bohemia (now the Czech Republic), a treaty was signed: amidst the text was the following:

> "I Richard, by God's favour, King of England, France
> and ruler of Ireland, salute all as affected by this
> document."

To this day that treaty and commitment to defend against aggression has not been rescinded.

Michel, with tongue firmly in cheek, began to chuckle whilst saying: "As the treaty has not been revoked, we Bohemian descendants ought to be entitled to offer our services to the King of England in these perilous times."

It was on June 22nd 1940 that an announcement came over the ship's radio that all Czech pilots stranded in France were to, one way or another, make their way to England; we breathed a collective sigh of relief. Such information proved that we were on the right track – well ahead of the lagging, official line. A day later, enveloped in a thick fog, the 'slow ahead' speed that was ordered did not worry us unduly – we were prepared to wait as long as it took for the Royal Air Force to accept us to fly alongside them towards the ultimate victory.

The following day, the weather turned so rough that some of the mothers and children became petrified; we moved our bedding nearer to them and literally held their hands. There were some who could speak French and after telling them that we had endured much worse sea conditions than at present, they calmed down. Albin and I took to caring for one mother who had a boy of five and a daughter of eight and when I told her that photography was a hobby of mine, she presented me with a tiny 35mm Lumier camera, insistent that I have it; and to Albin she gave a scarf.

By Monday June 24th everyone aboard the ship, including our own charges were looking decidedly happier and even more so at the sight of the Irish coast with the vividly green grass fields stretching towards the shore. Thereon, good progress was made towards the harbour at Belfast where the anchor was lowered early in the afternoon. For the first time since boarding, everybody was on deck.

It did not take long for five blue-uniformed officials, actually Royal Naval Police, to come aboard. Just what they were searching for we were not to know but after a quick look over the ship and a chat with the captain, they departed, with some of the passengers following. Among those who disembarked were the women who, suffering from complete exhaustion, were helped off the ship by Red Cross nurses and some ever-willing crew. Watching from the deck, we saw them ushered into waiting ambulances.

All those remaining on board were provided with a substantial hot and tasty meal with a choice of drinks. The children, who during the rough passage from Verdon, had not been eating very much, were now offered all they could manage to eat. They were spoilt by the ship's crew who acted like fathers, giving them chocolate and other delicacies that were not available previously.

The important duties completed, and with the food, drink and the ever so peaceful surroundings soothing everyone, the captain made the announcement that sometime that evening the ship would sail for Liverpool where everyone aboard would be allowed to disembark. After the information over the ship's loudhailer the captain came down from the bridge, walked among us, and shook everyone's hand, paying particular attention to the children. He spoke French and English as well as his native tongue. Not a single word of English was yet engraved on my brain and Jan, Michel, Tony and Albin were similarly deficient.

When the captain departed, the Jewish doctor and a group of other men and women climbed up to the bridge. We had no idea what motivated them to do so and when the five of us were also summoned to the bridge, we wondered why. We were ushered into a lounge and brought before the captain – who days earlier, had placed his illustrious name and address in my diary. He shook our hands and said – in French – that he had been pleased to have us on board his ship during the voyage and how much he, and his crew, had valued our help during the difficult circumstances. Overwhelmed by his praise, we told him that we considered ourselves to be very fortunate to have been allowed aboard and taken such good care of. The captain mingled with all his guests, making sure of introductions, the doctor offering a particularly firm handshake. One person in the party, speaking to us in perfect Czech, happened to be a famous pianist – his name was Lampel. Later on I asked him to sign my diary, he gladly obliged by writing a short musical score (see opposite), under which he wrote – "This was how the sea hummed to my friend and pilot, Frantisek Mares, we have arrived, we will succeed!"

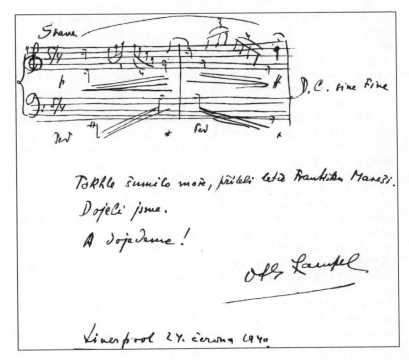

That evening of June 24th, the anchor of our ship – *Ville de Liège* – was raised and the last leg of our tumultuous journey from Verdon in France to Liverpool in England had begun. We let our strained nerves and limbs relax and mental tiredness took over. Curling ourselves up in our straw nests, separated by a couple of hanging blankets from 'our Mum' and her two lovely children, sleep came almost instantly. At 10am we woke up to find the ship was gently wallowing at the end of a massive chain cable and moored just outside the harbour of Liverpool.

On the west side of the mouth of the River Mersey was a lighthouse, standing ahead of another town called Bootle. The river was busy with incoming and outgoing ships of all sizes navigating past us with eager efficiency. There was some smoke hanging over Liverpool but the air that we breathed was fresh and warm. Our thoughts at this time were much the same as had bothered us over the past year – yet another challenge was beckoning. Somehow though, I had an uncanny feeling of confidence that from now on, our progress towards joining a fighter squadron would be efficiently handled. The RAF would be ready to enrol us into their ranks and a Hurricane was already waiting for my company.

This confidence was reinforced when it was announced that a

smaller boat was on its way to take us to Liverpool harbour where we would disembark. It arrived at 8.30am on June 26th and the speedy efficiency of our transfer impressed us. It was carried out without any shouting, only expert and courteous handling was evident. Those who were unable to walk the narrow gangway, which had been lowered between the two ships, were given assistance. Captain Isachsen and his crew cheered us on our way.

When everyone was safely aboard the boat that was to ferry us to Liverpool docks – we were either accommodated inside the saloon or, if preferred, on the deck. The two vessels then parted. Our vessel executed a very proficient 180° turn without any audible commands reaching our ears – as if the crew communicated by telepathy.

The transfer from the ferry to English soil was a very emotional experience as was my first sight of two British policemen, who, we learnt were affectionately known as 'Bobbies'. It was just about 11am when these two 'Bobbies' guided us around a corner where a group of soldiers was waiting for us. Those among our group, who were unable to walk, stayed behind at the dock and were probably moved to a hospital. Three buses parked at one end of the square, took us to a railway station which was so near that it could have been reached on foot. The unhurried, courteous way we were being dealt with since our arrival in England was a world away from the chaos we had endured in France where no one seemed to be in charge. In France we had felt as if we were held in limbo all the time – quite different to the efficient and dignified way of getting things done in England.

In Liverpool, the handling of our arrival, disembarkation, the transfer to buses and trains, was carried out as if we were part of, or perhaps watching, a silent movie. The thought came into my mind that perhaps after all it would not matter that I could not speak or understand the English language – communication, here in England, was by means of telepathy! It was something that the more volatile and demonstrative Europeans would have to get used to. When I came to fully appreciate and understand the reserved attitude of the British – known as a 'stiff upper lip' – I realised that the more temperamental Czechs were overdoing the gestures of appreciation, albeit sincerely felt, and were in danger of being called a creep, or in more diplomatic terms, patronising. Please let me assure my readers that my fond appraisal of the British came straight from my heart.

The journey by train from Liverpool took us mainly through built-up areas. Small parcels of open country were either cultivated or laid down with lush green grass. Our destination was unknown so whether we would be surprised or disappointed would be revealed upon our arrival. Our growing curiosity was satisfied after three quarters of an hour when the train stopped at a small station from where, after a short bus ride, we arrived at a large green field covered with tents. Some tents were already occupied, mainly by uniformed men who were standing around, expressing their curiosity as to what sort of refugees were spilling out of the buses. A large number of them were Polish whom we were able to understand and we had no problem identifying those of Czech origin. One of the tents, designed to accommodate six servicemen and their kit, was assigned to the five of us, leaving some room to spare. Inside we found a pile of blankets, enough in fact, to keep an Eskimo warm in an igloo. Whilst we were attuning ourselves to our new surroundings, the canvas door was drawn to reveal a British Army officer. He spoke excellent Czech and, after welcoming us to England, he enquired whether the facilities were acceptable and gave us the news that a stay of only one or two nights was planned before being moved on to a camp with more civilised facilities. Without waiting for our reply he indicated a building, standing at the edge of the field, and said: "Over there you will find a room where you can freshen up before going to the restaurant to have some nourishment." Looking at his watch he added: "It is almost 2pm, please make sure that you are back here by 4pm when further instructions will be given." The meal provided was hot and very tasty, and was followed by a bowl of stewed fruit under a thick layer of a creamy substance – called custard. The first course was later identified as a steak and kidney pie, which as time went by, became my favourite dish.

With the feast over, we had a spruce-up in the washroom before taking the long route back around the field perimeter, and talking on the way to some of the uniformed Polish soldiers; some of whom displayed wing badges which indicated they were pilots or aircrew members. They too had suffered some hard times in getting to England and, like us, were relieved to have arrived. The stories that were related by a few of our Czech compatriots were very similar to our own experiences although their route had been via Spain or from ports further south than Verdon. Everyone seemed thankful to be in Britain after the calm and reassuring reception.

We arrived punctually back at our luxury detached tent, awaiting further orders. The same Czech-speaking officer introduced us to a blue-uniformed man who requested to inspect all of our possessions. Making an apology, he explained that everyone entering the country from abroad, whether arriving by boat or aircraft, had to declare any items that duty might have to be paid on. It took only a few minutes for him to cast his keen eyes over our precious items which included the small (spy-like) Lumier camera that had been presented to me aboard the *Ville de Liège*. Nevertheless, with a "Thank you – that is all", he departed.

The shape of the facilities that we were making use of, suggested to me that it might be a sports centre and this was later proved correct when I was told that it was the venue for horse racing. It went by the name of Haydock Park. I was anxious to discover the name as it was this piece of land that formed my initial bond with Great Britain. My first close encounter with British civility and the broad-minded ability not to humiliate made an enormous impression on me. Despite our dishevelled state, our treatment was as dignified as one could wish for.

The customs inspection over, the Czech-speaking English officer explained that the stay at Haydock Park was intended to be brief – if it was at all possible we would depart the next day. He was aware of our wish to join the RAF and he told us that acceptance was only a matter of formality. Sensing traces of doubt in our eyes, he left, only to return with an RAF officer whose uniform had wings sewn over the left breast, under which were some ribbons. With the help of our translator, the RAF officer confirmed that there was no doubt about us becoming pilots in the RAF and, subject to us taking a conversion course in flying, it would not be long before we joined an RAF squadron.

These assurances were so convincingly delivered as to leave no trace of doubt in our minds – at last we were confident that our mission to take a viable part in liberating our country was within reach. That night we slept, no longer dreaming of our worn clothes but of being dressed in the RAF uniform with the pilot's wings and sergeant's stripes sewn on, brass buttons with the royal crown on each, shining brilliantly. We did not even wake to the sound of the high flying German bombers or the dense anti-aircraft guns firing at them. Our sleep was that of babies, blissfully happy in the arms of their mothers with not a worry to disturb their innocent minds.

The following morning, feeling refreshed and with our minds and bodies rested, we queued for access to the washroom before enjoying a breakfast at the restaurant that was worth waiting for. A message came that everybody had to attend an assembly at 10am in the centre of the field. The weather was brilliant, the warm sunny rays doing their best to evaporate the remaining traces of diamond-like dewdrops. The assembled company were divided into cultural groups, each under the charge of an English officer with an interpreter.

Albin, Tony, Michel, Jan and I, along with our other compatriots, totalling twenty-one persons, were all acquainted with the Czech-speaking officer. The purpose of our segregation was in order to speed up the necessary documentation process. We had not been issued with flying logbooks in France so, in order to assess our potential as pilots, all our past flying experience had to be written down. Every detail was recorded. Once the meeting was over we spent most of our time queuing for meals, none of which were to be missed. Those in charge did not leave us in the dark; more information was provided before we retired to our canvas abode that night. Subject to all the arrangements being completed, our transfer to another camp was due to take place without further delay; probably by 3pm the following day. Just to keep us well in the picture, we were also told about a bombing raid that had taken place during the night, 'somewhere' in England.

True to the promise, our departure from Haydock Park was by bus to Liverpool railway station where a train was waiting for us to board. A very comfortable compartment was allocated and, no sooner had we settled, then the journey began. Upon leaving the city that had been so welcoming, fond memories were engraved on our minds, particularly the English Army officers and the men who had taken so much care of us at Haydock Park. Our faith and our optimism, which had been at a low ebb when we arrived, had been fully restored. Any remaining doubts that we did have were dispelled by the hope that the train was heading towards a RAF airfield where fighter planes, with loaded guns, were just waiting for five eager Czech patriots who had a thirst for vengeance on the Nazis coursing through their veins.

We were told that our immediate destination was a camp by the name of RAF Bridgnorth, it was left to our own speculation as to whether it was a flying base or not. The duration of the journey was five hours, including two changes of train. Although we had eaten before setting off, by the time we arrived at the base we were a bit peckish. Once more, we found the native population very friendly. As we waited for our bus at the station several civilians offered us cigarettes.

The camp was a large one with many timber huts, all arranged in rows. Inside they were spotlessly clean, containing bed frames with springs, and a mattress made up of three sections, with blankets, sheets and pillows neatly arranged on top. Other furniture consisted of lockers, a table and chairs. Along the corridor were doors leading to flush toilets, a wash room with separate cubicles for baths and showers. There was even hot water. A luxury indeed! Like the living quarters, everything was clean and ship-shape. After freshening up we walked to the mess for a meal where everything looked so tidy, I could perhaps have been excused for thinking that we were at a holiday camp.

Much to our joy, our Czech friends who we had met from time to time since crossing the Czechoslovakian border into Poland occupied some of the billets. Among those I recognised were Venca Slouf's brother Karel and also Mirtl, Jilek, Koukal, Fishera and Benes. Mr Benes was the very man that I had flown in a Praga Air Baby from the Pilsen Aero Club, in order to drop his message over the town of Klatovy. He, with others, had arrived in England from Bordeaux or Agde and each had their stories to tell.

Spending a holiday at Bridgnorth, England was not what we had sought when escaping from our homeland, however. Though very appreciative of having such an easy time at the camp, we desperately wanted to be in on the action. Having failed in France, here in England there would be no more retreating as the British were obviously determined not to give in. The RAF fighter pilots were in the forefront of the effort and the British prime minister, Winston Churchill, roaring like a lion, was warning Hitler that from now on he had to deal with the British – a very resolute, peace and freedom loving people who, if necessary, would fight to the last man or woman.

In the evening, with permission granted, Albin and I, needing to clear our heads, walked into the town of Bridgnorth. It had been built on both sides of the River Severn with the houses, as if on display, on the slightly rising ground. It was past 6pm and there were not many people about – all the shops were closed and their windows were all criss-crossed with tape as a precaution against flying splinters, should a bomb blow them in. Since our arrival in England we had become used to the clean and tidy conditions and Bridgnorth was no exception – a homely place and undoubtedly worthy of fighting for. People in the streets gave us friendly smiles and wished us 'Good Luck' although, at the time, we could not understand what they were saying.

After the first comfortable night of sleep since staying with Madame Fournier in Paris, we breakfasted and then answered a call to assemble on the camp square. The Czech-speaking officer informed us that on the following Monday we were to be moved again to a place called RAF Innsworth in Gloucestershire where RAF uniforms would be issued. The Czech contingent was to be issued with shoulder-flashes that would read 'Czechoslovakia' and those of us who had been promoted to the rank of sergeant in France, would retain the same rank in the RAF.

Once again, the subject of when we could expect to start flying was diplomatically avoided yet, we felt that to doubt the integrity of our informants by asking further questions would not have been the ideal thing to do at this time.

On Sunday June 30th, preparation for our scheduled departure the following morning was unhurriedly carried out. The need for this move had not been adequately explained but we thought that someone, sitting in an office somewhere, completely unaware of the urgencies that existed, was wielding a pen as if a baton – the resultant orders were impossible to comprehend and generated a waste of time and valuable resources. The word I was seeking was 'bureaucracy' – if only I had an English dictionary!

Albin and I, in need of some relief from the time-wasting drudgery, set off to pay our last respects to Bridgnorth. At a cosy pub, a couple of beers acted as a tranquilliser to pacify our troubled minds. Another glass of beer arrived at our table as if by magic. The waiter refused to take our money and indicated our benefactors. By raising our glasses to them they understood Czech!

The morning departure from the base was carried out in the customary super-efficient British manner. A bus took us to Bridgnorth railway station for a pleasant journey of one and a half hours before arriving at Gloucester. We reached the camp after a thirty-minute walk, to find that the place was still under construction. This was Innsworth and, by the look of it, it appeared to be almost a replica of the camp we had left some two hours earlier. To tell the truth there was very little to complain about except, perhaps, not being offered a second helping of the very tasty meal; that would have been very much appreciated. Thereafter the company was divided into two groups of potential fighter or bomber pilots, navigators, observers and gunners etc. The five of us gave thanks to providence at being assessed as fighter pilots and were directed to our billet – Hut 36.

CHAPTER 12

FLYING WITH THE RAF

Settling in at RAF Innsworth was easy and apart from some regular assemblies, which I took to be a military discipline training requirement, and the start of lessons in English, we were well fed and generally spoilt. In spite of the holiday-style life at the camp, the 'ungrateful five' were getting very impatient. There were frequent air-raid alarms, which resulted in German bombs dropping very near by; the explosions reverberating in our eardrums. The flashes of the explosions during night-time raids and the burning fires which followed made the clouds above glow red in anger. Surely, I felt, this evidence of the savagery of a raging war should prod those responsible for action into hastening our applications to fly with the RAF. We were ready, able and very willing to fight – to the death if necessary, preferably to the death of our common enemy – Hitler's Nazis.

I would have swapped all the present comfortable living conditions for a barn full of straw and a chance to fight, and I knew my companions felt the same. My prayers were for my thoughts to be read and acted upon so that we could get on with the task we had set ourselves when escaping to England. Hopefully the bureaucracy would cease to offer promises that were not being kept.

Yet another parade was called, this time to appease a group of high-ranking English, Polish, Belgian and Czech brass, so it was obvious that my messages were not getting through! The purpose of the assembly was not really explained – if only it was to give us our 'wings' we could make haste to then prove such an action was a right decision. A rumour was spreading that our president, Dr Eduard Benes, now exiled in London, was to pay us a visit, preceded by a visit of a Major Berounsky who was the former military attaché at the Czech Embassy in Paris. All he brought with him was another pile of promises: that three Czech fighter squadrons and one Czech bomber squadron were to be formed in England, but it did nothing to excite me at all.

All I wished for was to serve with the RAF pilots in an RAF squadron – and the sooner the better. Michel had previously been promoted to officer rank which bugged me as I felt that as a sergeant pilot I would fly just as efficiently as if I had been a pilot officer. Promotion had to be earned and to do this the enemy had to be fought. Yet, a discord amongst us would not achieve anything. The major did tell us that it was proving very hard to get released those Czech nationals who were serving in the foreign legion in Africa. At least we were fortunate not to be in that situation.

On July 12th it became evident that our entry into the RAF was being seriously considered, when all of us were obliged to undergo psychological tests. I began to wonder if the necessity for such testing was due to my being considered too enquiring or of a distrustful disposition, or even unstable. These self-generated suspicions were quickly dispelled with the announcement that I was acceptable for entry.

Finally my prayers for some action were answered. Nineteen of our contingent were told to attend the stores to collect our RAF uniforms. We responded to the order at the double and were issued with brand new gear including underwear, but were told not to wear the uniform until officially instructed.

My lethargic optimism gained some impetus with the 'shrink' examination, the issue of a uniform and now the news that the potential RAF pilots amongst us were to be given a thorough medical check-up, which was to take place at RAF Uxbridge. Gathering all our kit, nineteen of us left RAF Innsworth on Thursday July 18th in a truck, which took us to the railway station in Gloucester. Despite three changes of train our journey was in comparative comfort, reaching London early in the afternoon. With time to spare before catching the Uxbridge train, the 'five musketeers' wandered outside the station just to see what London looked like. What little could be seen looked old, quaint and welcoming. With Albin as my close companion we stood on the corner of two streets where I offered up my grateful thanks to whoever had been listening to my past pleas for help.

Later that afternoon, having arrived at RAF Uxbridge, a meal was provided and rooms allocated for the night. The medical probing began. I was inspected from the top of my dark curly hair to the tips of my toenails. In between there was some prodding which proved to be either embarrassing or ticklish. It took three hours to evaluate my health and that of my companions before the medical expert's conclusion was announced. Although previously very confident that I would have no difficulty in passing as 'A1', the final announcement still came as a huge relief. Tony, Albin, Jan, Michel and I were declared fit and ready to fly.

That evening, after another satisfying meal in the mess, we decided to acquaint ourselves with the streets of Uxbridge before retiring for the night. We soon found evidence that a merciless war was being waged against Britain when we noticed a large gap in a line of houses. The roofs and windows of the adjoining properties were also badly damaged, some had been hurriedly repaired. Contrary to what one might expect, the people we saw in the streets did not look downhearted but were busying themselves as if in defiance of the maniac responsible for such tragedy. My immediate thoughts were for vengeance on their behalf.

After another comfortable night and an unhurried breakfast we were driven to the railway station at Uxbridge, where we were ushered into a reserved carriage. Some vague information had reached us that our destination on this occasion was RAF Cosford, which would be our last posting before being sent to an air station at which our flying training would take place. Much to our surprise, we did not go directly to Cosford but stopped at the RAF fighter station at Duxford where, once again, we became objects to be registered with yet more papers placed on our records. The idea that we had come to Duxford to fly was quickly dispelled although we derived some small satisfaction at the sight of Hurricane and Spitfire fighter planes taking off and landing at frequent intervals. I touched the planes on the ground and was encouraged to sit in a cockpit, so for me at least, the trip to RAF Duxford was worth while. Whether I would end up flying a Hurricane or a Spitfire did not bother me unduly, both had many guns fitted, a meaningful gun-sight and a firing button on top of the joystick. Our general observation led us to believe that the majority of pilots at Duxford were officers so, to meet some non-commissioned pilots in the mess, was an honour, especially when they treated us to a drink.

The admin office confirmed to us, on the following morning, that all nineteen of us would be put on a train and taken to Wolverhampton and thence to the RAF base at Cosford. Having no idea what assignments awaited us at Cosford, we could not understand why our presence at Duxford was to be so short lived. I impatiently asked for further explanations and added: "We are getting rather concerned that this is the fourth posting since our arrival in England." The officer to whom I addressed the question looked down on my impertinence. The translator appeared embarrassed when uttering: "You will definitely start flying at Cosford or a station that you may be posted to – please believe me." I did my very best to look like a believer.

With our kit now swollen by the addition of the RAF uniform which, so far, we had not been allowed to wear, and with each one treasuring a neat parcel of food for the journey, we boarded the train. While the wheels of our train rolled ever onward I began to be concerned with what might be awaiting us at Cosford. Would flying be on the agenda, if not, how much longer was it going to take?

On reaching Wolverhampton, a short ride by bus brought us to our destination, a very large camp indeed. We arrived at 6pm. As we had come to expect, the transfer from the bus to our allocated billets was accomplished with the help of several friendly souls in RAF uniforms. While the accommodation and facilities at previous camps had been very good, by comparison RAF Cosford was the 'Grand Hotel'. Our room had adjoining facilities which included a large swimming pool and a cinema. Our reception was both friendly and dignified.

Our appreciation was openly expressed and sustained until being handed over to some Czech officers who were based at the camp. Remembering their Prussian-style, we promptly obeyed their military orders. No sooner had they taken charge when one of them confiscated my Lumier camera. I was aggrieved that it was never returned to me. There became frequent and unnecessary assemblies on the camp square with meaningless speeches given by one or other of the Czech officers. The crowning occasion was a speech, delivered by a visiting Czech general whose misguided mission was to cheer us up. He announced that those of us who held commissioned rank in the Czech Air Force would retain that rank on enlistment into the RAF – the remainder of us, including the sergeants, would have to start life in the RAF as AC2 (Aircraftsmen 2nd Class). Before he could finish he had an uprising on his hands and it was only his luck that saved him from leaving the base unscathed.

Monday July 29th 1940 was my twenty-first birthday, and I realised that in all the time since I had escaped from my rightful home, from a subjugated country, where my parents and all those living in parts of Europe were being trampled on by the Nazis and the evil-inspired Gestapo, my resolution to succeed had remained unshaken.

The day of my birthday also brought me a reminder of how fortunate I was to have four loyal companions, especially Albin. He was good for my, at times, angry disposition, and remained patient and philosophical. He sensed how my birthday was affecting my mood, and remained close by. That Michel was pining for Madame Fournier was evident by his saddened eyes. Jan remained Jan, and Tony was the nicest friend to be with except when drinking too much, which was as frequent as temptation came his way.

An earlier rumour reappeared and took hold, that a visit by President Benes, was imminent. This was confirmed when our panic-stricken top brass ordered a general 'spruce-up' of ourselves and the billets. We were told that an inspection would be carried out during the following morning – Friday August 9th – and to expect our president to arrive at about 3pm. He would address us from a podium, which was being erected in the centre of the parade ground.

There was no need to remind us to show respect and to please our president – it was our natural instinct. The billets sparkled; not a speck of dust was missed. Everyone was ready for inspection well before the time of his arrival. We managed to cut each others hair and presented ourselves as a very trim outfit, our French uniforms cleaned and pressed, and our patriotic hearts beating in step as we marched to the centre of the large parade ground. When I began to sing a rousing song, everyone joined in the chorus.

Our president emerged from a large service limousine, while all on parade continued singing and then suddenly, without a word of command, we sang the Czech national anthem – "Kde Domov Muj – Kde Domov Muj" – "Where is my home? – Where is my home?" When the Czech national flag was hoisted to flutter alongside the British flag, I felt honoured to be in England.

Afterwards, the president, in company with high ranking British and Czech officers, took the salute as we marched past, then stepped down and bade us form a loose circle around him. He spoke honestly about matters everyone was most anxious to hear and willingly gave answers to many pressing questions. I entered a few of the president's words in my diary as follows:

> "I am absolutely convinced that England will not lose the war. It will not be easy, every effort will have to be used and sacrifices made. The war will become very fierce in 1942; great battles will be fought over and across the English Channel, mainly on French soil. Your presence in Britain is valued, of that you can be confident. There exist historical ties between England and the Czechs – Bohemian links remain unbroken. Please have patience; your turn to serve your country has now come here in Britain. I wish you good luck."

After his address he moved amongst us, listening carefully to what we were concerned or unhappy about, promising to consider all the points and to see what could be done to resolve the matters bothering us. As with his dignified arrival, he was cheered on his departure.

From our point of view, life at RAF Cosford returned to unacceptable normality. Some of our group of pilots who had more experience than us, began to receive postings to either Fighter or Bomber Command, Jan was among them. Our morale was uplifted only to sink again as the four of us remained.

Whenever it was permitted to leave the camp, Albin and I made excursions to the town of Wolverhampton. The town centre, marked by a statue of a knight on a charger, was uncluttered and the streets wide, and full of grand old buildings. There was a population of 45,000 and when we narrowed these down to a selection of young ladies, our visits became very interesting. It was worth going to town as often as time and money would allow. The young ladies' interest in us must have been enhanced by our best uniforms, which had been specially tailored in Paris. The sergeant's stripes, two pilot's badges and our peaked caps, worn at a slight angle, must surely have made us more attractive to them.

Flirting with pretty girls helped to quell our impatience at not getting posted. We rejoiced when we learnt about the successes of the Czech pilots already serving in RAF squadrons, scoring victories against the enemy. The Battle of Britain raged above our heads and there were frequent soundings of air-raid sirens and bomb explosions followed by the glare of fires.

On the last day of August 1940, an unforgettable, extraordinary event occurred when Albin and I were in Wolverhampton. Looking into a shop window was an elegantly dressed and attractive looking woman, accompanied by her teenage daughter. When the lady spoke to us, neither Albin nor I could understand a word she said on account of her strong Scottish accent. We understood her name to be Mrs Cousins and her daughter's name was Mary – it was not only the accent that stumped us but to be addressed in the street by such a gracious looking woman. Had Albin or I been able to speak perfect English, the occasion would still have rendered us speechless.

Mary was conscious of our bewilderment and rescued us from our embarrassment by slowly re-introducing herself and her mother. With the use of a few words that were familiar to us, we understood the word 'come' and the wave that indicated – 'follow us'. They had a black Hillman Minx car only a short distance away. With mounting excitement we could not refuse the invitation to join them.

A journey of no more than ten minutes brought us to their Tudor-style house standing in an exclusive area of the town. The surrounding garden was nicely laid out and well maintained. It was not until we entered their home, which was furnished and decorated to match the elegance of our hosts, that Albin and I had the manners to introduce ourselves. Delayed or not, the gesture was accepted by two welcoming smiles. Apart from the interior elegance there was a feeling of homely comfort. It was not long before Mary managed to loosen our tongues which, supported by gesticulations, soon had a flow of communication going on between us. Feeling more at ease we were encouraged to have our very first English afternoon tea, the contents and presentation were certainly an eye-opener.

Mr Cousins arrived in time to join the party. A medium-built man with light brown hair and the bluest eyes I had ever looked into. He too, was elegantly dressed in a dark brown lounge suit and, noting his soft hands, I could tell he was not used to manual work. Like his wife and daughter, he made us feel at home and it became absolutely clear from this first encounter that their home was, for the duration of our stay in Britain, ours also. As days passed into months, months into years, their friendship remained strong right up to the time of their deaths. My diary contains much more about them, all of which is unforgettable.

When Albin and I decided it was time to leave, there were protestations from our hosts but Mr Cousins decided to take us back as far as the bus station, or so we thought. In fact he had other ideas. Belonging to a golf club that was more or less on the way to Cosford, Mr Cousins proudly introduced us to several of the members there who were propping up the bar. Drinks were generously offered and gratefully accepted. On the large billiard table a game of snooker was being played and it fascinated me. I had a notion as to how billiards was played but was not conversant with this new game. With the passage of time, I learned to play, becoming quite good at it, to the extent that I could eventually beat Cliff Cousins. We eventually returned to our Cosford base at 9pm in a carefree mood.

On September 1st, yet another assembly was called for the thirty-five sad souls that still remained at our camp. Our immediate response was one of unwillingness but when we learnt that an English officer was in charge, our apathy turned into keen interest. The assembly hurried into place and formed a smart and orderly presentation just like a short stretch of railway track. Three airmen marched towards the assembly and stood to attention behind the officer. The airman in the centre carried the Union flag, which fluttered above his head, and we soon realised that an important and serious function was about to take place.

With the aid of an interpreter, we were required to repeat that we swore our allegiance to HM King George VI – we did so willingly. From that solemn moment on, we became members of the Royal Air Force and were entitled to wear the uniform. Furthermore, those of us who had been promoted to sergeant pilot in France would retain this rank, entitling us to wear the appropriate stripes. Before the order for dismissal was given, the officer congratulated us and affirmed that our days at Cosford were numbered. A posting to flying duties was anticipated before the end of the month.

In no time at all, our sergeant's stripes were sewn on as well as the Czechoslovakian 'flash' on top of the sleeve. When this was done, we packed away our French uniforms and made our way, in accordance with the standing invitation, to Wolverhampton. The Cousins family was pleased to see us again but saddened by the prospect of us leaving Cosford so soon, to what we hoped would be an engagement with the enemy. We left our French uniforms with them.

When I received a letter from Venca, who did not reveal his whereabouts, all of us who knew and respected him were cheered by his news. He wrote that he was a proud member of 242 Fighter Squadron, which included several Canadian pilots whose skill he praised. The squadron was commanded by the now legendary Squadron Leader Douglas Bader, who walked and flew wearing false legs and who was the most inspiring and courageous pilot he had ever met and admired.

Top left: Frank's father.

Top right: Frank's mother.

Bottom left: Frank age fourteen.

Bottom right: Tomas G Masaryk – President 1918 to 1935.

Top: Zamyšel – where Frank lived until aged six.

Bottom: Làny – the president's summer residence.

Top: Much to learn in so little time. Frank third row back, fourth from right.

Bottom left: Truth Triumphs.

Bottom right: Frank's first girlfriend, Jarka.

Top: A Praga Air Baby at Pilsen. The type Frank flew in with Mr Benes.

Bottom left: Frank's flying tutor at Pilsen, Mr J Rais.

Bottom right: The author's good friend from Pilsen, Squadron Leader Venca Slouf.

Top: National service in the Czech Air Force – Hradec Kralove. Frank second row, third from left.

Bottom left: The unforgettable Albin Nasvetter.

Bottom right: The *SS Kastelholm* – making good their escape from Poland.

Top left: Frank's French identity card.
Top right: Frank in French Air Force uniform, aged twenty.

Bottom: A Hanriot Trainer, the type that Frank flew at Bourges.

Top: In the French camp, Frank first left, back row.
Bottom left: Vive la France. A 'Thank you' presented to Mme Fournier.

Bottom right: Stetka, the fundraising diver.

Top:
Airacobra
aircraft of 601
Squadron.

Middle:
RAF uniform.
L to R: Joe Pipa,
Venca Slouf,
unknown.

Bottom:
RAF parade.
Frank third
from left.

Top: President Eduard Benes visits an RAF station, accompanied by his wife.

Middle: President Eduard Benes inspecting the RAF parade.

Bottom: Duke of Kent visits 601 Squadron based at Northolt.

A selection of photographs featuring
the author during his time with 601 Squadron.
Finally flying Hurricanes, he seems to be
having a bit of trouble preparing to scramble!?

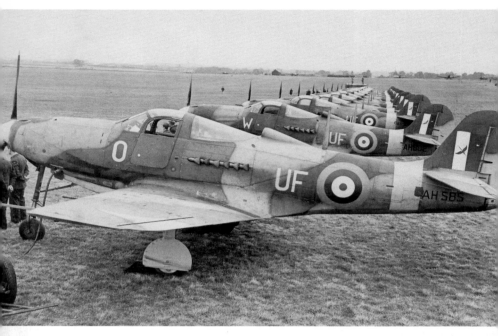

Top: 'Look nice but no sting in the tail.'
American Bell Airacobra AH576.

Bottom: Spitfires on their way to escort the
RAF's bombers. How many will come back?

ADMISSION

000041

NO. 601 COUNTY OF LONDON
(FIGHTER) SQUADRON
AUXILIARY AIR FORCE

A

SQUADRON DANCE

WILL BE HELD AT

TOWN HEADQUARTERS

54, KENSINGTON PARK ROAD, NOTTING HILL, W.11

ON

1 DEC 1941

Left and below: Despite the intensity of war, there was always time for relaxation.

Bottom left: Frank's very good friend Cliff Cousins.

Bottom middle: Mrs Cousins and her daughter Mary.

Bottom right: The Cousins family home.

Right, inset: 312 (Czech) Squadron's crest: 'Not Many but Much'.

Middle: A Spitfire of 312 Squadron taxiing at RAF Harrowbeer.

Bottom: Harrowbeer ground staff re-arming a Spitfire of 312 Squadron.

Top: On standby at RAF Bolt Head.   *Bottom:* Flight Sergeant Mares presented with the DFM.

Above: Frank's logbook with a personal note from his squadron leader.

Right: Frank's logbook and medals. Clockwise from top: Distinguished Flying Medal, Czech Military Cross, French Air Force Pilot's Wings, Czech Air Force Pilot's Wings, Czech Medal for Gallantry.

Other news included the loss of four Czech pilots during the recent air battles with enemy fighters.

The radio told of the horrendous news that London was bombed for five successive days and nights. Although being badly mauled by RAF fighters, wave after wave of German bombers were inflicting dreadful damage and on September 11th 1,500 people were killed and over 3,000 injured. Other awesome news was that RAF bombers were now retaliating by bombing Berlin where innocent civilians were paying the ultimate price for the deeds of their mad leader and his Nazi followers. I hope that I may be forgiven for repeatedly mentioning the distress that the bad news brought to those of us who remained inactive at RAF Cosford. Anguish and anger are indeed bad companions to share life with. The RAF was suffering heavy losses of precious pilots and planes whilst I, for one, if given the chance, was ready to unleash my pent up anger upon the enemy – "Oh gran, please stir things up and do something about it." These prayers were finally answered on September 26th, just when the last vestige of my patience was exhausted and the anguish was unbearable.

My gran must have stirred up a hornet's nest because our departure was so immediate that there was no time to pay a visit to our adopted English family. The train we boarded left at 11am for RAF Benson in Oxfordshire. When passing through Birmingham, the sight of the damage by indiscriminate bombing was the worst that I had witnessed so far. While I am easily motivated to anger, deep inside I am truly sensitive and the evidence of the cruel world I saw through the windows of the train brought tears to my eyes.

A brief halt of the train allowed us an opportunity to admire the historical university town of Oxford but our momentous journey continued until the small town of Wallingford welcomed us with a quiet grace. We then stretched our legs by walking to a waiting RAF bus. The approach road ran along the full length of the airfield. Behind a boundary fence, the aircraft were aligned and awaited us patiently; their sleek bodies glistened in the afternoon sun, some being tended to with engine cowlings undone. The bus leaned to one side as we all jostled in our seats and craned our necks to see them.

The bus, now trimmed back to a normal attitude, passed through the main entrance gate to RAF Benson, and came to rest besides a long, two-storey building that was to become our sleeping quarters which, only the day before, had been vacated by some Polish airmen. After following instructions to freshen up, we walked across the parade ground to the sergeants' mess to have a late lunch of sausages, chips and baked beans followed by something covered by custard – and finally a cup of tea.

After a short rest the sergeant who was taking care of us suggested that we might like to look over the planes; the larger of which, from the

bus, I took to be Hurricanes but were later identified as Fairey Battle Ts
– a converted trainer version of the light two-seat bomber. The smaller,
low wing monoplanes were Miles Magister basic trainers and I had not
expected to fly these but I was proved to be wrong!

Our next task was to attend the administrative building to repeat what
we had already done at previous RAF stations; to give all our personal
details including all those specific to our past flying experience. Lastly,
we eagerly visited the stores building to be issued with flying suits,
helmets, boot, gloves and jackets. By now we were hungry and returned
to the sergeants' mess for another meal and to make the acquaintance of
others in the lounge. Later, feeling tired by the events of a crammed full
and memorable day, our optimism was at its peak and we returned to our
billets for the last necessity of the day – sleep.

The following morning, at an assembly on the parade ground all the
new arrivals were officially welcomed by the station commanding
officer who, after the formalities, spoke to us individually to explain
why we had been posted to his station. He listened to our questions and
was obviously sensitive to our patriotic enthusiasm.

The next formality was that our group became split up between the
three squadrons. We had no choice in the matter and I was allocated to
a squadron together with Novotny, Dubec and Dolezal. The rest of the
Czech pilots, including Albin, were divided between the other two
squadrons. With that sorted out, the instructors explained the purpose of
our being at RAF Benson. It was to undergo a short familiarisation
course in getting used to flying in England and how to handle the
planes; the Fairey Battle in particular. The course also included use of
the R/T (radio/telephony) which was something we had not been
familiar with. It was most important that we understood the flying
discipline and strictly obeyed it.

We now found ourselves, one by one, being seated in the aircraft
whilst the instructors explained the position and function of all the
controls, the instruments, operation of the radio and the sliding hood.
During a briefing-room session, with an interpreter present, the plane's
characteristics came under review, consisting mainly of take-off,
climbing and cruising speeds; as well as the speeds at which to lower
the undercarriage and operate the flaps. Finally, the stalling speed was
given and we were told how the aircraft behaved in a spin and during
the recovery. Finally there was an open discussion with questions
eagerly asked and answered – the translator being in great demand.
Before dismissal, we were informed that the weather forecast for the
next few days was as good as could be wished for and that the flying
programme would commence early the next morning.

Back in our billets, and all in an excited mood, we spent the time
checking and trying on the flying clothing; fitting the earphones into the
helmets; the microphones and the oxygen tubes into the face masks

together with radio-socket connection cables. The rest of the evening was devoted to a study of the plane's instruction manual, committing to memory the concise explanations, the photographs and diagrams.

Like the previous morning, our impatience was rising. We had a quick 'splash' followed by breakfast in an otherwise empty dining room and then flexed our muscles by heaving two Fairey Battles out of the hangar. Whilst waiting for the instructors we sat in one or other of the planes, performing imaginary take-offs and landings. My instructor was a Pilot Officer Fisher DFC, who was about twenty-five years old with stern looking eyes, softened by a thin face and a smiling expression. His voice, whilst not dictatorial, was one to be listened to and obeyed. After a suitable introduction he said: "OK, let's see what you can show me." He remained standing on the wing, leaning over to watch me carry out the pre-engine start procedure. This was a discipline that had, by now, become second nature to me. Before giving the all clear to press the starter button, he climbed into the seat behind me. I began to feel my heart rate stepping up a beat as he said: "OK, let's fly."

Permission to taxi, line up and take off was granted by the flying control tower over the R/T so, with the propeller pitch set at fine, I opened the throttle to its fullest extent. By the feel of the controls I knew the instructor was not taking any chances and was holding onto the dual control. With the wheels off the ground, which I remembered to retract, I raised the flaps when at 300 feet. I was then given a 'free hand' for the rest of the flight. Use of the radio seemed strange at first but the voice of flying control was reassuring. It was even more so when flying solo and later, during operational flying, a lifesaver.

Gently climbing, the Rolls-Royce Merlin engine was purring sweetly – but my feelings of confidence were jolted by the voice of the instructor through the earphones, telling me to level off at 1,500 feet, I obeyed as soon as the altimeter indicated that height. From thereon I enjoyed myself during the flight, comparing the Battle with the Dewoitine that I had last flown in France. The sensitivity of the Battle's controls was about the same as the Dewoitine's. Capable of cruising at 200 knots, it was a little bit faster and generally easier to fly. I landed – wheels down – strictly on my own, and the instructor seemed satisfied. The entry in my logbook for my very first flight over England read:

> 29.9.40. Fairey Battle No.R7380 – P/O Fisher/Sgt Mares
> – Dual – 1 hour.

The following morning, the weather obligingly remained perfect; I flew with the same instructor in Battle R7406. During the forty-five minute flight I carried out various exercises including the vital recovery from a spin and a stall.

Without further ceremony, my instructor sent me off on a solo flight that was sheer bliss and a just reward for having had to wait impatiently for so long. I was given an hour to float around the sky, so I flew near the town of Oxford as if to offer it an assurance: "Here I am to protect you." More solo flights followed. Detailed to practise the spin and stall recoveries, I was very tempted to perform the forbidden flick-roll, instead I did an ordinary slow-roll. Not satisfied, I repeated the roll until pleased with the result.

After my initial solo flights at RAF Benson, intensive flying followed each day and there was no time to feel discontented. All flights covered the use of the R/T and its procedures, together with formation and instrument flying, some with an instructor but mainly flown solo. By October 11th, our training at Benson was complete, having flown fifteen hours in the Battle; one hour forty minutes in the twin-engined Avro Anson V5672 with a Squadron Leader Soames; and one hour fifty-five minutes in the little Magister – a flight that was to prove noteworthy.

On the very last day of the course there was a short assembly at which the station commander thanked us all for our diligent flying, above all, for not 'pranging' any of the planes. He then said that one trainee, Sergeant Mares, who had, upon arrival made it quite clear that he wished to become a fighter pilot – nothing else would do – would, at 2pm demonstrate in the Magister, just how good he is, adding: "I shall be watching." To say that I was shocked would be to put it mildly.

At 2pm precisely, obeying the order to fly the Magister, I climbed to the prescribed 3,000 feet during which time I composed myself and decided upon the sequence of aerobatics that I would perform. The entry and recovery from a spin was easily accomplished. A loop and a barrel-roll followed, also successfully, however during a following loop I ran out of the necessary speed when in the inverted position. The dirt from the cockpit flew past my head; I was prevented from following by the seat straps. The controls not responding, I thought that the world had toppled over. The over-used saying: "There I was, upside down, nothing on the clock" had been especially tailored for me. The conclusion to my predicament was decided by Mother Earth's gravity; neither the plane nor I had any say in the matter, we just fell out of the sky. The training I had received in Czechoslovakia, France and in England had taught me how to recover from 'unusual attitudes' so I still managed to execute a safe landing. When I reported back to the station commander, expecting to be stripped of my rank and shot, he was laughing his head off. Recovering his composure at last, there was no expected reprimand but a shake of his hand. What he said was hard to discern through the laughter but I did hear the words "Fighter pilot!"

Our friend Jan had somehow contrived to get himself posted from RAF Cosford to RAF Duxford and was sadly missed when, on 14th October, the remaining four of our group were posted to 6 Operational

Training Unit at RAF Sutton Bridge. This station was situated some four miles south of the Wash and there my first dual flight was in a Miles Master (an advanced pilot training aircraft) powered by a Rolls-Royce Kestrel engine. The instructor for this thirty-minute flight was Flying Officer Down. The next thirty minutes I flew solo in the Master. This was deemed sufficient to send me up in a Hurricane fighter number L1601. After a flight of forty-five minutes, which I had spent months waiting for, the instructor briefed me to take off again and climb to 25,000 feet to become used to breathing oxygen, which had to be turned on at 9,000 feet. It took one hour and ten minutes from take-off to landing. Apart from the natural difficulty experienced in speaking into a microphone at that height, everything went smoothly.

CHAPTER 13

OPERATIONAL AT LAST
WITH 601 SQUADRON

The very first time that I saw a Hurricane fighter at close range was at Avord in France where one had made a forced landing. It had British roundels on the wing and fuselage. I was drawn towards it as it was being refuelled, with an uncanny feeling that it was not the last time I should see such an aircraft. Had I been able to speak English I would have spoken to the young RAF pilot who was impatiently waiting to fly back to his base – provided that in the meantime, the Germans had not occupied or destroyed it.

My premonition was that the Hurricane and I would, in the future, become as one. This proved to be correct from the very first Hurricane flight that I made at RAF Sutton Bridge. Somehow a bond was formed; the characteristic behaviour of the plane suited my nature. Generally, the Hurricane's performance was dependable yet, at times, when pushed too hard it would display a temperament. If properly harnessed however, it would secure a victory or survival during combat.

The scheduled operational course of ten days was condensed to a ruthless training programme in order to turn out a future fighter pilot. There was not a single day that we did not fly; even bad weather was not allowed as an excuse to ease off. It was at Sutton Bridge that I learned to shoot 'from the hip' and 'fight like a dog' – savagely. Formation and instrument flying also figured very prominently on the course. My instructor, Flying Officer Down, gave me another thirty-minute check flight in a Master and then, both flying Hurricanes, we performed a simulated combat. He taught me sufficiently well that I managed to 'shoot him down', my reward was a pint of beer. From Flying Officer Down I also learnt the importance of using the rear-view mirror which was mounted at the top of the plane's windscreen, the instructor's advice was: "Use it properly and it will save your life – it is not there just for you to admire yourself."

On the eve of our posting from RAF Sutton Bridge came the tragic news that our Jan had been killed whilst flying a Hurricane at RAF Duxford. It was not hard to understand that the four of us were shattered by the announcement. When the posting details arrived, Albin and I were unfortunately sent to different operational squadrons. This was upsetting but there was nothing that we could do to alter things – we made a vow to keep in touch with each other and with our family at Wolverhampton.

My flying logbook showed that a total flying time of thirty-one hours and thirty minutes had been achieved at Benson and Sutton Bridge. The record of training was countersigned by the station commander and the flight commanders, bringing my fighter training to an end. I did not have to wait long before being told of my and Michel's posting to 601 County of London Auxiliary Squadron which was based at RAF Exeter. The squadron, 'licking its wounds' after being decimated during the Battle of Britain, was short of serviceable planes and badly in need of some fresh pilots.

At last, I had become a fully trained fighter pilot, ready to fulfil the promise I made to myself, to my country and at RAF Cosford to HM King George VI. From now on there was some serious flying to be done.

Michel and I duly reported to the CO of 601 Squadron, determined not to show how tired we were after such a long journey. It was late in the afternoon of Sunday November 10th and a warm welcome awaited us at the dispersal hut office. Though our English was still very rusty, we got the message loud and clear from the strong handshakes and the often repeated words of 'welcome'. I was assigned to 'B' Flight, Michel to 'A' Flight and told that none of the flying personnel were billeted at the base but dispersed amongst private homes in the nearby city of Exeter. Our hosts turned out to be Mr Petherick, a Lloyds Bank manager, and his wife Christine.

My new squadron was one of the RAF's famous auxiliary units, formed back in the 1920s at RAF Northolt, just north of London. Its first CO, Lord Edward Grosvenor, had been able to pick his own officers, so these tended to come from the 'well-to-do' of the time, young men with time and money, as well as a sense of adventure. These weekend gentlemen forged a solid bond however and although in some quarters they were sometimes referred to as the 'Millionaire Squadron', they had nevertheless done well in the first year of the war. Of course, by this time, most of those early officers had long since left but had been replaced by similar young men; men like Max Aitken, the son of Lord Beaverbrook who was the Minister of Aircraft Production. Then there had been Willie Leefe Robinson DFC, the son of a First World War VC holder. He had been among the last to die in action in September 1940 just before 601 Squadron was withdrawn for a rest. His brother-in-law Richard Demetriadi, son of Sir Stephen, was lost over the English Channel in August. The American anglophile, Billy Fiske, had died in August also, landing back after being terribly burned in combat. He had been the son of an international banker and captain of the US Olympic bobsleigh team, as well as driving in the Le Mans race when just nineteen years old.

These and others like them had now passed into history and 601 Squadron was becoming a different type of squadron. One might say that they were letting anyone in – even me! However, we knew we had a tradition to follow. We would do our best. For the moment the squadron was a 'C' Class unit, pulled out of the front line in order to rest and to train new pilots. While it remained operational, no more than a quarter of its pilots were deemed as such. The rest of the pilots were still training but we gradually became operational as either the CO or his two flight commanders considered a pilot ready to join the rest of the nucleus.

My new CO was Squadron Leader Sir Archibald Hope who had succeeded his father as the 17th Baronet of Craighall in 1924, when he was just twelve years old. He had learned to fly with the Oxford University Air Squadron and had signed up for the RAF in 1931. It was not surprising that he joined 601 Squadron, considering its penchant for having the famous within its ranks.

As if to emphasise the training state of the squadron after we had joined it, several accidents befell pilots within days of our arrival. On November 21st, Pilot Officer Jimmy Hoare-Scott crashed about half a mile from the airfield soon after taking off. Four days later Sergeant Erik Hetherington just failed to clear a small but well camouflaged car sitting at the edge of the runway and broke an undercarriage leg. However, he made a well executed crash landing without hurting himself. Erik later found fame over Malta but was unlucky to die in a Liberator crash at Gibraltar in 1942 whilst on his way home for a rest. Then on November 28th, Sergeant Johnson, whose flaps were not properly down, overshot on landing and put his Hurricane onto its nose but he was not injured.

The regular transportation to and from the base was by a camp bus or a large Humber station wagon – the latter taking us directly to the house where our hosts were expecting and waiting to welcome us. Mrs Petherick ushered us into a large twin bedroom, the comfort of which exceeded our expectations. We were provided with food at the base but there were times when Christine's hospitality could not be overlooked. On the rare occasion when flying was not possible, Mr and Mrs Petherick showed us places of interest in the city which included an opportunity to pray at the cathedral. During a visit to the Guildhall, the Lord Mayor's chain of office was placed around my shoulders. As well as being introduced to their friends, an opportunity to fraternise with a few young ladies, of their choosing, provided a pleasant distraction.

My first flight as a 601 Squadron pilot was on Wednesday November 13th 1940, consisting of practice formation flying for two hours. The CO, as well as the flight commanders, deemed this to be a priority in view of their experience during the Battle of Britain. Training flights were vital and up to four hours every day was spent in putting into practice all that we needed to know. There was much fighting to be done before the Germans could be defeated, therefore the CO was making sure that the squadron remained a potent adversary. We flew regardless of the weather. I was learning fast, from those who had survived so far, how to beat the enemy in the air, shooting down Nazi bombers or fighters or even strafing them on the ground.

The experienced pilots demonstrated their skill to us in the air, and on the ground I became a compulsive listener as they proved time and time again that they really knew what they were talking about. To make sure our English was up to scratch an old fashioned, hand-wound, gramophone was provided and on it we played a specially produced record. All the vital R/T procedures and messages were repeated until we clearly understood them all such as: 'vector' (course), 'angels' (height), 'bandit' (enemy aircraft) and 'bogey' (unidentified aircraft); all vitally important. The word 'scramble' did not have any connection with the preparation of eggs but, to pilots in operational readiness, it meant moving as quickly as possible from the dispersal hut to our own particular Hurricane fighter in order to take off and chase the bandits. The vector and angels were transmitted to us from the operations room by those 'guardian angels' in uniform, the indispensable WAAFs (Women's Auxiliary Air Force).

The very first operational scramble that I was involved in with 601 Squadron at RAF Exeter was as a member of 'B' Flight, flying at the rear of a 'V' formation led by Flying Officer Whitney Straight, an American and confirmed anglophile, who had seen service in Norway and the Battle of Britain. He was soon to add the DFC to the MC awarded him in 1940. He later became a famous name in RAF history. Our task was to intercept a bandit, so we climbed as quickly as possible on a vector of 260°. The visibility was good with a broken cloud ceiling at just over 6,000 feet. We had just about reached that height when the leader shouted over the R/T: "A bandit ahead, Tally Ho!" and began to give chase. The enemy aircraft was a Junkers 88 flying at some 1,500 feet higher than us and heading south-east. Spotting us, the enemy pilot opened his throttles and dived for safety in the clouds beneath. Our pursuit turned out to be a failure. During the chase, some of it in the clouds, our formation split up and when I emerged I found myself alone in the sky. I descended to below the cloud base and began to circle looking for my squadron of Hurricanes and to establish my position. Neither of these two objectives were achieved, I began to panic, telling myself that I had failed my flight leader and the squadron.

By continuing to circle I became disoriented and on looking down, the ground appeared strangely desolate. A sense of shame overtook my common sense and I stubbornly refused to radio my base and simply ask for a course for home. Much to my relief, when descending through a hole in the clouds, a coast line came into view which enabled me to establish that my position was now over the southern fringes of Dartmoor. I was happy to realise where I was but still ashamed of letting my flight commander and the squadron down. I imagined that they were still chasing the Junkers – and may even have shot it down; whereas I was thinking about setting a course for my base. I searched the area for another twenty minutes hoping that I might be able to reunite with my flight but my petrol gauge was indicating that it would be a good idea, regardless of how I felt, to return to land without further delay. After obtaining permission to land, I decided that there was no other choice but to face my flight commander. Parking my dear Hurricane, I offered it my humble apologies. I entered the dispersal hut, fully expecting my squadron mates to turn their backs on me, instead of which they all seemed in awe, waiting to hear the heroic deeds that I might have performed. The flight commander, instead of issuing a reprimand, praised my tenacity for chasing the enemy for so long. Apparently, they had given up the hunt twenty-five minutes before I had.

Thereafter, the training flights gave way to operational flying which was in response to scrambles or to escorting bombers across the channel, continuing until the squadron was moved to RAF Northolt. Having flown a total of fifty-one hours on Hurricanes, my reputation untarnished, I was a happy member of 601 Squadron.

Squadron Leader Hope left the squadron in December 1940. Our new commanding officer was Squadron Leader John Anthony O'Neil, who always signed himself as Anthony. He was twenty-five years old, had already been in the RAF for five years and had started the war as a bomber pilot flying Armstrong Whitworth Whitleys with 58 Squadron. He had flown a leaflet raid over Germany on the first night of the war and had remained with his unit until June 1940. He had then become OC Flying at the Central Landing (Parachute) School at RAF Ringway and was decorated with the DFC for his work with Bomber Command. Squadron Leader O'Neil was very welcoming to the Czech arrivals, which was in contrast to the Prussian-style of our former pre-war Czech commanders. His only concern was for our sad lack of English, he seemed to have no doubts about our abilities as pilots. I imagine he knew that as soon as the squadron was ready it would be leaving RAF Exeter and returning to 11 Group at RAF Northolt. I remember two things about him. First he was a good organiser; second, he really kept us busy with constant formation and other flying practice; almost to the point of exhaustion.

To transfer a squadron from one base to another is a complicated undertaking, requiring expert planning and execution. Whilst it may have seemed to some pilots that a move happened as if by magic, I took nothing for granted and remained very impressed by the whole process. It was not simply a matter of fuelling the Hurricanes and flying them off to the new base. The squadron adjutant and his capable (usually WAAF) staff, in liaison with the station commander, the squadron commander, the flight commanders, the technical officer and the highly efficient ground crews, were busy long before the squadron took off. This hive of activity, which included the loading of equipment and stores, was done quietly and kept, as much as possible, under wraps by the intelligence officer.

The squadron pilots were spared the worry and concern of these vital procedures but they remained on operational duty, ready to scramble and intercept or chase any intruding enemy aircraft. The Hurricanes were always in a fully fuelled and serviced state regardless of the impending departure to RAF Northolt. On the morning of Tuesday December 17th, the whole squadron, with spare aircraft, some of which were brand new, set course for Northolt. I was flying one of the new planes. The flight was being treated as an operational sortie, all the guns were loaded, primed and the firing button catches well oiled. Our destination was on the western fringes of London, the approach to which was easy to find except that great care had to be taken to avoid the menace of hundreds of barrage balloons tethered to the ground by steel cables. Avoiding the maze of steel wires, we made our approach via a 'corridor', something that we all had to get used to and respect, especially in bad visibility or at night. In these situations, our survival was entirely dependent upon the uniformed 'angels' in the operations room to guide us down.

As the squadron aircraft took their turn in obtaining permission to land, I felt proud indeed to be a fully operational member. The unit was fully restored to its efficient fighting capabilities, including the supporting officers and ground crews. The flying crews, led by a very capable CO, consisted of a couple of Australians, three Canadians, an American – the first to join the RAF – one Nigerian, the Czechs and of course, the English, Irish and Scottish nationals, all of whom were proud to constitute the mainstream of a British squadron.

A safe landing at RAF Northolt had brought us to an old and well established base that was steeped in aviation history. All its facilities, whether technical or personal, were the very best and buzzed with meaningful proficiency. The sergeants' mess contained an accommodation block in which Michel and I were housed; and we found it well up to our expectations. When the air-raid sirens sounded their alarm – it was as if to warn the Huns: "Beware, 601 Squadron has arrived – keep clear of our sky or be shot down." That they stayed clear on this occasion made it a memorable day.

Just as if we had never left RAF Exeter, the next morning the order was to take off in three formations of four and climb to just below the clouds to form into flights of six planes. 'A' Flight and 'B' Flight would enter the clouds on different vectors in order to practice the skill of formation flying in cloud. With this very demanding exercise fulfilled, the order was to intercept each other at 8,000 feet above the clouds, relying on radio guidance from the ground. Being guided down through the clouds to end up precisely in line with the 'balloon corridor', was really exhilarating and a very prudent practice to get us used to flying in and out of the base via this narrow flight path. Sufficient warnings not to take chances were received when several pilots had collided with the cables and consequently lost their lives. It was essential, particularly in bad weather, to obey the flying controller's instructions, thus for the next couple of days, similar training was continued.

From thereon, each squadron sortie was an operational mission but without a close encounter with any enemy planes. The exception was when we took part in an operation – codenamed 'Circus' – over Calais and Boulogne. The objective of a 'Circus' was to provoke the Hun into coming up to fight but only a few responded, resulting in the loss of one Messerschmitt (Me)109 which was shot down by a member of a Spitfire squadron. The 'Circus' consisted of three squadrons, including 601, who formed a 'wing'. Much to my disappointment, I had yet to prove my combat skills.

On Christmas Day morning 1940, Michel and I were not rostered on duty, and after an especially good breakfast, we returned to the billet to write some letters and for me to update my diary. I had heard no news from Albin or Venca, so I wrote to both of them as well as the Cousins family at Wolverhampton. Michel's concern was for Madame Fournier so he wrote a letter to her. Another year had passed since Albin and I had prayed for peace in the cathedral at Bourges and the prospect remained very uncertain. At this, the second Christmas away from home, I began to feel homesick.

Since arriving in England and the start of flying training at Benson, Sutton Bridge and Exeter, I had been kept very busy with my efforts to become a fighter pilot worthy of the RAF. Now, with 601 Squadron in particular, there was little time for reminiscing. However, this Christmas Day, at RAF Northolt, with no flying pending, felt strangely unreal. Outside the billet there was no sound of take-off or landing aircraft or even any engines being tested. There were no air-raid sirens giving their warning of approaching enemy planes – even the wind was giving itself a rest. Michel, sitting at the table, had a writing pad in front of him just waiting for his pen to put his thoughts down on paper. In spirit he was not in my company – I was alone, shouldering the heavy burden of a traumatic past and a very uncertain future.

England was on the verge of being invaded and to celebrate

Christmas in the manner I was used to at home, forgiving and even loving the enemy, would be a betrayal of the faith that good would triumph over evil. The good had to be fought for; the evil mercilessly destroyed. It was not possible to condone the madness of Hitler and his warmongers simply because they were giving us a Christmas Day free of the daily murderous bombing of cities, towns and villages. To do so would have condoned their madness. Michel, at last 'coming to', joined me in deciding that, after the Christmas lunch in the sergeants' mess, we would go for a walk to the nearby church and try to join in prayer and thought with our loved ones, wherever they may be enduring life at Christmas time. I also gave thought to Albin and felt the presence of my spiritual gran.

During the phoney respite from war, the squadron operational sorties gave way to training flights that took place every other day. On one of our off-duty days, Michel, myself and Dubec, the other Czech member of our unit, took an underground train for the first time to visit the centre of London. We emerged at Piccadilly Circus in mid-afternoon and walked to Trafalgar Square to look at Lord Nelson's statue on top of a high column. He looked as if he was sending a message to the German Navy that he was still to be reckoned with. Then we went inside St Martin-in-the-Fields church for a spell. Suitably rested, we continued to the bank of the River Thames and along to the Houses of Parliament; that cradle of democracy I had heard so much about at school. Finally, accompanied by the chimes of Big Ben, we reverently entered Westminster Abbey. While inside, I vowed to come again as often as possible in order to feel the presence of the magnificent past and to pray for an equally proud future.

The winter's early darkness curtailed our sight-seeing so, by pooling our resources, we hired a taxi, which took us to Bedford Square where we had heard there was a Czech club, renowned to serve traditional meals. We were not disappointed except when the time came for us to descend to the depths of the nearby underground station. Walking the length of the platform, I was struck-dumb by the sight of all those London citizens who had gathered there, not to board any train but to spend their night sleeping on the utility bunk beds that were fixed to the platform walls. Such were the numbers that many had to make do with the stone platforms on which to make their beds.

In order to escape the indiscriminate bombing of London night after night, they crowded into the underground and gained my admiration for the cheerful and philosophical way they endured the situation. It fortified my faith and lifted my morale that, in spite of all the discomfort, they never looked downhearted. They chatted with one another, played games and sang with the help of a small band of buskers. The echoes bounced off the curved walls. I was sure that had we decided to spend the night there, space would have been found for us. I took these people into my heart to dwell alongside those that I truly loved.

On Sunday December 29th, London suffered a most horrendous night of bombing and the many incendiaries dropped raised a holocaust of fire. My thoughts and prayers were with those who had no chance to survive and with those brave souls deep underground.

The next day the squadron flew two operational sorties which, for me, was a great relief for my tormented mind. I just had to give vent to my explosive feelings. Unfortunately the guns of my Hurricane remained silent, the daylight proving too risky for the enemy airforce.

At 6pm on Tuesday December 31st, the entire squadron personnel, including Michel, Dubec and myself, were transported to the long established 400 Club, based in London, to bring in the New Year of 1941. We made comparisons between the celebrations held in our country and England, coming to the conclusion that the English tradition was equally intoxicating. The singing of 'Auld Lang Syne' brought memories of the precious past. Future happiness was worth fighting for and when the kissing began, I was very happy to be deeply involved.

For the most part of January thick fog curtailed the flying from RAF Northolt. When we did fly, it was mainly escorting our bombers as far as Boulogne or Calais, often in a combined operation with other fighter squadrons. On Monday January 6th, I was detailed to carry out a twenty-four hour duty as the station control pilot with responsibility for all the ground facilities being in working order. With so much fog prevailing, my vigilance was not put to the test.

When, on Wednesday January 8th, the CO gave me four days off, I made a quick telephone call to alert the Cousins family in Wolverhampton. It was a very cordial reunion, almost as if I had been their own kin. There was good food to be enjoyed and the comfort of the house to relax in. I was also taken to a concert given by Maurice Winnick and his Hawaiian Dancers, performing at the town's Hippodrome Theatre. In the evening, Cliff and I played some snooker at his golf club. We talked of Albin, who Mary had fallen for. As a member of 1 Squadron, he was busy participating in similar operational sorties to those conducted from RAF Northolt. Mrs Cousins was very pleased to be addressed by me as 'Mum' and shared her worries about Albin and me with her family. While I enjoyed every minute of my stay, I was well aware that my responsibilities were, for the duration of the war, to be at readiness at all times.

From January 13th until the end of the month, flying from Northolt was still hampered by the thick fog lying over London, at times shrouding the whole of south-east England. Under these conditions, London was bombed at night as well as during the day. Some bombs exploded at or close to our base and as the squadron was not able to take any retaliatory action, my frustration built up to explosive proportions. When we could fly during the day, the daylight bombing raids stopped. When the RAF fought and won the Battle of Britain, it was an act of self defence, using every plane available. The survival of Britain depended upon a few brave fighter pilots. Lessons were learnt on both sides and Goering's Luftwaffe now only flew at night, or when fog grounded the RAF fighters.

On the occasions when flying from RAF Northolt was possible, our missions were to provide a close escort to the Bristol Blenheim light bombers who were to attack targets along or beyond the French, Dutch or Belgian coastlines. On the approach to each target it was necessary to fly through sky blackened by exploding anti-aircraft shells (flak). As the fighter aircraft were able to take some evasive action the danger of being hit was not so perilous but it was deadly for the bombers who were trying to hold a steady course before dropping their lethal load. Those pilots and crews were the brave ones. If any enemy fighters appeared they were usually chased away by our higher escort fighter planes.

The month of February 1941 began with much improved weather and thankfully no fog! Operational flying by the squadron continued on a daily routine of providing escort to the Blenheim bombers. The losses or damage to our planes was mainly from the flak and quickly patched up, or, if more seriously damaged, reserve aircraft were brought into action.

On Wednesday February 5th the target to be bombed by twelve Blenheims was near St Omer in France. The bombers were to be escorted by three fighter squadrons. As with all these operations it was planned to the last detail, the fighters being divided into close, mid and high altitude protection. My squadron took up its usual position, which was closest to the bombers, and this particular mission had us flying through the heaviest anti-aircraft barrage I had ever experienced. It was a one hour and fifty-five minute nerve shattering operation which resulted in the loss of five planes. The squadron was fortunate in that all twelve members returned to base with only a few wounds to lick. For the four days that followed we mainly patrolled the Channel, the threat of invasion rippling its surface. The operations room fighter controllers, in whom we had implicit trust, gave no reports of enemy fighters in the vicinity.

Flying exercises continued, as well as the pre-planned or sometimes spontaneous operational sorties. It became necessary for longer flights over the English Channel to such places as Dieppe, Le Havre and the longest of all, to Brest where the German submarine depot was located. Equally long flights over the North Sea to reach targets along the Dutch coast were now common place. To a flyer, the sea is a hostile environment, to me personally the thought of crashing or having to parachute into the sea was terrifying!

When I was about ten years old I had nearly drowned in a lake named Bolevak, near Pilsen. I was under water after going down a slide and was kept under by several people following and dropping onto my head. Gasping for breath, I was rescued by a nearby swimmer. During the following winter, the lake was frozen over and whilst skating I witnessed the drowning of two young brothers of about my age. The ice had broken and during the rescue attempt the weight of the rescuers who had fetched a boat, cracked more ice, some of which was under me – I was fortunate to be rescued once more. These memories made me very wary when flying over water.

I always took good care of my parachute and before donning the Mae West life-jacket made sure that the inflation canister, (together with the sachet of yellow dye intended to colour the sea in an emergency) and the whistle, were all in place. The dinghy, attached to the parachute, formed a cushion to sit on; its discomfort was a constant reminder that it was there. Other aids we carried included a knife (hidden inside the flying boots, which was to be used to convert the boots into shoes), a silk map sewn into a shoulder pad and a compass hidden in one of the brass tunic buttons. Added to all this was my determination to escape from enemy territory and hopefully return to base and later to write a book about my exploits!

Monday morning, 10th February – our squadron commander, Squadron Leader O'Neil, a battle seasoned pilot and respected leader, briefed us that the squadron would take off at 9.30am to once again escort six Blenheims who were to bomb a target near Calais. Our assignment, no longer a surprise, was close escort duty and the CO's final instruction was that, in the event of enemy attack splitting us up, we were to reform over the sea but, if still separated, the vector for home was 310°.

Shortly after the briefing, we climbed in brilliant clear skies to a height of 6,000 feet to join the bombers over the Channel. With this achieved, the target was clearly visible ahead. On approaching the French coast the sky began to turn black with exploding, well-ranged shells, which spelled disaster, forcing us to exercise evasive manoeuvres and lose our hitherto close formation with the bombers. Although there were no enemy fighters to be seen the heavy flak was enough to make the task highly perilous. As far as I was aware, no bombers were destroyed but it was evident that some of our Hurricanes suffered damage when we reformed. I joined the CO as his number two (Red 2) and later, when about half way back across the Channel, he instructed me to peel off and take a reciprocal course to search for one of our pilots apparently in difficulty and, if I found him, to escort him back to base.

Promptly obeying the order, I flew back towards the French coast, searching the sky. Some ten minutes into my reciprocal flight I spotted a plane at a height of 3,000 feet with a vapour trail and closing in I identified the aircraft as one of our Hurricanes. It was flying in perfect trim, gently descending and maintaining a straight course with its engine running. When alongside, I could see the pilot, his head up looking straight ahead but there was no response to my radio calls or even glances in my direction. I flew ahead and gave him the 'follow me' sign of wing waggling, only to be ignored by the pilot who remained as if frozen in his seat. The aircraft maintained its straight course, gradually losing height whilst I remained close at hand for protection, calling repeatedly on the radio. Even at the minimum height to bale out, my call was ignored. Just a few feet above the calm sea the pilot still appeared motionless, the nose of the aircraft rose slightly before touching the waves. The instant the Hurricane made contact with the sea it tipped on its nose and sank within fifteen seconds. I circled the spot for a while, which was marked by a slight disturbance and when I was sure that the pilot did not surface I climbed to 2,000 feet and made a radio request for a 'fix' that would locate the scene of the crash. Receiving no reply to my call, I set course on 310°, as briefed, expecting to reach the English coast in ten to fifteen minutes.

After flying for half an hour on the prescribed course, my fuel was running low and I had cause to worry as there was no sign of the coastline ahead. Flying as economically as possible with the propeller in coarse pitch I climbed gently looking for a ship, over which I might bale out. I remained reasonably calm and after a quick look at my map, felt that it would be a good idea if I altered my course to fly west on 270°. As I reached 10,000 feet the petrol gauge indicated zero. It was with great relief and in answer to my prayers when a thin line of the coast appeared, as if by magic, in the hazy distance.

I throttled back the engine to idling speed, gliding towards the coast, and hoping to find an airfield to land at. There was much to pray for and when the engine began to splutter, I turned off the fuel cock, switched off the ignition and, selecting a suitably large area of ground, lowered the undercarriage and landed. The landing point was adjacent to a village named Occold, due south-east from the small town of Diss in Norfolk. The farmer, on whose land I had 'squatted' was kind and helped by phoning the nearest RAF base which was Martlesham. The station commander responded by arranging for the plane to be guarded overnight whilst I was whisked off to be de-briefed at the base and then to have a good night's rest. The following morning, preceded by a petrol bowser and a servicing crew, the station commander, together with a retinue of officers, made good company as I was transported back to my well guarded plane.

The Hurricane was refuelled and serviced and then, at my request, was pushed to the furthest corner of the field and turned to face the gentle breeze. I kept the brakes fully on and the wings and tail were held back during the build-up of engine power. Flaps were fully down and at the pull of the engine emergency booster, and on my nod, they all let go. Releasing the brakes, the aircraft shot forward and after a few bumps I was airborne. The original plan to fly directly to RAF Northolt had to be abandoned owing to severe engine vibration. Instead I landed at RAF Martlesham where the cause of the vibration was found to be the result of a missing tip on one of the wooden propeller blades.

As another propeller was not immediately available, a piece was made to match and glued on. The glue took two days to set so I stayed at RAF Martlesham until the morning of February 14th. After only ten minutes into the flight towards Northolt, the engine began to vibrate again. I decided to nurse the plane back home regardless. I set the propeller to a coarse pitch, lowered the flaps to five degrees and throttled back the engine to fly at just above the stalling speed. That I made it back safely was not solely due to me but to my prayers being helpfully answered.

During the de-briefing at Northolt, I learnt the name of the pilot that I had seen plunge into the sea. It was a Flying Officer R C Lawson who had been a member of 601 Squadron. Long after the war, in 1990, my wife and I had the pleasure of meeting Norman Franks, a well known author of books about the RAF. I told him the story of my escort duties on February 10th 1941 and the tragic loss of the pilot. He later sent me some further information. Richard Chester Lawson was the son of Admiral R N Lawson CB and, before joining the RAF, had been an officer in the Royal Tank Regiment. He had been posted to 601 Squadron in September 1940. He has no known grave but his name is recorded on the Runnymede Memorial.

I also learnt that I had not been the only one who had failed to make it back to base that day. Sergeant Hubbert and Pilot Officer McKelvie had both been forced down at Rochester due to fuel shortage. One problem we faced after the Blenheims had bombed was that they then split up into two formations of three, which necessitated our squadron splitting up to escort them. The heavy flak had made things more unpleasant, although luckily it was only accurate for height, not direction.

I wondered how I had ended up being so far off course during my return flight after I had seen Flying Officer Lawson's Hurricane plunge into the sea. I concluded that having failed to ascertain that his Hurricane was on a north-easterly course, had I continued to fly on vector 310°, I would more than likely have drowned somewhere north-east of Yarmouth. All my radio transmissions requesting a fix and a vector for base remained unanswered. Whether this was due to my R/T being damaged by flak or some other fault having developed, I never did discover.

CHAPTER 14

ON THE OFFENSIVE

For the rest of the month of February and the whole of March, our operational flying continued to be escorting Blenheim or the American-made Douglas (DB-7) Boston bombers to targets often well beyond the coastline of France, Belgium or Holland. Most of these sorties were carried out at heights of 30,000 feet or higher, making the use of the oxygen equipment a necessity. At these heights we also breathed sighs of relief for being outside the range of enemy anti-aircraft shells, it was a pleasant change not to be regularly blasted by flak. The enemy fighters mainly kept their distance or turned tail if chased. On some occasions our high altitude patrols were over designated areas. One such sweep was over Boulogne and Calais at 28,000 feet in company with aircraft from 303 (Polish) Squadron, and produced no reaction at all from enemy fighters. The occasional convoy patrol was interesting except in bad visibility, when the ships' crews became somewhat trigger-happy and the balloons they tugged along had to be given a wide berth.

The Duke of Kent's visit to 601 Squadron was a very welcome event. The Duke stayed for over an hour and spoke to each one of us individually. I thought that it was an appropriate gesture when he also chatted with the ground crews.

Although I did not fly with the squadron on March 29th, Squadron Leader O'Neil led a sortie to the French coast. It was the forerunner of operations we later called 'Rhubarb' but at first were named 'Mosquito' because they were planned to be a nuisance and an irritation. These could be exciting missions, usually flown in poor weather conditions by pairs or at most, a section of four machines. They were flown at low level and were therefore, not only exciting but extremely hazardous. Later in the war, they were virtually banned.

In early 1941 Mosquito (and then later, Rhubarb) missions were flown with much enthusiasm. Letting young men loose in a high-powered fighter with guns at their fingertips was exhilarating stuff. On

147

this occasion, the CO spotted twelve Me109s on an airfield near Dunkirk. He peeled off and made a strafing run and then attacked a motor barge he found off the French coast. The object of these missions was to cause as much damage or disruption to enemy targets as possible, using cloud cover to avoid trouble if it came our way.

Flight Lieutenant Whitney Straight and Sergeant Norman Taylor circled the Belgian city of Ghent at 20-50 feet, skimming the rooftops and flying down the main street. They were greeted with waves and cheers from the inhabitants. When they then spotted a small party of German soldiers, they were unable to open fire for fear of hitting innocent Belgians, so flew off to vent their frustrations on a flak-ship they found off Knokke, Belgium.

Flight Lieutenant Mayers left us about this time. He went to North Africa where he commanded a Hurricane squadron. He won a Bar to his DFC and then a DSO, ending up as a wing commander. On one occasion he gallantly landed to pick up a downed pilot, flying off again, seated on the lap of the other man. On a later mission, as a wing commander, he was reported missing and was never heard of again.

Our new 'B' Flight commander was Flight Lieutenant Humphrey T Gilbert. He had been with 601 Squadron since August and maintained the tradition of the squadron as he was a descendant of Sir Humphrey Gilbert of Revesby Abbey, Lincolnshire. He had been wounded with the squadron in the Battle of Britain but later returned.

On Friday April 4th, I was detailed to practise a dog-fight with Flight Lieutenant Gilbert, the 'B' Flight commander and renowned English aerobatic ace. I felt inferior to such a master of the air, my feet turned to jelly inside my flying boots. I had no choice when, at 5,000 feet above the thick clouds, we set to battle it out. The flight lieutenant was soon on the tail of my Hurricane. My simulated fate of being shot down was not easy to accept. After steadying my nerves I used the technique I had learnt in France, that of the flick-roll in order to get out of serious trouble and I too scored, my confidence returning. Thereafter the two of us embroiled ourselves in a kind of fight that became equally strenuous to bodies and planes. When my tutor waggled his Hurricane wings I formed tight alongside and saw him pointing to the microphone mounted on his oxygen mask, it meant that his radio was out of order. After my thumbs up acknowledgement, I led him down through the cloud and the balloon corridor to base, over which we split up. Having come out of the cloud, Flight Lieutenant Gilbert suddenly shot ahead diving towards the door of the squadron dispersal hut – at the last moment he pulled his aircraft up into a number of spectacular slow and flick-rolls, then turned round into another dive. Once more he repeated the rolls, this time, low over the aerodrome. As he came round for the third time I was just slightly astern of him and to starboard, I caught him looking across at me. Thinking that I had better not show any sign of cowardice, I followed Flight Lieutenant Gilbert by performing a series of rolls, nearly killing myself in the attempt.

Due to my inexperience in dare-devil aerobatics I lost height. I remember vividly that during my third slow-roll, whilst on my back, I could see trees and some rooftops flash by either side of me. Those on the ground, watching my 'brilliant' display may have been thinking how skilful a pilot I was, but with due modesty after landing, I hurried off to change my underpants. There and then I vowed that I would never again do aerobatics below the prescribed height of 3,000 feet.

Flight Lieutenant Gilbert left 601 Squadron in the summer to take command of the first American Eagle Squadron (71 Squadron RAF) and later he took command of 65 Squadron and received the DFC. Bearing in mind his predecessor's feat of successfully taking off after rescuing a downed pilot, Flight Lieutenant Gilbert had an unfortunate end. He decided to go to a dance and to take the station controller with him. He elected to fly a Spitfire with himself and the other man in the cockpit. They crashed and both were killed. Flight Lieutenant Gilbert was due to be married the following Saturday.

In April 1941, Fighter Command intensified its offensive posture using Rhubarb missions. The first of these missions came on April 12th and naturally every pilot wanted to be chosen as the first to go and begged the CO, Squadron Leader O'Neil for the honour. Eventually, in fairness, all the names were put into a hat and to Flight Lieutenant Whitney Straight's and my delight, we were the two chosen. Like everyone else I wanted the opportunity of having a crack at the enemy. Flight Lieutenant Straight immediately turned to me, shook my hand and said: "OK Frank, let's make a good show of it." I felt very privileged to fly with him on this special sortie, there was something about him. He was very friendly to everyone regardless of rank and there was, as the British might say, no 'side' to him. I don't remember him as an exceptional pilot although we all knew of his earlier exploits. I felt that I wanted to keep up good relations with him as all the pilots held him in high regard. He was very enthusiastic and always liked to remind us that he was one of the first Americans in action, long before the USA came into the war. After a briefing, when the purpose of our intrusive mission was divulged, we both flew from RAF Northolt to RAF Manston where our fuel tanks were topped up and our guns and equipment checked.

We wasted no time and took off in good visibility. At 900 feet, we climbed into the dense, moisture laden 10/10 cloud (full cloud cover), which was excellent weather for the Rhubarb operations. The visibility in the clouds was very poor and I had to keep tucked well in behind my leader's starboard wing, heading off on the agreed and timed course and aiming to emerge below the cloud close to the German fighter base at St Omer. Maintaining our position and strict radio silence, we finally emerged from the clouds and opened our formation to begin a search for suitable targets. Within a couple of minutes, Flight Lieutenant Whitney Straight began a steep left hand diving turn onto a reciprocal course and that was the last I saw of him until I struggled back to base.

My opportunity for some action came near Hazebrouck where I spotted an oil or gas storage tank among some trees to my right. I immediately dived and fired but when no flames or explosion ensued, I attacked again. During this second dive, firing all my guns at the target, I was hit from behind, bullet holes appeared across the starboard wing and a cannon shell exploded behind my seat, the shell fragments smashing into the cockpit and instrument panel. Powdered glass and cordite made my eyes sting and then I became aware that my right arm had been hit. My mirror revealed that a Me109 was trying to shoot me down and there were three more waiting to help my assailant. With my Merlin engine responding to full throttle, I went into a very tight loop, and my Hurricane started vibrating when, with the joy stick hard to my groin, I kicked the right rudder. Flicking from the top of the loop to the right, the Me109 dived past me and provided an easy target when no more than 50 feet from the ground, I let him have all my guns blazing and I was still firing when the aircraft turned onto its back, spewing smoke.

For many years I had nurtured the thought that my assailant crashed but I now know that the Me109 pilot, from the Stab Staffel of JG 2, managed to get his Me109E-4 (Werk No.1982) back home, albeit heavily damaged. My other antagonists that late morning were from III Gruppe of Major Werner Mölder's JG 51. Feldwebel (Sergeant) Leusch was the Luftwaffe pilot who scored hits on my Hurricane (Z2803) and actually claimed me destroyed, obviously believing I could not possibly get back across the Channel.

When another volley of bullets hit my plane I took a quick glance into my rear view mirror, which almost led to disaster. When I looked ahead, blades of grass were being thrown into the air by the tips of my propeller, I yanked back on the stick to prevent an imminent crash, and my tail wheel hit the ground hard. The Hurricane lurched violently, the engine died, and I was petrified as the prop was silently windmilling. Next I was crashing through high voltage electricity cables and as the steel pylon flashed by, instinctively, my hands and feet let go of the controls and I prayed! Once more, at ground level, just about to crash, my guardian angel took over and suddenly and miraculously the engine burst into life. I was still on the deck, the Me109s were behind and the shells were ripping into my aircraft. In sheer desperation I decided to hug the ground and began weaving around trees, scattered buildings and other such obstacles. My instrument panel had been smashed and, worst of all, so had the compass and there was no sun to guide me. Somehow, as if my brain had been implanted with a homing device I managed to get on to a north-west course towards the English Channel. Bullets were still smashing into the Hurricane and churning up the sea ahead of me as I crossed the French coast. As there was nowhere to hide except in the clouds above I pulled the engine emergency power boost lever, sending the aircraft into a steep climb, praying that the Me109s would not catch me before I reached the clouds. I made it but with the flying instruments smashed I had to fly by the seat of my pants for fifteen minutes.

As I emerged from the clouds the welcome sight of the English coast was a little distance ahead of me – bidding me to find the nearest airfield on which to land. After selecting my undercarriage down, I did feel a movement but no green light of confirmation came on so I had to trust my luck. The flaps did not function and during my approach there was a distinct feeling of instability in the aircraft. I made three very hairy attempts at a safe landing. Finally down, I managed to get out of the cockpit onto the ground in spite of the severe pain in my right arm and my flying suit sleeve was heavily bloodstained. My plane was an unbelievable sight. The damage sustained consisted of over 240 holes, there was a fifty-foot length of finger thick HT cable hooked around the Hurricane radiator cowling and there was no tail wheel.

My emergency landing was at RAF Gatwick where I was attended to by the medical officer who removed several pieces of shrapnel from my arm and gave me a tetanus injection. With a de-briefing complete, the squadron Magister was flown in by Sergeant Frank Jensen, to take me back to RAF Northolt. As I was standing on the wing of the 'Maggie', about to climb into the passenger seat, Sergeant Jensen enquired as to the whereabouts of my parachute. With apologies, I pointed to my sad looking, abandoned Hurricane. Telling me to stay where I was, he walked over to the aircraft, climbed up and bent over the open cockpit, and began to pull hard at the parachute harness but had to summon help from an airman standing by. The two of them eventually succeeded in pulling the 'chute out. They could hardly believe their eyes when they found that five bullets had penetrated the belly of the aircraft and the pilot's seat into which the parachute fitted. The five bullets had been stopped in the folds of the parachute silk which had obviously saved me from an embarrassing injury.

Back at base, I received an appreciative welcome from the CO and the squadron personnel. The next day the following article appeared in one of the daily papers.

"Bagged Nazi from 50 feet! On an offensive patrol over Northern France yesterday, a Hurricane fighter pilot shot

down an enemy fighter from a height of only 50 feet.
Then he caught the ground with the plane at close on 300
mph. Momentarily out of control, states the Air Ministry
News Service, the Hurricane tore through some high-
tension cables stretched across a field. The engine picked
up and the pilot was able to climb clear. Although
wounded in his right arm and with machine gun bullets
embedded in his parachute, he made his way back and
landed safely at his base. The pilot was a Czech Sergeant,
a member of a famous Auxiliary Fighter Squadron."

Flight Lieutenant Straight, after attacking a small military convoy,
which was out of my visual range, had been unable to reach me by R/T
due to my bullet-ridden equipment. After his attack he had climbed into
the clouds, remaining there until over the English coast, landing safely
at RAF Northolt.

Despite the injury to my arm and some bother to my eyes from the
powdered glass (details of which I did not disclose for fear that I would
be grounded) I flew with the squadron the next day on patrols at 26,000
and 30,000 feet and, apart from feeling cold and suffering poor
visibility when the cockpit hood froze over during the descent, both
patrols were uneventful since no enemy fighter put in an appearance. It
was during a briefing session that the flight commander noticed that my
eyes were slightly blood-shot and ordered me to see the station medical
officer immediately. I had no choice but to obey and, much to my
dismay, was grounded for seven days in order to undergo some
treatment.

During my respite from harassing the enemy I received a telegram
from the Czech General Janousek, conveying his congratulations to me
and advising that an order (S.D.V.N. No 11/25.4.41) had been issued
which announced the award of the Czech Bravery Medal. I was also
promoted to the rank of 'Rotny', the equivalent of an English warrant
officer, but they made no mention of any extra pay! I felt really
honoured at the arrival of another telegram from the Cousins family,
Net (aka Christine), Mary and Cliff and I never did ask them just how
they made the right deduction from the announcement in the
newspaper.

Having been injured, I missed the show on April 16th when the
squadron escorted Blenheims once again. However the day was not one
of the best. It was a time when Fighter Command was beginning to
develop fighter wings and several senior officers were being considered
for this onerous task. It took certain skills to become a successful wing
leader and in the early days of 1941, the requirements were still an
unknown factor. At RAF Northolt, Wing Commander G S L Manton,
previously OC 56 Squadron and station commander at RAF Manston,

had been made the wing leader and he led the escort on this late afternoon operation. Fired with enthusiasm no doubt, even Northolt's station commander, Group Captain Theodore McEvoy, decided to fly. Even then, the group captain was suffering from curvature of the spine which forced his head forward but it wasn't going to stop this otherwise sprightly thirty-six year old from flying.

The Blenheims were from 21 Squadron, attacking the airfield at Berck-sur-Mer, a base that seemed to feature greatly in our operations. The Northolt Wing at this time consisted of 303 Squadron and ourselves. The raid was something of a success, with several Me109s damaged by the bombing but as the force retreated back over the Channel, disaster struck. Me109 fighters from both JG 51 and JG 53 pounced, JG 53 coming down on our Polish friends; shooting down two and damaging another.

Meanwhile JG 51, led by Major Werner Mölders himself, attacked 601 Squadron. Major Mölders claimed a Spitfire and a Hurricane, with two of his pilots each claiming a Spitfire and yet another pilot claiming a possible kill. His 1 Gruppe pilots claimed two Hurricanes, a IV Gruppe pilot claimed a third. Added to this, a JG 2 pilot claimed a Spitfire near Dover at midday.

The Poles did indeed lose two Spitfires and their pilots, with a third damaged and its pilot wounded. 601 Squadron only lost one Hurricane but very nearly lost three. Squadron Leader O'Neil claimed a Me109 destroyed but then he was attacked from astern and shot down into the sea off Dungeness, receiving some leg wounds. Fortunately he was rescued. Wing Commander Manton's machine was shot-up as well and he too crash landed, also having been wounded. Group Captain McEvoy sustained damage to his Hurricane, which forced him to crash land at Lydd. JG 51 very nearly wiped out all three of our senior officers.

Our new CO, who arrived on April 23rd was Squadron Leader E J Gracie DFC, known to everyone as 'Jumbo'. He was a little older than most of us, about thirty, but he had been in the RAF since 1937 and fought gallantly with 56 Squadron over France and during the Battle of Britain. He would remain with us until almost the end of the year.

CHAPTER 15

CHANNEL AND CONVOY PATROLS

For the whole period of my being at RAF Northolt, the German bombers were being kept at bay by either the RAF night fighters, the anti-aircraft guns, or by 601 Squadron when scrambled. When grounded by bad weather our time was taken up by sessions on the Link Trainer. This equipment simulated instrument flying and became obligatory in order to keep ourselves in practice. Our squadron shared the camp facilities with the Polish 303 Squadron, with whom I maintained great camaraderie.

On one occasion, a large four-engine aircraft landed and was parked close to our dispersal hut. I had not seen anything of this size before, and was later informed that it was a Stirling bomber. The Short S.29 Stirling was the first four-engine monoplane to enter service in the RAF and the first to be used operationally in World War II. It stood very high; nearly seven metres or twenty-three feet, on double-jointed undercarriage legs supported by huge wheels. It looked as if it had just been wheeled out of the factory, bristling with gun turrets at the front and dorsal positions, each with two .303 machine guns and four similar guns in the rear as the sting in the tail. The fuselage belly was capable of carrying a bomb load of up to a thousand pounds. While standing awe-inspired by this monster, I did not see the approach of a convoy of blue RAF limousines. They were heading towards the gleaming aircraft when two RAF policemen requested me to leave the scene. I obligingly moved myself to a distance where I was no longer an obstruction and watched multiples of high ranking RAF officers escorting some sombre dressed, bowler hatted men, to the Stirling. I could hardly believe my eyes when I spotted, among the retinue, the British prime minister, Winston Churchill. There was the man, with the voice of a lion, whom I had listened to and admired, and thought of as a saviour, standing no more than fifteen yards away.

I returned to our dispersal hut to find everyone astir at the thought that the American Ambassador to Britain, Mr Wynant, who had also been in the crowd of people viewing the Stirling, was about to leave the VIP party in order to visit a RAF fighter squadron. He wanted to see for himself just what a fighter squadron on full readiness looked like and to have a word with some of the pilots. Our CO introduced His Excellency to each one of us standing in line, each offering a polite handshake. I was introduced as the squadron's 'Czech' pilot, at which the ambassador's bushy eyebrows did a steep climb and, with an expression of surprise he said: "I did not realise that each RAF squadron employed a 'check' pilot." The CO diplomatically explained my status at which a broad smile of understanding spread over the ambassador's face. Almost as if prearranged for the ambassador, the phone rang and we were instructed to 'scramble'. Those of us on duty then gave a display of how to reach the sky in double quick time. After landing we were in no doubt that it had been a false alarm.

On Friday May 2nd, 601 Squadron was moved to the airfield at Manston, situated in the south-eastern tip of England, in the county of Kent. Just like Northolt, RAF Manston was a well established permanent RAF airfield and the closest one to the French coast and the town of Calais. The narrowest part of the English Channel was all that separated us from the German long-range artillery. As we had come to expect, the personal and technical facilities were excellent and functioned like clockwork. The operational dispersal hut was timber built and apart from the CO's and flight commander's small offices, the remaining space was furnished with chairs and some iron framed mattress-covered beds, which were for our rest when on duty. A telephone was permanently manned by an airman whose job it was to announce the order to scramble.

The transfer from RAF Northolt was achieved with all the usual calm precision and Michel and I found ourselves in the company of Pilot Officer Manak, a very likeable compatriot and a superb pilot. The remainder of the day was devoted to our settling in and making sure that we would be ready and operational by the next morning. This was all achieved without any orders being shouted at us.

In the first action, around midday on May 4th, Sergeants Scott and Fearn were escorting an air sea rescue Lysander off Deal, ready to help any pilots on a sortie over France who might be returning damaged. They were attacked by three or four Me109s. Sergeant Fearn turned to meet them, and saw his fire produce strikes on one Messerschmitt but he was then hit and wounded in the head and leg. He staggered back and made a good wheels-up landing at RAF Manston. Meanwhile, the experienced flight commander, Flight Lieutenant Mayers, was flying on a 'Sweep' over France and was attacked by a Me109 while on his way back over the Channel. He managed to get in view of the English coast when he found it was time to leave the aircraft, so bailed out. He came down in the sea uninjured and was later rescued, while his Hurricane (Z3087) actually crashed on land, at Eastry, near Deal. Flight Lieutenant Mayers was claimed by our old foe, Major Werner Mölders, while Sergeant Fearn was claimed by a JG 53 pilot. On the evening of the 7th Michel, in Z2912, with five others, climbed to attack two Me109s but there were two more loitering way above and they came hurtling down on him. His aircraft sustained damage but he bought it back to RAF Manston for a forced landing.

At the crack of dawn the first Channel patrol was carried out at a height of 5,000 feet, followed by two more, each of an hour's duration – at times flying close to and parallel with the French coastline. On one such flight, five Me109s approached but when tackled, fled off in a south-easterly direction. They were faster than our Hurricanes so any pursuit would not have been prudent. On May 5th, whilst on a patrol we were attacked by some Me109s and, during the ensuing dog-fight, my aircraft sustained some slight damage, how badly my opponent was damaged, was not easy to assess. From the 7th to the 14th, more Channel patrols resulted in many skirmishes. When two Me109s were shot down our efforts proved worthwhile. Our duty in protecting Britain required some hard flying; our revengeful muscles flexed in readiness for whatever the Nazis could come up with, including the invasion with which they threatened Britain. We also performed other duties which included escorting Supermarine Walrus or Consolidated Catalina aircraft during their air sea rescue operations to pick up pilots, who had been shot down and bailed out to end up in the drink. German pilots were always ready to attack these mercy mission planes and consign them to the deep.

We continued with the Channel patrols, which were mainly carried out by pairs of Hurricanes at one and a half hour intervals. An experienced pilot from 'A' Flight was shot down on one of these sorties, as was a Sergeant Fearn from the same flight. Sergeant Fearn was hit by an Me109 but fortunately both pilots were able to bail out and were picked up. On another occasion, Sergeant Briggs of 'B' Flight was shot down, parachuted into the sea and was saved by Pilot Officer Manak who shot down the Me109 that was trying to destroy the Walrus aircraft. Michel also sustained hits from another Me109 but made it back to base to carry out a forced landing.

Shortly after 3pm on Friday May 16th, Sergeant T A McCann and I took off to carry out another Channel patrol, which was, in the words of officialdom: "Designed to combat the hit and run raids by the German raiders over the south-east and southern coast of England." Our patrol line was between Ramsgate and Dungeness, flying at 4,000 feet in a clear, cloudless sky. I took station as planned, some distance behind McCann's aircraft and performed 'S' turns which we called 'weaving' in order to maintain a 360 degrees scan of the area. Shortly, low down over the sea, I spotted a monoplane heading for the English coast but at my height I could not identify it positively, so I kept it under scrutiny. Suddenly the machine went into a steep climb and headed for

McCann's aircraft, which was about half a mile ahead of me, on a westerly course.

My suspicion hardened that it was a Me109. I recognised the shape and then the tell-tale bracing struts beneath its stabilisers, followed by the black cross on its fuselage and the yellow nose prop spinner: it was indeed an enemy. He had obviously not seen me as he had Sergeant McCann firmly in his view. I throttled back slightly, tactically allowing him to get ahead of me, knowing that he was still out of range of my companion. I waited for him to set himself up, checking behind me and switching my guns from 'safe' to 'fire'. Finally as the Me109 drifted in front of me, I called to Sergeant McCann: "Break leader, bandit on your tail." Sergeant McCann whipped into a break and all I had to do was press the gun button, the Me109 being no more than 100 yards in front of me. So intent was the German pilot on his target that he failed to observe the golden rule of checking behind him. Had he done so he would have seen me closing in. He paid the price. As soon as my first salvo hit him he turned 90 degrees towards the French coast and foolishly went into a steep climb to the left, hanging on his prop. I followed, hanging onto my prop too. I pulled the boost knob and surged forward, firing again from about fifty yards into his belly; he did not stand a chance. Bits began to fly off, smoke started to stream back from his engine and after a while, with me still firing short bursts, he suddenly went down and dived straight into the sea not far from Folkestone. I circled for a while and then regained some altitude and some composure. I felt terrible rather than elated. The man hadn't seen me; I hadn't had to fight for this victory, he just set himself up in front of me and all it needed was a little bit of thinking, to remain cool and to fire before he could open up on Sergeant McCann. Having gained height I immediately returned to base. Instead of being praised by my CO, he severely reprimanded me for not continuing my patrol.

Of course, by the very nature of things, one rarely knew one's opponents on these occasions. This only really happened if a pilot or a member of a bomber crew was captured and was, perhaps, in a nearby hospital where he might be visited briefly. Only today can our historians and researchers find out a little more of the men against whom we were matched during the war. It seems that on this day, I had shot down Oberleutnant Gerd Sprenger, the Kapitän of 1 Staffel, JG 3. He had been flying a Me109F-2 and therefore it was one of the first 109F versions of the Messerschmitt we had seen.

My combat report on this occasion records:

> "At 1505 hours I sighted a Me109 attacking Green 1 from astern. I had been weaving above the Me109 and Green 1. I immediately took up a position behind and above to deliver a one second burst. The enemy aircraft turned

quickly left in the direction of France. I followed and gave the enemy aircraft a three-quarter second burst and saw bits off the tail and smoke. I then saw the enemy aircraft crash into the sea. Both attacks were delivered at 150 yards range.

I was flying Z2496, while McCann was in Z2745. The sortie was timed at 1430 and 1520 hours, seven miles south of Folkestone at 4,000 feet."

During May, I had flown thirty-two missions, totalling thirty-five hours and forty minutes. Our new CO, Squadron Leader Gracie, who had replaced Squadron Leader O'Neil, was also a very experienced pilot. Perhaps a little more formal than his predecessor when dispensing orders, but he quickly proved to be an exceptional leader. Whenever he flew, I was generally required to fly as his number two (Red 2).

The first day of June was highlighted when Pilot Officer Manak shot down a Me109F and was later awarded the Czech Bravery Medal. Tuesday 10th June the squadron lost two pilots while carrying out another Rhubarb mission. They were both shot down. Flight Lieutenant Gregory was killed and Sergeant Scales became a prisoner of war. On Friday June 13th I took part in a similar mission; this time with Sergeant Norman Taylor. I was flying a Hurricane Mark IIC that had two 20mm cannons amongst its armament. Once more I was weaving behind the leader when we were suddenly confronted with four Me109s coming at us head-on. Sergeant Taylor immediately opened fire but I could not do so for fear of hitting his aircraft. It all happened so fast but one Me109 was already streaming smoke when Sergeant Taylor dived after a second Me109. He was still right in front of me so I was unable to fire. The aircraft he was following had more than likely been hit since it went into some haze. I followed, only to see a large white patch on the sea where presumably the Me109 had gone in. Unfortunately we were mistaken.

It now seems that our opponents on this day were from the Stab (staff pilots) of JG 26, patrolling near Dover and in fact all four returned to their base at Audembert, although one had been damaged. One problem was that when attacked a Me109 pilot would open his throttle which tended to blow out a puff of black smoke from his exhausts so that an allied fighter pilot might believe his fire had caused massive engine damage when, in fact, nothing had happened to the Me109's engine at all. As the standard Me109 manoeuvre for getting out of trouble was also to half roll and dive, this tended to suggest a serious hit and that the Me109 was finished and going down. As to the disturbed water, I have no excuse – I had obviously seen nothing more than a breaking wave.

To be quite fair, Sergeant Taylor did not actually say that he had shot the Me109 down but somewhere between our reports, the report of the squadron intelligence officer and group HQ, credit was given to him. It was not an isolated case by any means. His actual report states:

> "I was Green 1 on Channel patrol, flying south between three and four thousand feet when I saw four aircraft flying head-on towards me at the same height, in wide echelon to port – yellow nosed, black 109Fs. Fired a one-second burst at the leader and saw black smoke pour out of it, confirmed by Green 2. Enemy aircraft (EA) passed to my right and I made a steep turn to get on their tails. The enemy aircraft then broke formation and I fired a three-second burst into all four of them as they turned towards the open sea. Two enemy aircraft went into a vertical dive and I followed them down to 1,000 feet, firing all the time. I saw strikes hitting both enemy aircraft. Pulled out of a dive and saw no more of the two EA who had dived. Green 2, who had followed me through the combat in line-astern, saw large white patch on the sea as he turned right out of the dive and the spot where EA would have crashed."

I had been flying Z3450, whilst Sergeant Taylor was in Z3257.

I recall Sergeant Taylor very well, including the time that he 'bent' the wings of a Hurricane whilst testing a prototype anti-G suit which was never on general issue. He was a ruthlessly brilliant fighter pilot who had fought in the Battle of Britain. Sergeant Taylor DFM, was later commissioned and won the DFC in 1942 for shooting down a Fw 200 Kondor (maritime patrol bomber) while engaged on MSFU (Merchant Ship Fighter Unit) operations. He destroyed a total of seven German aircraft during the war only to die sadly in 1948 as the result of a flying accident.

For the remainder of May 1941, intensive operational flying continued, mainly carrying out Channel patrols, flying from dawn to dusk. On 21st June, I was detailed to take off at dusk and escort a Westland Lysander – an aircraft that was capable of taking off and landing 'on a postage stamp'. The task was to cross the Channel where the Lysander would land to drop off, or pick up, British or French undercover agents. When it became too dark, I returned to my base as detailed. Although June was a month of victories, it became increasingly hard to bear the loss of any more squadron pilots, either killed or missing – each time it felt like losing a brother. It was no consolation that losses were inevitable.

On Tuesday June 17th, I received the news that my wartime best friend, Albin Nasvetter, who was serving with 1 Squadron, had died in hospital of horrendous burns. My sorrow reached the depth of my soul. Albin and I were very close friends and his passing left an inescapable gulf of torment. I received the news too late to attend Albin's funeral but I made a vow, that whenever possible, I would make a pilgrimage to his grave.

Albin, with 1 Squadron, had been on a sortie to intercept some enemy fighters who were about to attack our bombers. Albin survived the combat but another member of his squadron was shot down and bailed out into the English Channel. A Walrus air sea rescue plane was sent to pick up the ditched airman but was attacked by German fighters. Albin went to the defence of the Walrus and whilst tackling one Messerschmitt, was shot down in flames by another. He managed to bail out in spite of being badly burned, and was rescued from the sea. Unfortunately he died in hospital and was interred in the churchyard of St Luke's at Whyteleafe, Surrey, which was the nearest cemetery to his base at RAF Kenley.

Our 'adopted' parents at Wolverhampton were also informed of Albin's death and their grief was as if they had lost a son, Mary particularly, was heartbroken at losing someone she loved. I found myself wondering which of the three of us remaining would be the next to be grieved over. Our thoughts went out to all those loved ones at home who received news about the fate of their kin.

Ever since the squadron's arrival at RAF Manston, life at the base was one of considerable unease. This was due to the 'hit and run' indiscriminate bombing by German aircraft. After a bomb had hit the WAAF quarters, killing or maiming some of the brave 'angels', a kind of permanent alert prevailed, usually because the attacking aircraft had managed to fly under the radar and some were even missed by the observer corps in their coastal posts. Unfortunately, the air-raid sirens often sounded after the first bombs had dropped.

Early one morning, with the squadron on stand-by all pilots were in readiness inside the dispersal hut. All of us were wearing a Mae West and passing the time either reading or playing cards. Some, like me, were stretched out on their beds, longing for peace. Our Hurricanes were parked close by outside, fully serviced and with guns loaded. For speed and convenience each pilot had his own parachute on the wing of his plane from where it could be easily snatched and buckled on when the order to scramble came through. We were all keyed up and just waiting for the phone to ring which would announce the action. Often we found ourselves jammed in the doorway in our extreme rush to get to our patiently waiting Hurricanes and ground crews.

We were in this state of limbo when suddenly a mighty explosion occurred. The door to the hut, complete with its frame, caved in. The radio that was standing to one side, disintegrated after falling to the floor. The fire extinguisher that was usually hung on the wall performed a loop and landed on its striking knob. The extinguisher spout spewed white foam all over the place, turning the hut into a snow scene, and finally gurgling as if mortally wounded. Being well trained for an emergency, everyone inside the vibrating hut sprang into action by fighting for a safe place under the beds. Only the bravest ventured outside to investigate the cause and to tend to any one who might have been injured by the explosion.

It was an unbelievable sight that met our eyes, as there was our squadron commander's Humber station wagon embedded into the side of the hut. The vehicle's driver was behind the steering wheel, his mouth agape like a dummy – which he was. He was pulled out and after recovering from his transfixed state, was asked just what the hell he was up to. With rolling eyes and a trembling chin, he said, "I was bored and to pass the time, decided to teach myself to drive." We were all still laughing when the CO arrived who, after recovering from the shock, proved that he was in no way amused by the situation. The offender – a pilot, survived, but I will not reveal his name in case, like me, he is still around to tell his story.

News came from the squadron adjutant that my dear friend Michel and I were to be posted to 313 (Czech) Squadron which was based at RAF Catterick. We were not at all pleased and decided to take action. It was at Cosford when joining the RAF, that I swore allegiance to HM King George VI, promising to fly and fight alongside the British and this is what I wanted to do with 601 Squadron.

I promptly went to see my CO, Squadron Leader Gracie, who naturally was aware of the air ministry instruction and I pleaded with him to use his influence to have the posting squashed. Whilst he pondered, I added, with tongue in cheek, "After all sir, as your number two when flying, I shall be missed." Somewhat bemused, he agreed to see if anything could be done. He was successful.

However, on June 22nd Michel left for his new squadron, I was sorry to be parted from a very loyal friend with whom so much had been endured since our meeting in Prague two years earlier. We vowed to keep in touch with each other.

There was no respite from the operational flying over the Channel where, on the other side, we dared the Hun to come up and fight. The CO at times even used the R/T to make some uncomplimentary remarks, daring them to put in an appearance. If they did, it was only a brief visit and their departure was very fast. I carried out two more Lysander escorting tasks, each one at zero feet when the daylight was ebbing, making the flights strenuous but interesting. Whenever the squadron flew as a whole, we would intrude deeper into France or Belgium on provocation flights, which were known under the code-name of 'Jim Crow'. This was intended to point out to the Nazis that they need be under no illusion – their past superiority in the air no longer applied – the RAF were now on the attack and pilots, especially me, were seeking revenge.

Just by way of a change, on June 28th, Flight Lieutenant Himr and I were detailed for a dusk take-off to provide a night escort for a single Blenheim bomber.

When the details of the mission were revealed in the briefing room, I felt that the prospect of my staying with the bomber was very slim and the venture likely to be 'hair-raising'. I had not really been trained to fly at night and since sustaining the injury to my eyes on a Rhubarb flight in April 1941, my night vision was not all that good. For me to take off in the pitch dark alongside the bomber, was enough to make me feel apprehensive. It would be necessary to keep the bomber in sight at all times when attacking the target, regardless of his manoeuvres, thus making it a very tall order indeed.

Feeling somewhat inadequate to fulfil such an important task, I told the CO about my concern. He asked how much flying I had done so far, to which I replied "410 hours". Squadron Leader Gracie thought that this was perfectly adequate and told me he had no doubt in my ability to cope.

Before taking off at 3.30am, I had a word with the pilot of the Blenheim who agreed to take off with his position lights (one on either side of the fuselage) switched on so that I could glue my eyes to them. After take-off, when at 200 feet, these lights were switched off and I had to rely on the glow of the Blenheim's starboard engine exhaust. The night was very dark, my fear of failure equally impenetrable.

I was determined not to lose sight of my charge and when at 3,000 feet we crossed the French coast, the Blenheim turned to the left onto an easterly direction, aiming to follow the coast from the proximity of Calais along as far as Walcheren in Holland. While on the way back to base, if a suitable target was found, the Blenheim would drop his bombs and then scarper back home. On reaching the Dutch turning point, the flak and searchlights fully illuminated us. I was blinded by the lights, petrified by exploding shells and I lost the bomber I was entrusted to look after. Flying by the seat of my pants and avoiding the searchlight and flak, I began a search for the Blenheim and the other escorting fighter but it was hopeless. Failing to find either, I set my compass to a westerly course only to be caught, once more, in a shaft of light and some flak which was much too close for my comfort.

When my eyes began to settle down after the unwelcome attention from the ground, a chink of the dawn was very welcome. I recognised Calais to my port side and I decided to make another attempt at finding my protégé. After ten wasted minutes I set course for base where, before I landed, I noticed the Blenheim squatting close to the reconstructed dispersal hut. After landing, I taxied my Hurricane at a very leisurely pace in order to delay facing the music.

I was de-briefed in the presence of the CO, the intelligence officer and Flight Lieutenant Himr who also admitted losing the Blenheim outside Calais when the bomber turned east. The bomber returned to base directly from Walcheren, landing half an hour before I did. To my surprise I was not reprimanded or even criticised for my persistence. Only a total of four of these missions were carried out, mine being the last one. Only on one occasion were any bombs dropped and even then the result was uncertain.

Tony, like Albin, was separated from Michel and me at RAF Sutton Bridge. He had not kept in touch and my letters to him had not been answered. Sadly, he was tragically killed when flying a Percival Proctor communication plane P6275 on July 10th 1941. Apparently it happened somewhere in Lincolnshire when he was flying in thick fog. He lost control and crashed. I could hardly believe the news. Tony was buried at St Andrew's Church, Cranwell. To my shame, I have yet to pay my respects to his grave but who knows – I may go painting with him again.

Since 601 Squadron moved from RAF Northolt to RAF Manston, we were kept intensively busy with flying and this pressure was only relieved by some brief but enchanting encounters with the base WAAF population and the occasional visit to a café in Margate where a 'secret' steak, with a fried egg sitting on top, could be enjoyed. When an order came for the squadron to take up residence at RAF Matlask, an airfield situated about fifteen miles north of Norwich, we thought that the change of air would do us all good. We felt that victory was now certain as the war had flared up between Germany and Russia. That the conflict would help to relieve the pressure along the Western Front was morale-boosting news for everyone engaged in fighting the Nazi enslavers of freedom.

At Matlask, as with the previous RAF bases, it was very easy to settle in and our welcome by the permanent station staff was very cordial. All of us in 601 Squadron quickly concluded that this new base was not a holiday camp. On July 3rd we became fully operational and ready for action. There were frequent convoys of vital cargo-carrying ships that required our protection from the low flying Junkers or Dornier bombers that, at the last moment, would climb above the convoys to drop their bombs and then flee eastwards. Our regular sorties had us crossing the coast well behind the convoy, flying for ten minutes before making a 90 degree turn in the direction the ships were heading. Another 90 degree turn towards the coast kept the convoy in a 'box'. Any enemy planes sighted were tackled before being able to deliver their fatal load.

Such patrols were frequent, with take-offs often at dawn or after the sun had long vanished behind the horizon. On one occasion the mission was carried out in response to a scramble, and our take-off occurred during a thunderstorm. We flew as a formation of six Hurricanes and strained to remain together in the most turbulent conditions. We were being blinded by flashes of lightning that were instantly followed by thunder, louder than the faithful beat of our Merlin engines. That we managed to stay together, despite the violent conditions, was an achievement that only RAF-trained pilots were capable of. How we avoided hitting the balloons towed by the convoy ships and not be shot down by their guns blazing at us, was a miracle. We were assisted in our landing by our much-relied-upon WAAFs in Air Traffic Control. The WAAF handling my approach deserved a hug of appreciation, but I was too tired after landing at midnight.

My fear of drowning was at its worst when I was detailed to carry out a sea search for airmen thought to have bailed out or crashed. Usually flying singly or possibly as a pair, these flights were long and stretched far from the English coast as we strove to find, make a report and, if possible, stay on the scene until a rescue could be made. My unease would only diminish when those who were subject to the search were found – only then would the feeling of satisfaction outweigh my fears.

During the whole of July and through to the middle of August, there were frequent convoy patrols; escorting bombers to more distant targets; offensive sweeps over France, Belgium and Holland and, at times, even crossing the German border. There were many scrambles to intercept bandits, some proving to be friendly intruders. So, all in all we became very tired – certainly too tired to render our appreciation for the services supplied by the WAAFs that we admired and trusted.

One very special sortie that stays so vividly in my mind was when, as a squadron, we provided a close escort for six Stirling bombers on their way to bomb a target near Lille in France. I was inspired and thought myself privileged to be part of the operation. In my imagination, these giant bombers flew with the special blessing of Winston Churchill and this made me very determined to protect them at all costs. When two Spitfire squadrons joined us in mid-channel I felt that my squadron was not alone in having such a notion. The monster-sized British bombers were carrying a serious message to the Nazi evil perpetrators to 'beware'; the might of British determination was on its way to defeat them. Whilst the bombs were being dropped a Me109 appeared but, after a brief scrap, quickly got the message and fled. I was not called upon to operate my trigger finger and our charges were able to fly home unscathed and empty bellied, leaving behind them an obliterated target.

On August 20th, I took a flight of some significance which was in an American Bell P39 Airacobra (AH576), a fighter plane that had been flown in by a US pilot. In spite of the difficulty in understanding the

American accent it was possible to follow his briefing. I gave the plane a thorough inspection from nose to tail before I flew it in order to pass an opinion on its capabilities. It was a very sleek looking fighter aircraft of unorthodox design. The engine was mounted amidships, behind the pilot's spacious cabin, driving a three-bladed CV propeller, through the centre of which protruded the nozzle of 37mm cannon. Two machine guns were carried in each wing. The Allison engine was powerful enough to propel the plane at speeds in excess of 400mph. It stood on a slender looking tricycle undercarriage. The very roomy cockpit contained an array of switches, some with puzzling functions that I tried to understand. I was familiar with the instruments but their positioning would need some getting used to.

Like any flight in a plane for the first time, I was keen to sample the feeling and thrill of the Airacobra characteristics. I liked the precise light and responsive controls which gave the feeling of agility. There was a queue of squadron pilots waiting to have their go so it was only possible for me to have four flights before the end of the month; I didn't manage to try it out at high altitude but did discover that it was a beast when in a spin. It entered a spin too eagerly and objected to come out of it unless 'kicked in the ass'. I found it easy to land on its tricycle undercarriage and there was particularly good visibility from the cockpit when taxying. One disadvantage of the fighter was that it was necessary to cock the machine guns from inside the cockpit before firing.

Not long after my arrival at RAF Matlask, one of the squadron pilots, an officer with whom I could talk about cars in a way that some describe their women, told me he not only had an expensive Lagonda Saloon but also, at his home not more than seventy-five miles away, he had a Wolseley Hornet special coupé. Apparently, this car was standing in a barn and as he had no use for it he offered it to me for the sum of £20. Accepting his assurance that the car was road worthy, I counted out all my savings which amounted to £18 and struck a deal. He arranged for one of his farm employees to bring the car to me and, I must say, I was not disappointed.

The Wolseley Hornet was black with massive Lucas headlamps mounted on a gleaming chrome bar. The side and rear lamps, including the radiator grill, were when cleaned, also finished in shining chrome. The hood and removable Perspex side windows confirmed the car's age and the hard use that it had had. There were only two seats but a hard board behind them was sufficient in which to squeeze, with some discomfort, a couple of WAAFs, a space which was often accommodated. I 'x-rayed' the engine, using my experienced ears and eyes and pronounced it very healthy except for the vacuum petrol pump which, at times, had to be coaxed for it to behave. The tyres were a little on the bald side so I set aside a period to accumulate the necessary funds. The one thing that I could not do much about was that petrol was rationed. If any of my highly valued and respected ground staff wished to borrow the car, they were very welcome to it provided that they supplied the fuel and made sure that it was returned with sufficient in the tank for my future use.

On one of our rare days off, I decided to go into Norwich accompanied by another Czech pilot, Joe, who had recently joined 601 Squadron. It was a city that we knew well from the bird's eye point of view but had yet to sample at ground level. Our first thoughts were of regret that we had not made the visit earlier, if only to admire the serene and gracefully aged buildings and to appreciate the company of the inhabitants. After an enjoyable walkabout, including a short visit to one of the churches, we came upon a restaurant where afternoon tea was being served accompanied by a lady on a piano. Thinking ourselves to be in need of some culture, Joe and I decided to grace the establishment with our presence. No sooner had we entered than we caught the eyes of two very pretty WAAFs, one of whom was a member of the squadron's administrative staff. Our bid to join them was successful and the afternoon tea most enjoyable. My offer of a lift back to camp was accepted and the two lasses were very welcome company.

Having to be back in camp before nightfall we set off at 5pm, and the four of us squeezed into a car designed for two. The drive was expected to take about half an hour but possibly longer if the countryside along the way proved irresistible. Driving along in a carefree manner and failing to halt at a country crossroads, I hit the offside running board of a huge, chauffeur-driven Rolls-Royce. After the impact, one wheel of my car wanted to turn left, the other in the opposite direction. Our dear companions saved themselves from being ejected by their strong embrace of Joe and me. The silence that followed did not last long enough for the ground to swallow me whole.

A very refined lady, having been helped out of the Rolls-Royce by her chauffeur, walked around and demanded to know if any of us were hurt, especially the WAAFs. I meekly gave an assurance, which was met by a stern look in the lady's eyes. Was I about to be deported? It was evident that we were dealing with a real English lady when, as if by spiritual materialisation, a policeman appeared on the scene and immediately tried to take control of the mess that I was in. "What are you doing here, George?" the lady said; "I have not sent for you, but as you are here, make yourself useful and go to the garage for help to remove that wreck, and be quick about it!" "Yes Ma'am" was all that he could utter before mounting his bicycle and pedalling off as if in a race.

As the accident was partially obstructing the crossroads, the chauffeur was detailed to act as a traffic policeman whilst we trembling souls were told to follow her into the Rolls-Royce. Before the expected, and probably deserved, reprimand came from her lipstick-free lips, I managed to apologise and assured her that I had consumed no alcohol that afternoon. Some questions were asked in a firm manner. After generalities had been disposed of, her enquiries were directed at Joe and me who, by the flashes on our tunics, she could see were from Czechoslovakia. Probing questions into our past followed and she wanted to know what it was that drove us to leave home. By the time the cross-examination was over, I could detect a distinct mellowing and before the garage break-down vehicle arrived I knew that I had been forgiven.

Telling us to stay in the car, she approached the garage proprietor. To see my car being towed away, the front end hanging on chains, almost broke my heart. The damage to the Rolls-Royce was minimal, only a slightly rumpled running board. I was given no say in the matter as the four of us were driven a short distance before turning through open wrought iron gates, drawing up alongside a large mansion where we were invited in. A servant ushered us into a lounge, the beauty and elegance of which I had never seen before. In my imagination, I thought that the gates we had recently passed through were the gates of heaven and the past encounter at the crossroads was only a dream.

My guilt-inspired illusions were disturbed when asked to sit down by her ladyship and two maids tip-toed into the lounge. "Refreshments can now be served," she said, and was acknowledged by a curtsy and a "Yes Ma'am". It did not take them long to reappear with trays laden with sandwiches, cakes and a beverage that was poured into cups so fragile that I was scared to one pick up. A very mellow conversation followed whilst taking the refreshment. This boosted my confidence that, despite my crime, I would be allowed to live in order to inflict further punishment on the Nazi maniacs who were now determined to invade Britain and destroy the kind of democracy I was now enjoying with our aristocratic hostess.

Before we were driven back to our station in the Rolls-Royce, the lady of the mansion told me that I would be informed when the repairs to my car had been carried out and that I was to wipe that worried look from my face. On arrival at the camp gates the guards rushed outside and stood to attention, preparing themselves to present arms or salute. When they realised that there were no dignitaries or high-ranking officers among us, the only salute given, as we disembarked, was by the bemused chauffeur.

Two weeks later, my car was brought back to me by one of the garage mechanics who told me that the bill had been settled and I was to forget that the accident ever happened. Some time later I drove to the mansion to make enquiries about the cost and I was told that her ladyship was away and that it had been her pleasure to have the car repaired at her expense. She felt that it was the least she could do for someone, like us, fighting for Britain. On the drive back to camp, I was in no doubt that, had I attempted to change the mind of her ladyship, I would have lost the battle.

CHAPTER 16

INTENSE OPERATIONS AND AEROBATICS

Operational flying continued in our reliable Hurricanes but on August 13th 1941, I was detailed to give the Airacobra another evaluation flight of unlimited duration. I climbed, for the most part tediously, to 35,000 feet, quickly levelling off as I realised that at that height the Airacobra was 'out of breath' and, had I encountered any enemy aircraft, survival would not be possible. The controls were sluggish and the plane wallowed like a duck on a rippling pond. It was my opinion that 25,000 feet was the maximum operational height. Below 10,000 feet it was very nice to fly and, with the nose down slightly, capable of a speed of 370 knots. It was possible to perform some aerobatics but doing a spin was not to be recommended. My wariness about the plane's unwillingness to come out of a spin was proved valid when, tragically, one of our pilots was unable to bail out after entering an inverted flat spin. I was taken to the site of the crash where the plane was lying upside down, crumpled in soft ground but still in one piece. The cockpit had been crushed, breaking the pilot's neck.

After performing some simulated dog-fight manoeuvres, the engine developed a 'cough and a splutter' but I did manage to land back at RAF Matlask. Given a choice between a slower, less comfortable Hurricane or the Airacobra, I would certainly opt for the well tried, faithful and reliable Hurricane with its 'never miss a beat' Rolls-Royce Merlin engine!

The ever more frequent take-offs at dusk and consequent night flying was causing a great strain on my eyes which felt as if they were full of grit. I kept this information to myself, hoping that the condition, if not clearing, would at least not get any worse. I had joined the squadron to fulfil all the allotted tasks but the grit in my eyes, plus the shrapnel wound on my arm, were personal reminders that the fight must continue until all the nations now under the Nazis, were liberated and peace reigned once more.

The squadron's intensive and, at times hazardous, flying from RAF Matlask came to an abrupt end on August 16th when, at very short notice, we were moved to RAF Duxford to continue operational flying in Hurricanes and commence intensive training flying Airacobras. The prospect that we were about to become equipped with this American aircraft was not one that I, and several other pilots, welcomed.

RAF Duxford was a modern base with comfortable accommodation, which I shared with Joe. The sergeants' mess facilities and food was as good as the officers' mess. My first operational flight from Duxford was to patrol in a Hurricane between the base and RAF West Malling. It was uneventful, as was another scramble to intercept a bandit at 15,000 feet.

An opportunity arose that allowed Joe and me to drive to Cambridge which was seven miles north of the base. I enjoyed the atmosphere of the historic university town. Joe was not as good company as my never to be forgotten pal Albin, his prime interest was in women with whom he claimed to be very successful. By today's standards, the stories he told in the mess whilst having a drink, would create a best seller.

Towards the end of August, the Airacobra flying training became a priority as our Hurricanes were being taken over by another squadron. My disappointment was shared with several squadron pilot friends when the Hurricanes were flown away.

By now, my eyes had become very inflamed and were giving me severe pain and there was no option but to see the station medical officer. I was declared unfit for operational flying and on informing my CO, was given three days off and permission to have the squadron's Magister R1920 to fly myself to Wolverhampton. Net, Cliff and Mary did their very best to make me feel at home but they had serious concern for my dreadful looking eyes.

On my return flight, when about half way back, a rapidly developing fog forced me to land as quickly as possible on the nearest field that I could find. After two hours the fog cleared and with the help of the local policeman, I took off again to later land quite safely at RAF Duxford.

Using the medical officer's prescribed treatment, my eyes improved but not to the extent to be rated operational. My consolation was that the squadron's American fighter planes were also non-operational, I was not missing any bomber escorts or duels with Me109s, instead I was requested to ferry the two-seater Hawker Cygnet; a light all-metal aircraft, with a triple fin, which flew rather like a brick. On another occasion I was flown in a Blenheim to collect a de Havilland Hornet Moth which was a delight to flirt with.

During the month of September 1941, 601 Squadron remained bogged down with technically troublesome and often unserviceable aircraft. My eyes were not improving and headaches were accompanying the pain, so the medical officer dispatched me to the RAF hospital at Ely to undergo some tests and treatment. There was some improvement which made me feel happier, although I was still unfit for operations. My CO kindly allowed me to have the Magister again, which enabled me to seek the comfort of my adopted family at Wolverhampton.

The belief that problems always arrive in threes was somewhat borne out by the arrival of a letter from a girl at Exeter named Elizabeth (Beth). I had been introduced to her by Mr and Mrs Petherick. The letter suggested that I ought to marry her, which was a shock, and took me some time to get over. As a man of honour, I replied forthwith.

By October 1st my eyes had become so bad that any flying was now out of the question. I was driven to the Princess Mary's Hospital at RAF Halton to undergo a month-long treatment. The hospital was a large unit, staffed entirely by RAF doctors, nurses and ancillary personnel who were there to treat members of the Royal Air Force. My bed was one of twelve in a spacious ward where, soon after my arrival, the treatment of my inflamed right eye began. It consisted of various eye drops, ointments and injections, one of which was a painful application of my own blood jabbed into my buttock. Later on I was relieved of an eye-tooth and also my tonsils were removed. The improvement to the eye condition was very slow and the reoccurrence of the inflammation is still something I worry about.

On November 30th, I was sent to a convalescence unit at Blackpool which, in view of the dismal weather, I found to be very bleak. The rest and regular application of eye drops seemed to be effective though and following a medical board check-up, much to my relief I was deemed fit to fly.

I resumed flying duties on December 13th with the Airacobra but the squadron was still considered non-operational. By the end of the month I had flown another five hours on training flights which included air-to-air and air-to-ground firing practice.

Over the Christmas period I reminisced about my kin and grew more pessimistic about the chances of my survival. My thoughts centred on Albin, Jan and Tony who were the first three of our party to die. I was out of touch with Michel and even Venca was probably too busy flying to find time to write. I was certainly not forgotten by my Wolverhampton parents, and I had a pile of letters from them to prove it. My correspondence with Beth was also mounting.

Had it not been for the frequent lion's roar of Winston Churchill's voice over the radio, I would have been worried about the threat of invasion to Britain. Freedom and democracy was being destroyed all over Europe, yet the United States was still unwilling to fight for something with which they themselves were blessed. There was also bad news from the Russian front. My squadron was, in my opinion, wasting valuable time playing with Airacobras. There was not much to be cheerful about.

On January 4th 1942, the squadron, Airacobras and all, was moved once again to a grass airfield, RAF Acaster Malbis, situated three miles south of York. My morale was at a very low ebb but my prayers were eventually answered, when on March 13th, like a bolt from the blue, we were equipped with the Spitfire Mark VBs fitted with a 20mm cannon and two .303 machine guns in each wing. The next eight days were devoted to familiarisation flights in the Spitfire. I thought it to be the best fighter plane in the world. The Airacobras, no longer required, were collected, and we understood they were being dispatched as a gift to the Russian Air Force. They also went with my blessing.

RAF Acaster Malbis was the most primitive place that I had been stationed at since joining the RAF. The accommodation huts were of wooden construction and the beds had a frame standing only six inches above the ground. The ablutions and catering facilities resembled a camping site but it was impossible to be disheartened when the Spitfires arrived. The heating in our billet consisted of two paraffin lanterns. On one very cold evening the lanterns were left on when Joe and I decided to pay a visit to York. Upon our return, the room, including the beds were all covered with a layer of black soot. The beers we had partaken of in the beautiful city helped us overlook the dismal scene and we turned in.

The partnership between myself and the Spitfire was quickly affirmed, its flying characteristics were very refined and more tolerant than the Hurricane when flown close to its limits. If about to stall, at either high or low speeds, a warning was given by a shudder. It was much more manoeuvrable and faster than the Hurricane. When on the ground, the narrow undercarriage and the poor forward visibility made taxying difficult but in the air the Spitfire was a gem and in combat it was deadly.

After nine days of training, 601 Squadron was moved on March 25th to RAF Digby, situated twenty-seven miles west of the Wash and some six miles north of Sleaford in Lincolnshire. The stay was of short duration as another move came through – this time to Malta. Joe and I were not allowed to leave the British mainland and so we were posted to 610 (County of Chester) Squadron which was based at RAF Hutton Cranswick, some three miles south of Driffield in Yorkshire and about ten miles from the east coast. This squadron was also equipped with the Spitfire VB and was in a fully operational state. The CO was a Squadron Leader G Haywood. My first flight was in a Magister on March 28th followed by an operational scramble in a Spitfire VB on March 30th to search over Hornsea for a bandit.

Squadron Leader Gordon Stanley Haywood was yet another pre-war airman. He had been flying with 616 Squadron prior to moving to 610 Squadron as a supernumerary, until he took command on March 9th 1942. The two flight commanders were Flight Lieutenants Denis Crowley-Milling DFC and Ronald Courtney who were usually referred to by their nick-names of 'Crow' and 'Buck'. Flight Lieutenant

Crowley-Milling had flown with 242 Squadron in France and the Battle of Britain, while Flight Lieutenant Courtney had seen action with 151 Squadron over Dunkirk and the Battle of Britain. We were both part of the Coltishall Wing, commanded by Wing Commander P P Hanks DFC. Wing Commander Prosser Hanks had seen considerable action during the Battle of France flying with 1 Squadron. After a period as an instructor, he commanded 257 Squadron then commanded the Duxford Wing prior to taking over the Coltishall Wing in February 1942.

My flying at RAF Hutton Cranswick continued daily until the end of the month when 610 Squadron, including Joe and myself, were moved to RAF Ludham on April 1st, a well established RAF fighter station which was thirteen miles north-east of Norwich and only seven miles west of Winterton-on-Sea. The squadron embraced me into its friendly fold as an experienced pilot. Although I held the rank of flight sergeant, on many important missions I took the lead of formations, which included officer pilots. Our CO took the view that rank took second place to flying experience and ability. The squadron became fully operational as soon as it touched down at RAF Ludham and the first patrol was carried out on April 2nd under the codename 'Balbo' (a large formation of fighters). I flew in my usual place as number two to the CO.

When the CO took part in any operational sorties such as scrambles, he expected me to take off in a very tight formation with his Spitfire and land likewise, as if the planes were tied together. Squadron Leader Haywood was quite a character and was held in the highest respect. However, the close formation flying he insisted that I do with him was a real problem as I felt that I could never compete with him at aerobatics. It was the first time that I realised how scared I could be in the air. He really insisted I tuck myself in close but I did not find it enjoyable, just hazardous, especially when doing a tight-roll at low level!

Apart from a few days of bad weather in the middle of the month the operational flying was very intensive. On some days, two or even three missions were carried out, 90% of which were over the North Sea. The convoy patrols were shared with some long distance 'Jim Crow' intrusions towards and up to Ijmuiden on the coast of Holland. On April 13th, I was carrying out one such flight, flying at zero feet with, as my number two, Pilot Officer Wright. The purpose of these long distance flights was to find and report on any shipping or unusual marine activities close to, or along, the Dutch coast. It was essential to fly as low as possible in order to avoid detection by German radar. It was while our aircraft were being fired at in the proximity of Ijmuiden that my number two lost control for a split second and his propeller touched the surface of the sea. Realising his predicament, I turned and set course for our base; flying at the lowest possible throttle setting in order to ease the strain on my number two's plane. We made a safe landing at RAF Ludham. Inspection of Pilot Officer Wright's Spitfire found that eight inches of all three propeller blades were bent backwards. Had one of the three broken off, it would not have been possible to make such a long flight back to base.

Another unforgettable, and to me unforgivable, flight took place on April 27th 1942 when, just before midnight, the squadron was ordered to patrol over Norwich at 5,500 feet. Being pitch dark each one of us took off individually and after levelling off had to keep our eyes strained to avoid colliding with other aircraft while circling the town. When I saw flashes followed by fires burning, I immediately reported the situation over the R/T to the operational controllers, asking for further orders. Their prompt reply was: "Continue your vigilance at present altitude," an order I obeyed with the uneasy feeling that we were possibly orbiting Norwich at the wrong height instead of being given a free hand to search for the evil German bombers. While the town was being ripped apart and set on fire I remained at the stipulated altitude, completely impotent. The anti-aircraft defences were unable to shoot for fear of hitting the Spitfires circling above. When ordered back to base it was disclosed that the bombs that had rained on the town were dropped from a height of 1,000 feet. I wondered whether I should have disobeyed the orders given. The city was badly hit and many people had been killed or maimed while I complied with (what I thought were) misguided instructions.

One evening, several days after the bombing of Norwich, Joe and I drove into the town where we were able to view the damage. We were both hesitant to enter a pub in fear of the reception we might receive, but when the bartender met us with friendly gestures we realised that they were just as grateful for our presence as before and our two pints of beer were on the house. After leaving the pub, and on our way back to where the car had been parked, the air-raid sirens sounded seconds before the first bombs exploded. They were so close it was as if the attack had been aimed directly at Joe and me. Walking past a row of terraced Victorian houses, as we dived down a few steps to seek shelter, a the basement door was opened by an old woman who beckoned us inside. There was no time to argue. She said in a quiet, calm voice: "Quick, get in there," pointing to a space under the stairs where two very young children were huddled. While the exploding bombs were shaking the foundations of her house, the old woman's calm voice and gentle manner protected us and soothed the children. It was at this time that I learned a great deal about the true meaning of the word 'brave'. Had I some medals in my pocket at that moment, I would have pinned them on her.

Squadron Leader Haywood and I undertook a shipping recce on May 3rd; he in his usual Spitfire DW-E (BL564) while I was in DW-B

(W3128). We took off at 1025 hours, and passed over the Norfolk coast three minutes later just to the north of the port of Yarmouth. Flying at 200 feet on a course of 105° for thirty-one minutes, we then turned to starboard ten miles off the Dutch coast when we were two miles north of Ijmuiden, at 1059 hours. Visibility was good, up to thirty miles, but with cloud at 10/10ths at 1,000 feet. Then we spotted two small tugs, sailing north in line astern about three miles off the coast. Tugs didn't just 'swan-about' for their health, they must be looking for something to assist. Continuing on, at 1108 hours, just off the Hook of Holland, I spotted five ships, all anchored as we could see no smoke or steam. There were two E-Boats, two more small tugs, and what appeared to be a tanker of about 1,000 tons listing to one side.

Our job was not to make any sort of attack; merely to observe and report back. Others more suitably equipped would be sent out if it was deemed necessary. The damaged tanker was obviously the target for the two tugs we had seen shortly beforehand. At this point, we just turned back, re-crossed the English coast north of Yarmouth, and landed back at RAF Ludham at 1145 hours, to report our findings.

Every mission that I participated in during May 1942, whether singly, in pairs, flights of six or as a squadron, was purposely operational. We responded to many scrambles, convoy protection patrols or long haul escorts of our bombers to targets deeper and deeper into Germany, Holland, Belgium and France. If we or the bombers we were protecting were attacked, our response had to be quick and effective and the attackers destroyed or chased off. Whether those bombs found, damaged or destroyed the target, we rarely had time to find out. If a bomber was hit, the horrendous sight of it being blown out of the sky with no parachutes emerging, made me feel numb.

On May 9th, responding to a scramble, I was ordered to intercept a bandit at 36,000 feet. On my approach its guns started firing at me – I was about to retaliate when, in a split second, I recognised it to be a huge American Boeing B17 Flying Fortress, bristling with gun turrets. That I was not shot down was due to providence alone.

For the next ten days and nights, flying continued without respite, providing plenty of action against the Nazis. On May 14th I flew four sorties; the third of which was as number two to my CO, who had a definite hunch that it would prove interesting. Squadron Leader Haywood seemed to have some sort of built-in radar when it came to these things. This was demonstrated to me when a scramble was called. The duty section would become airborne but the CO would keep himself and me back for a while and then about five or ten minutes later would turn to me and say: "Right, now it's time for you and me to go." Soon after our synchronised take-off, he headed eastwards whilst climbing to 4,000 feet. It was a brilliantly clear day, the sun shining on the back of our heads, the sea below remarkably calm. There were no ships in sight and I was no longer maintaining close formation having eased my Spitfire back from the CO's flank. I was gently weaving and scanning the bright blue sky above and below and straining my eyes towards the horizon and the vast expanse of sea. My vigilance was rewarded when, well below us, flying in the opposite direction was a twin-engine bomber which I immediately recognised as a Junkers 88 – an evil bandit. With lightning speed I switched on my R/T and called my leader: "Red One – Red One, an enemy bomber at 3 o'clock below, heading west." Seconds later came his reply: "Yes I can see him – Tally Ho!" and he began a steep spiralling dive after the foe – myself following in quick pursuit.

When our aircraft came within gun firing range, the Junkers rear gunner opened fire; his aim too good for my liking. My CO fired the first salvo from his Spitfire's two cannons and four machine guns and then pulled into a very steep left turn climb. By the time he was clear of my line of fire the Junkers was spread-eagled across my gun-sight, my right thumb pressed hard on the firing button. While my plane's guns were spitting fire, the tracers raking the enemy bomber, I had no feeling of remorse. The Junkers was my personal enemy! During the attack by my CO, the enemy bomber was turning tightly to the left and then settled on an easterly course. I pressed home a second attack while the bomber, flying with throttles fully open, tried to escape my wrath.

After firing a second salvo I saw flames coming from the bomber's port engine and pieces falling from it. Then I received a distress call from my CO stating that he had been hit. I immediately broke off the engagement with the bomber and escorted him back to base. After our individual landings I was relieved to learn that Squadron Leader Haywood had not been injured but his plane's engine had been damaged and was spewing oil. After a quick re-fuelling and a re-arming of my plane, I flew back over the sea zig-zagging to where I thought the action had taken place. I searched for possible survivors but found nothing. The CO claimed the Ju 88 as being destroyed and awarded a half share to me.

On May 14th, Squadron Leader Haywood was flying his 'E', I was again in 'B'. He said:

> "I was Red 1 of Red Section, 610 Squadron and took off at 1830 hours with Flight Sergeant Mares (Czech Red 2) to patrol over the sea at Lowestoft. At 1845 hours a Ju88 approached from the south at zero feet. I attacked it and fired three bursts of cannon and machine gun and on final burst of machine gun only, from 200 yards astern, and saw strikes on fuselage and port engine with latter three bursts. These were confirmed by Red 2, who then fired a 3 second burst of cannon only at bandit as I broke away.

I saw strikes on port engine, which streamed white vapour until last seen, when bandit was losing height from 50 feet. I claim half of one Ju88 probably destroyed".

My report was as follows:

"I was Red No 2 of Red Section, 610 Squadron, and took off at 1830 hours with Squadron Leader Haywood, Red 1, to patrol over the sea at Lowestoft. At 1845 hours a Ju88 approached from the south at zero feet and was engaged by Squadron Leader Haywood who fired four bursts at it from astern. I saw strikes on port engine and fuselage. As Red 1 broke away I fired a 3 second burst from 200 yards from fine port quarter, flying at 50 feet and saw strikes on port engine which then streamed white vapour. I then broke away and followed Red 1 who I believed to have been hit. When last seen, bandit was losing height from 50 feet with engine still streaming white vapour and I claim half of one Ju88 probably destroyed."

As has already become evident, I am a believer in guardian angels and destiny and that important events in life come in groups of three. Details of the following events may make my reader a believer too.

On May 15th, the squadron was scrambled and was led by one of the flight commanders, Flight Lieutenant Courtenay. The CO, having another of his hunches, stayed on the ground; so I was obliged to do likewise. Ten minutes later we got airborne and climbed into the sky with me tucked alongside his Spitfire. Just like the previous day, we flew on a 090° course for at least forty miles over the North Sea when, this time, I saw a Dornier 217E-2 heading towards the English coast. After reporting the sighting, my CO took first crack at the enemy after which I pressed home a broad-side attack which had his starboard engine coughing out black smoke and flames licking the outside. We were then joined by two more aircraft from 610 Squadron, each one having a go at the now doomed Dornier. The enemy was now heading on an easterly course with no chance of making it back home, yet it flew on with its engine burning and when the port side propeller stopped the bomber pancaked onto the smooth sea. That was when I realised that I was the only witness to the end of yet another Nazi attempt to deliver bombs on a British target. My Spitfire was performing impeccably, largely thanks to the ever-faithful ground crew. So, with enough fuel in my tanks, I circled over the still floating plane, to observe the crew emerge from the port side fuselage door. While they huddled together, with some remorse in my heart, I took my plane up to 2,000 feet and requested a 'fix' and reported the facts to the operations controller. After setting course for Great Yarmouth, I was assured that my message had been duly acted upon and a marine vessel had been sent on its way. I altered my course to land safely back at base.

My CO, Squadron Leader Haywood, along with Pilot Officer Hokam and myself were credited with having destroyed one Dornier 217E-2. During the de-briefing I told the intelligence officer of the crew and the lifeboat proceeding to rescue them. My CO decided that he and I should drive in his official Humber station wagon to Great Yarmouth. His intention was, if an interpreter was available, to have a word with the Dornier crew. We arrived some hours after the plane had ditched and to my distress were told that all the crew were now dead. They had been stripped of their clothes to allow close scrutiny to be carried out by the intelligence department. The CO and I returned to RAF Ludham in a very sombre mood; I don't think a word passed between us. In spite of this close encounter with the dead crew of the Dornier and the powerful impact it had upon me, I remained steadfast in my resolve to accomplish my original mission. I was helped enormously by the bulldog-like determination of the British to get ever closer to the jugular vein of the Nazis. The Dornier was from the second staffel of KG 40 (Werk No 1190) and its code had been F8+LM. Oberfeldwebel Martin Kalisch and his crew were reported missing.

Squadron Leader Haywood later made out this combat report:

"Together with Yellow Section we engaged a Do217E-2 approximately 15 miles north-east of Yarmouth at 1805. I made three attacks and saw strikes on fueslage confirmed by White 2, F/Sgt Mares, and I claim one quarter of this Do217E-2 destroyed. Bandit was seen to strike the sea and sink."

My report stated:

"I was White No. 2... together with Yellow Section we engaged a Do217E-2 approximately 15 miles north-east of Yarmouth at 1805. I made three attacks and saw a piece fall off the tail of bandit and saw his port engine catch fire. I claim one quarter of this Do217 destroyed."

A third member involved in this combat was our wing leader, Wing Commander Prosser Hanks. No doubt due to our recent successes and engagements over the last couple of days, he too wanted a piece of the action and had taken off to join in the fun. Not only that but the Canadians of 412 (RCAF) Squadron from Martlesham had been sent off over the North Sea. Our squadron diary records the day's events well:

"White Section, 1845 – 1935 hours, visibility ten miles. Section flew over convoy NUMERAL at 3,000 feet after making R/T contact and orbited five miles east of the convoy for three minutes, then turned due south. Three minutes later, at 1900 hours, White 2 called White 1 – "Below in front!" White 1 identified a Ju88 approaching head-on from the south at zero feet, one mile ahead. Made a head-on attack from 500 feet firing long burst closing from 300 yards and passed 50 feet above enemy aircraft. White 2 saw strikes on fuselage from nose to tail. Return fire experienced from the nose of enemy aircraft and from dorsal position saw the port wing of White 1 penetrated by a machine gun bullet. Fire from the dorsal gun was stopped by attack by White 2. As White 1 passed over bandit, White 2 made an attack from astern with a two second burst of cannon and machine gun from 150 yards and saw strikes on port wing and engine, although cannons then failed to function. White 1 circled and attacked again from the starboard quarter to astern until his ammunition was finished but saw no strikes. White 2 then attacked from 150 yards astern until ammunition was finished, firing one burst on starboard engine and one on cockpit. Port engine streamed smoke and dorsal gun ceased firing. White 1, believing his ammunition exhausted, flew alongside bandit at 1,000 yards for ten miles at 200mph IAS (indicated air speed), during which time enemy aircraft tried to gain cloud and saw Wing Commander Hanks approach five miles behind at sea level and make a feint attack on enemy aircraft which dived back to sea level in front of Wing Commander Hanks who made his attack from astern, after which White 2 made a final attack on bandit hoping his cannons would function but he was unable to fire them. When last seen, both engines of the bandit were smoking and two oil streaks seen on the sea in pairs at regular intervals and it is doubtful if enemy aircraft regained its base. Camouflage of enemy aircraft was dark grey. Sergeant Mares believes the cross on the fuselage was enclosed in a circle and the space between the cross and the circumference was painted red. Squadron Leader Haywood and Sergeant Mares landed 1935 hours."

The bandit was shared between three of us as a probable and we certainly believed the bomber would not have got home for it had a long way to go to regain the enemy coast. With its engines spewing out oil and both smoking, they would not have been able to function for much longer. We now know that there were no Ju88s lost on this day but that two Dornier 217E-4s of KG2 failed to get back from sorties at this time against the convoy. One Dornier was definitely brought down by the Canadians of 412 Squadron, just before 7pm.

One Dornier (Werk No.5373) was coded U5+BL, the other was (Werk No.5378) U5+CL, flown respectively by Oberfeldwebel Karl Fischer and Oberleutnant Karl Berges. They and their crews were reported missing and no other Fighter Command claims were made on this day in this area. Did we mistake the identity of our adversary? In the heat of battle it often happened that one's eyes saw what one wanted to see and it is no secret that often fighter pilots failed to correctly identify other aircraft in the air. Dorniers were identified as Me110s and Ju88s, Hurricanes mistaken for Me109s, Beaufighters for Ju88s and so on. Often, intercepting pilots, on being told what to expect to see, saw exactly that; which resulted in friendly aircraft being shot down. Our bomber was low down, well camouflaged in dark grey, blending with the sea, chucking out smoke and oil, while we were dodging return fire in the initial stages. Perhaps it was a Dornier and not a Ju88.

At 5.15pm on May 16th, the CO, with me as his loyal twin, climbed the ladder of success of the previous two days, and set course several minutes after the bulk of 610 Squadron had been ordered into the air. At a height of 3,000 feet plus, we crossed the coast at Lowestoft, maintaining a south-easterly course – this time directed by the CO's intuition towards another of Hitler's Ju88s on its way to kill innocent people in Britain. After spotting us, the Junkers' crew, overwhelmed by the sight of two Spitfires, got the message before we were within range with our combined firepower of four canons and eight machine guns and promptly made a 180 degree turn and streaked off. They were making for some haze, which was hanging over the blue sea. With our Merlin engines at full throttle the CO and I were in no mood to let him escape. When we had caught up, the tail gunner of the bomber was somewhat disoriented by the low western sun and his tracers presented no severe threat to us. We began to fire almost simultaneously; myself from line astern, the CO slightly to port, aiming at the nose of the bomber. One of the engines blew up, its fragments passed my plane a little too closely. It continued to fly on whilst being shot at until, at zero feet, it was swallowed up in a bank of fog. Our guns empty, we set course back to base. When we were over the airfield, I disobeyed Squadron Leader Haywood's orders to 'stick like glue' to him and performed a victory roll a safe distance behind.

During the de-briefing, I noticed a distinct touch of respect from Squadron Leader Haywood for my active participation in the combat of the past three days. Our claim of yet another German deliverer of carnage was duly noted and recorded. When the CO received an air ministry order that I was to be posted to 313 Squadron at RAF Fairlop, he did his utmost to have the order cancelled but unfortunately for me, his genuine efforts failed, leaving me very upset indeed at having to leave. I pleaded desperately with the CO of 610 Squadron to find a way for me to stay, which he promised to try to do. When he realised that the order was politically motivated and the Czech squadrons badly needed pilots, especially those experienced in battle with the enemy, I had to go.

Meanwhile, to stop me brooding, the CO and I were kept very busy on operational sorties. I was also instructed to fly the squadron's Magister and deliver a Sergeant Creagh to RAF Acaster Malbis for his posting. I enjoyed the return trip in the delightfully light plane and practised aerial ballet.

Squadron Leader Haywood wrote the following commendation in my logbook on May 20th 1942:

> "F/Sgt Mares has been with me for nearly two months and has flown as my number two during this period. On three days we downed one Dornier 217 destroyed and two probable Ju88s. He has proved himself to be an exceptional pilot of great prowess.

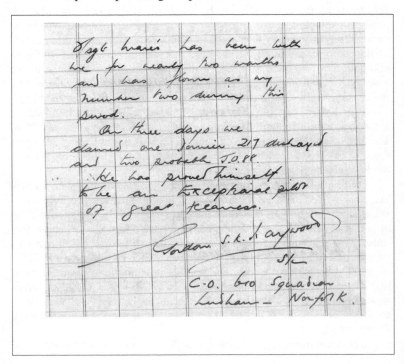

CHAPTER 17

CZECH SQUADRONS

On the sad day of my departure from 610 Squadron at RAF Ludham, I discovered that whoever had used my car last had failed to live up to the contract. Counting the petrol coupons that I was issued with by the station administrative 'Scrooge', I wondered whether I would have enough to carry out my journey to RAF Fairlop. I was also troubled by the knowledge that all the road identification and directional signs had been removed as a precaution in the event of an invasion. Unfortunately it was not possible to call control to give me a course for home. A strategy therefore had to be worked out. From previous experience and by tuition from fellow squadron pilots who also owned cars, the idea was to make frequent calls on the road-side filling stations, where a puffed up display of the pilot's brevet and medal ribbons, would be enough to grab the attention of the garage boss. At the same time, a look of desperation, although never overdone, would possibly result in an odd gallon or two being supplied without the necessary coupons. If one was lucky to pull in when a large lorry was being refuelled, the driver's generosity might extend to having the car's tank filled to the brim.

After having lost our way once or twice, especially when getting close to London, Joe and I arrived safely at RAF Fairlop on May 25th. The two of us reported to Flight Lieutenant V Hajek who was acting as the CO of 313 Squadron. Once more, Joe and I shared the accommodation, which was more than adequate.

As soon as I settled in my billet, I searched for Michel, who I knew had been posted to 313 Squadron some months earlier. I was absolutely stunned to learn that on March 27th 1942, while engaged on an operational mission over France, he had crashed into the sea about five miles west of Ostend. I wanted to know how it had taken almost two months for me to discover this sad news – it was unforgivable. This meant that I was now the only one remaining from the original five who had escaped from our Motherland in 1939. It was a blood curdling shock, which left me thinking that my chances of survival were very slim. Michel's name is inscribed on Panel 70 of the RAF Memorial at Runnymeade.

In contrast to life as a member of the RAF's 601 and 610 Squadrons, in 313 Squadron there was a gulf between the officers and other ranks. However, as I came looking for action against the Nazis, this did not bother me unduly, I merely wanted to be noted for my flying capabilities.

The reader may wonder why I was so against joining a Czech squadron and being with my fellow countrymen. The truth is that my memories of serving in the Czech Air Force before the war were so incompatible with my life in the Royal Air Force. The difference between receiving orders from RAF officers and from Czech officers was considerable. If you were a non-commissioned officer, as I was, or even of lower rank, the gulf between you and the officers was very, very wide and strictly observed. During the war when the Czech squadrons were being formed in England, I joined as an NCO so that this gulf affected me. One rarely got to know such men as Wing Commander Alois Vasatko, our wing leader, other than by his orders. I judged our officers only by the way their orders were handed down.

However, by this period in WWII the Czech officers had mellowed a little, having experienced and learned how the RAF leaders did it in Britain. When I joined the RAF squadrons the CO personally welcomed me. He introduced me to everyone and from then on I became part of a very efficient team. I was never afraid to talk to him or the flight commanders, using their christian names, which I wouldn't dream of doing in the Czech hierarchy. Nevertheless, Wing Commander Vasatko was a highly intelligent man and a respected person whose orders I willingly accepted.

Some time previously, whilst still serving with 610 Squadron, I had been recommended for a commission, eventually to be told by the CO that it had been refused on political grounds and that he had no power to do anything about it. In the Czech forces one could not become an officer unless of a high grade education. In the RAF, during the war, men were commissioned on merit of achievements; an NCO could lead, often having a less experienced officer as his number two. While serving with the Czech squadrons, missions could only be led by officers, no matter how little experience they had. This was the policy in the Czech squadrons right up to the end of the war.

Joe and I soon became an integral part of the Czech squadron and were made to feel very welcome. My first sortie was a Sector Recce on May 26th. There was no flying of great importance until May 30th when, during the morning, I flew a one hour forty minutes Convoy Patrol with Sergeant Dehnal in Spitfire BM483. I then took part in a 'Rodeo' in the evening. A Rodeo was a fighter sweep over enemy territory without bombers. This mission saw four squadrons of Spitfires forming a patrol over St Omer at 25,000 feet, for the sole purpose of trying to lure enemy aircraft towards us whilst daylight bombing raids were carried out over Holland.

We took off at 2015 hours, led by our CO Squadron Leader K Mrazek DFC. This time I was flying BM322 behind my flight commander, Flight Lieutenant Hajek. The Hornchurch Wing, on this occasion, consisted of 22, 64 and 313 Squadrons led, not by a wing leader, but by Squadron Leader W G G Duncan Smith DFC, CO of 64 Squadron. We took off from RAF Fairlop and made a rendezvous with the Hornchurch squadrons over Hornchurch, then headed south, crossing out over Rye while setting course for St Ingelvert, where we crossed into France at 2100 hours. The thirty-six Spitfires then began to climb to 25,000 feet and once over St Omer, we turned to port. Heading back towards Gravelines we turned again, this time to Cap Gris Nez, where a final turn put us over Guines, from where we headed back to England.

Many times we were to fly this type of operation and see virtually nothing. The Germans normally knew whether we had bombers with us. Unless they felt particularly aggressive, they knew we alone posed no danger, so why mix with us. If they were unsure they might come up and look us over and, if no bombers were visible and they could see no straggling Spitfires to pick off, they would leave us well alone. They did so on this occasion. Eight Me109s and some Focke-Wulf (Fw)190s were spotted way above us, obviously giving us the once over. Although they dived down from 27,000 feet they did not engage and soon turned away. Who could blame them? We were thirty-six Spitfires, the best RAF fighter around and, although the new Fw190 was superior to our Spitfire Vs in battle, nothing is certain, so why risk the loss of a couple of Fw190s just to knock down a couple of Spitfires? At best we had diverted a few German fighters away from the main operation and hopefully saved some bombers from attack. After this bit of excitement, we headed back over the sea, reducing height gradually and after crossing the English coast at Dungeness, started landing back at 2145 hours, in time for a late supper.

During the first three days of June 1942, we flew five offensive sorties giving support to some Hurricanes who were dive bombing invasion barges – an assortment of small boats anchored along the coast between Ostend and Dunkirk. On another occasion their target was a silk factory at Calais and on each sortie we followed the bombing by pumping our cannon shells into the boats or nearby factory roofs. A heavy anti-aircraft barrage took its toll on the Hurricanes and even our Spitfires required some patching-up when we returned. These five missions represented seven hours of operational flying, of which at least two hours were spent dicing with death over the target.

After a very short spell with 313 Squadron I was posted to 312 (Czech) Squadron based at RAF Harrowbeer at Yelverton, ten miles north of Plymouth, South Devon. Joe did not get posted with me. Whether I had become surplus to requirements at 313 Squadron or was poached by 312 Squadron, I never cared to find out. Although I disliked the frequent posting from one squadron to another, as long as my flying time was filled with action and I was able to inflict my personal revenge on the enemies of peace and freedom, it was all OK with me.

For this posting to RAF Harrowbeer, I ensured that my car had a full tank and I kept a reserve petrol coupon in my wallet. I set off on June 12th for Wolverhampton to spend three days with Cliff and his family at their house. I was greeted lovingly and, as usual, they were determined to spoil me. Later that evening, Cliff took me to his club where my much improved snooker was remarked upon. I had been able to practise on the snooker tables at each RAF base and I was now a worthy opponent. I found myself challenged by their club snooker champion to a game in which I was offered a three black ball start. The challenger was a manager of a nearby Dunlop factory and Cliff, who knew that my car tyres were rather bald, suggested that the bet should be, if I won, that I would be provided with four new tyres. Whether it was a fix or not, that particular evening I played like Joe Davis and beat my opponent fair and square and two weeks later the tyres were delivered to Tavistock railway station. Tavistock was a lovely ancient town six miles north of my new base at Harrowbeer.

On my way from Wolverhampton to Harrowbeer, I called on Beth in Exeter with whom I had corresponded ever since being introduced by Mr and Mrs Petherick. Beth was one year older than me and lived with her parents – retired farmers – in a nice house named 'Katomba', situated on the fringe of the town. She worked as a clerk for a firm of solicitors in Exeter. Beth was pleased with the surprise visit, as was her mother, a short, slightly portly lady. During the couple of hours that I could spare, I clearly understood that I had become the man chosen for Beth, at least by her mother! I left with my head in a spin, absolutely confused with the perplexity of the situation.

RAF Harrowbeer had been built hurriedly in March 1941 and became officially operational on August 15th of the same year. The very first plane to land was a Blenheim bomber. A Blenheim squadron arrived in September, which was replaced in October by 302 (Polish) Spitfire Squadron led by Squadron Leader Julian Kowalski. In May 1942, 312 Squadron arrived with their VB Spitfires led by a former regular Czech Air Force officer, Squadron Leader Cermak. He was an officer everyone respected; he had an aura about him. He was a good leader, not just in the air but also on the ground. You always felt you would profit by listening to what he had to say. He was a man I really liked for the gulf between officers and NCOs was never observed by him, and he was friendly to one and all. I, and others, would have given our lives for him and followed him anywhere.

As ordered, I reported for flying duties at RAF Harrowbeer on June 16th, being cordially greeted by the CO of 312 Squadron who assigned me to fly with 'A' Flight. The billets and the mess facilities were to the west of the airfield, in and around the small village of Crapstone. In no time at all we found the friendliest, quaintest pub by the name of 'Who'd Have Thought It' in the village of Milton Coombe.

One of Harrowbeer's three runways was very close and running parallel with the Plymouth to Yelverton main road and, to make things more interesting, the approach from the south was marked by a thirty foot high rock, fraternisation with which was not recommended. Following my first operational flight on June 17th, which was to carry out a 'shipping recce', 'A' Flight was detached for three days to RAF Bolt Head – an airstrip situated on the edge of a headland about two miles south of Salcombe. There we were at a constant state of readiness on a grass strip with a steel mesh laid over to form a runway that headed out towards the sea below. It only took ten minutes of flying time from Harrowbeer to Bolt Head, where there was tented accommodation and a field kitchen, providing all that one could wish for on a camping holiday.

There was a seriously urgent need to maintain the Spitfires at readiness, so that we were capable of being scrambled within seconds of a red signal-rocket being fired. It was normal practice to keep a couple of aircraft parked at the top edge of the runway; the pilot remaining strapped into his seat and the engine being kept warm by starting it up at fifteen-minute intervals. When the scramble came, those on readiness were required to be airborne within seconds to catch intruding German fighter-bombers intent on dropping their bombs on the coastal towns and villages. Speed was vital to take off, intercept, give chase to, and if possible destroy, any Hun that appeared. The order was imprinted upon my mind, stirring my commitment to succeed. The Fw190s were faster than our Spitfire VBs, therefore any seconds lost in getting airborne would mean a failure of the mission or even worse, getting ourselves shot down.

On June 23rd 1942, 312 Squadron became part of 10 Group's 'Ramrod' 23 in the late afternoon. A Ramrod was a bomber escort mission. Six Boston aircraft were to bomb Morlaix airfield and the Exeter Wing, of which 312 and 310 Squadrons were a part, acted as a rear escort. 19 and 234 Squadrons were also involved. At 1830 hours, the formations crossed the coast at Start Point, flying at sea level and staying low for twenty minutes to avoid radar detection. They then began to climb, making landfall at Plestin at 9,000 feet. 310 Squadron maintained this height while 312 Squadron flew at 10,000 feet off to port. Meanwhile 313 Squadron was covering everyone at 11,000 feet off to starboard.

The Bostons went in and bombed the Morlaix airfield from the east and explosions were seen on the south-west dispersal. The flak was intense for some minutes. The formations then turned for home, crossing the French coast just east of the Ile-de-Batz. At that moment 310's CO, the veteran Squadron Leader Frantisek Dolezal, spotted a Fw190 preparing to make an attack on the Bostons. He attacked the Fw190 but saw no result. Flight Lieutenant E Foit attacked the same aircraft and it went down smoking. Flight Lieutenant Foit was ordered to reform but one of the Boston crews saw the Fw190 go into the sea.

There were more Fw190s about and several followed our formation back to England; obviously waiting for a moment to pick someone off. Squadron Leader Dolezal saw a Spitfire plunge into the sea about ten miles from Berry Head but he had seen no combat above nor did he see anyone bail out. In the skirmishes in and around the clouds and the bombers, three Spitfires of 312 Squadron were hit. Of those, Flight Lieutenant J Kasal landed at RAF Exeter with his fighter badly damaged; Flying Officer Perina had to crash land at RAF Bolt Head with battle damage; while Sergeant V Ruprecht also got his damaged Spitfire safely down at RAF Exeter. Squadron Leader P R G Davies, CO of 19 Squadron looked back and down to see some splashes on the sea. Going down to investigate, he found three crashed aircraft in the water. He also spotted a Fw190 that he attacked and damaged. However, 19 Squadron lost one of their Spitfires (W3644) flown by Sergeant Ridings and had another shot-up off Start Point.

While all this was happening, back at RAF Bolt Head four aircraft were at a state of readiness; two were from 312 Squadron and two from 310 Squadron. At 1908 hours we were scrambled to help protect the returning formation from being harried by Fw190s over the sea. Our meticulous training came into play. As soon as I pressed the starter button, the warm engine roared into life. Pilot Officer Strihavka, Flight Sergeant Drejtnar, my companion and I, began to move forward. When the cable connecting my Spitfire to the starter trolley was disconnected, the aircraft and I leapt into action; the right rudder fully on to make a line-up and take-off simultaneous. The throttle was at full setting when a mighty crash occurred. The propeller of my aircraft had sliced into another plane which had, at that moment, only just come into my view. When a Spitfire is on the ground the nose and wings completely obscure any forward vision thus I could only conclude that whoever parked the plane that I hit, must have been suffering a brain black out. I despaired, as if the enemy had shot me down. According to 310 Squadron, my BL512 crunched into Pilot Officer Strihavka's Bl265 before he had even moved, happily without causing him any injury whatsoever. After this misfortune, I flew another sortie on the same day, determined to even the score. To my disappointment, no German aircraft were intercepted. After that, I flew on eleven more occasions from the satellite airfield at RAF Bolt Head where the lesson of the crash was well and truly learnt so that I was always aware of where aircraft were parked.

However, the other two aircraft managed to get away but soon became separated as they headed for Exeter, where there were reports of German fighters over the English mainland. Over Start Point, Flight Sergeant Drejtnar saw the wing's Spitfires heading in and down towards the airfield at Exeter and then spotted a lone Fw190 at 10,000 feet above them. He immediately gave a 'Tally-Ho' but then lost sight of the Fw190. Climbing to 18,000 feet, he caught sight of it again but this time the German fighter turned and came down on him, more or less head-on. Both fighters began firing at about 600 yards apart and Flight Sergeant Drejtnar saw hits, almost at the same time that his Spitfire was hit in the starboard wing and pieces were blown off. A splinter wounded him in his arm as his aircraft went into an uncontrollable spin from which recovery proved impossible. Finally Flight Sergeant Drejtnar had to bail out at 5,000 feet, landing heavily at the village of Black Dog near Witheridge, twelve miles north-west of Exeter, sustaining a simple fracture of his right leg. He later reported that the Fw190 pilot circled around him as he dangled in his parachute before flying off.

As the events of the evening unfolded, it became apparent that the missing Spitfire and the one that Squadron Leader Dolezal had seen crash into the sea, was that flown by our wing leader, Wing Commander Alois Vasatko DFC. He was a legend, a graduate of the Military Academy in Czechoslovakia and had commanded a squadron during the German occupation. He had fought in France, winning the French Légion d'honneur, Croix de Guerre with five palms and four stars. In addition he had also received the Czech Military Cross with two bars.

As soon as the Spitfire had been seen to crash, Squadron Leader Dolezal had alerted the air sea rescue service to find our missing commander. Aircraft hunted over the grey sea and hopes were raised when a dinghy was sighted, however, the occupant turned out to be a German fighter pilot. It later transpired, when this German was picked up and interrogated, that he had collided with a Spitfire and had had to bail out. Wing Commander Alois Vasatko was never found and had obviously gone in with his aircraft, Spitfire BM592 which, as with all RAF wing leaders, was marked on the fuselage with his initials 'AV'.

We now know that the Fw190s were from JG 2 and were obviously feeling rather more aggressive on this evening. The German 'ace' Oberleutnant Egon Mayer (who would end the war with 102 victories) was leading and he claimed two Spitfires. The pilot who collided with Wing Commander Vasatko was Unteroffizier Wilhelm Reuschling of JG 2. Other JG 2 pilots had witnessed this and he was credited with the victory.

A significant event of the day involved the pilot who shot down Flight Sergeant Drejtnar. Oberleutnant Arnim Faber, adjutant of JG 2, after downing Flight Sergeant Drejtnar, had flown west instead of south, crossing over the Bristol Channel rather than the English Channel. Either his compass or his sense of direction was faulty. Once across this expanse of water, he believed he was over France, whereas he was actually over South Wales. Probably getting short of fuel by this time, he spotted an airfield and landed. Unfortunately for him, it was not a German base in north-west France but RAF Pembrey, near Swansea. The luckless Oberleutnant Faber was quickly taken prisoner, having presented the RAF with a perfect example of the Fw190A-3. The RAF, in fact, had been so desperate to secure data on the latest version of the Fw190 that they had been considering a plan to drop someone near a German airfield and steal one! Oberleutnant Faber's mistake made this unnecessary.

After the loss of Wing Commander Vasatko, a former CO of 313 Squadron, Squadron Leader Karel Mrazek was promoted wing commander to take over the Czech Wing.

Following my collision on the ground at RAF Bolt Head, it did not take too long before two more aircraft were available to assume readiness duties. An Fw190 had shot down one of the replacement pilots that flew the next sortie, who managed to bail out but broke a leg on landing. The sad result of the events was one pilot injured, out of action, one Spitfire lost and a further two damaged.

It was to my shame that as a result of the accident, the 'A' Flight commander wrote the following reprimand in my logbook:

> "At Bolt Head, about to take off on an operational sortie,
> failed to ensure that the runway was clear – collided with
> another aircraft. Over anxiety to take-off quickly was the
> cause of carelessness."

For the remainder of June 1942, and on until September 11th, the majority of the squadron operational sorties carried out from RAF Harrowbeer consisted of convoy protection patrols or searching for ship movements along the enemy coast. On the occasion of enemy aircraft putting in an appearance they were usually, after a short skirmish, driven off, some times in a damaged condition.

On August 6th, Beth and her mother came from Exeter to spend a few days with me and stayed at The Rock Hotel at Yelverton close to the airfield. Their arrival diverted my brooding after the event at Bolt Head and their presence helped me to regain my self-confidence, not only as a fighter pilot, but also as a desirable young man! Because I was flying every day, sometimes up to four sorties, I could only be with them in the evenings of their short stay. During this time Beth's mother did her utmost to show me how desirable a girl her daughter was.

On August 19th, the squadron carried out two separate patrols over

Dieppe, and it was on the second of these patrols that we were attacked by a large number of Fw190s, a great battle ensued and a few were shot down. I fired a long burst into one of them but I saw no evidence of serious damage and made no claim. At a lower altitude I caught sight of two Dornier 217Es and made an attack. One of these was claimed by Flying Officer Keprt and the other by Sergeant Liskutin who, as war progressed, scored several victories. All of us landed back safely at Harrowbeer, elated by the success of the missions.

The Dieppe raid, of course, was an important event for Fighter Command as well as the whole combined operations team under Lord Mountbatten. Much has been said and written about the raid on this French port, which cost so many casualties amongst the mainly Canadian raiding force. It was never meant to be anything but a probe, to see if a small force could capture a port for a day and destroy its installations. However the Germans reacted vigorously to it and although it provided much information for the future, the Canadians suffered terribly.

Fighter Command, on the other hand, welcomed this trial by strength, it being the biggest event since the Battle of Britain, two years earlier. Throughout the day, Spitfires, Hurricanes, North American P51 Mustangs, Bostons and Blenheims, tested the German air defence and believed they had inflicted severe losses on both enemy fighters and a force of Dorniers that were intending to bomb the ships. We now know that the claims were optimistic and that the RAF lost far more aircraft than the Germans did, but it proved to be an exciting day.

For 312 Squadron, we claimed a couple of Dorniers, another Dornier damaged, plus two Fw190s probably destroyed and a third Fw190 damaged. Luckily we suffered no losses although Sergeant Tony Liskutin managed to bring his badly damaged Spitfire back with a huge hole in the starboard wing. However, in sharing a Dornier, he brought back a splendid sequence of camera-gun film showing the burning bomber on the water. I flew on two of the squadron's three sorties; the first between 1040-1225 hours in EP435, the second between 1450-1600 hours – both led by the 312 Squadron CO, Squadron Leader Cermak.

Another important sortie, also carried out in August 1942, was when the squadron provided the rear support to bombers carrying out a daylight raid on a target in France. During our rendezvous over the island of Guernsey, our bombers were about to be attacked by several Me109s. A battle ensued and one of the Me109s had its guns trained on me whilst I was in the process of engaging another Me109. The tracers proved much too close to be ignored and realising that the Hun was determined to dispose of me, I performed a flick-half-roll from a steep turn which then placed my adversary at the mercy of my guns as he spiralled down towards the sea. The prime duty of the squadron was to protect the bombers, so I pulled my stressed and shuddering Spitfire upwards to catch up with the other aircraft. Sweat was running down my face and there was time enough to feel scared.

CHAPTER 18

BACK DOWN
TO EARTH WITH A CRASH

On September 2nd 1942 I was told by the squadron adjutant to report
to the CO in his office. I immediately assumed that I was due another
reprimand for the incident at RAF Bolt Head and my resentment began
to take hold. As ordered, I presented myself to Squadron Leader
Cermak, who was very tense and stern faced but, instead of delivering
the expected admonishment he handed me a telegram, shook my hand
and expressed his heartiest congratulations. When I was able to
examine the telegram it read as follows:

> To: Harrowbeer – 312 Squadron – Exeter – 310 Squadron
>
> From: 10 Group
>
> P645 2/9 H.M. the King has been graciously pleased to
> award the D.F.C. to S/LDr F.Dolezal (82593A) (310 Sqdn)
> the D.F.M. to F/Sgt. Mares F. (312 Sqdn). These awards
> are not, repeat not, to be published.   A.OC extends
> his heartiest congratulations – 1055.

After my CO had elaborated on his personal pleasure that I had been so
graciously honoured by HM King George Vl, he handed me another
telegram, the contents of which read as follows:

> H.B.R.   GPJ NR KWY 605/2 Pass self to F/Sgt Mares
> 312 Squadron Harrowbeer Yelverton Devon.   From AM
> Czech Inspectorate Gen P4222 2/9 Best Congratulations on
> your D.F.M.   Good Hunting
>
>
>
> Group Captain J Schejbal = = = 1800/A
> Tinkler B+
> GPJ.   R2125A PJ VA+
> Passed F/Sgt Mares 312 Adj and Stn Adj.
>
>

The general understanding among RAF pilots was that to be awarded the Distinguished Flying Medal (DFM), the recipient had to have shot down a minimum of six enemy aircraft or carried out an extraordinary feat. The prestigious ribbon was worn under the RAF pilot's wings – my pride knew no bounds and certainly no words could adequately express my feelings.

On the day that it was my turn to carry out the search for the two elusive German pocket battleships – the *Scharnhorst* and the *Gneisenau*, Sergeant Motycka was flying as my number two. As we took off from RAF Bolt Head the visibility at only a few feet above the sea was perfect, with only the slightest haze above. My companion was keeping a safe distance and I warned him to be careful not to dip the propeller of his Spitfire in the briny. We flew on a vector of 210°, according to our brief, holding the course whilst maintaining a strict radio silence. When the ships were spotted it was time to climb quickly to 1,000 feet and transmit details of our find. Immediately afterwards, we were to fly back at full throttle to our base to urgently convey the full details to the leader of six two-engine, single-seat Westland Whirlwind light bombers that were standing by at Bolt Head.

About thirty-five minutes into the mission, I noticed a silhouette of an oblong mass in the distance at 2 o'clock. The closer we approached the more I thought that it could be a large ship. Whilst I remained unsure, my number two switched on his transmitter and excitedly declared: "There it is – There it is," and began to climb. Having left me no choice in the matter, the radio silence already broken and possibly detected by the Germans, I followed him in the climb and when at sufficient height, transmitted the information about our find. By the time we arrived back at RAF Bolt Head the six Whirlwinds had taken off. Details of our find had been passed to the highest RAF Command and the 'hornets' were buzzing – their sting ready!

I awaited the return of the bombers with cramp gripping my stomach, my reputation as a reliable RAF pilot was, once again, at stake. After fifty-five seemingly endless minutes, the Whirlwinds returned safely and after their leader had a short talk with the officer in charge Sergeant Motycka and I were summoned. Something told me that I was in deep trouble.

When we joined the group, the leader of the six bombers was, to my relief, gleefully retelling his experience and that of the Whirlwind crews. He explained that, just as I described, upon first sight of the large shape in the sea he too believed that it was a warship. When they climbed to the bombing height of 2,000 feet, their approach did not bring forth any anti-aircraft barrage and he realised, at the very last moment that the large shape was in fact a solitary oblong rock that had been cunningly camouflaged by the Germans to resemble a ship. Realising that the rock target was a ploy, they got out of the area as fast as their twin-engine Whirlwind bombers could carry them; the cargo of bombs remaining in their aircrafts' bellies. My conscience was relieved and the cramp in my stomach began to ease as forgiveness from the bombing leader and my own CO appeared unconditional.

Having logged a total of 232 operational flying hours which exceeded the prescribed 200, I was posted for a 'rest' to 2 Delivery Flight which was based at RAF Colerne; a well established camp situated three miles north of the spa town of Bath. Before taking up any full-time duties I was able to have a ten days' leave of absence which was mainly spent with the Cousins family at Wolverhampton. For the last two days, I chose to be with Beth and her parents, in their spacious home in Exeter. Once more I had the feeling that they were making plans for my future.

I arrived at RAF Colerne on September 22nd 1942 and reported for duty to the flight commander, Squadron Leader Howard Williams DFC. I offered the standard RAF salute and stated my name: "Warrant Officer Mares, 787653, reporting for duty, sir." The CO pondered for a moment, then, with a twitch of a smile, looked me straight in the eye and replied: "Ah! Are you by any chance the chap who sent six Whirlwinds to bomb a rock in the ocean?" My face sagged and a mixture of anger and surprise turned my smart salute into a sloppy wave. Hesitating, I made the reply: "Well, yes sir..." but before I could say any more, he shook my hand saying "Good show Warrant Officer Mares, a very interesting story indeed." I had a further boost to my confidence when I read the reference that my old CO of 312 Squadron had written for me: "He is an experienced and reliable pilot and during the period of his attachment to 312 Squadron, I have been well satisfied with him."

The function of this new unit was the collection and delivery of aircraft of all shapes and sizes, with the exception of the four-engine types. The aircraft were a mixture of new and old; some ready for the scrapheap, others to be flown to or from the maintenance units (MUs). In order to expedite the movement of the delivery pilots, three de Havilland Dominies were kept on strength to ferry myself and sixteen other pilots around. The Dominie was a twin-engine de Havilland Dragon Rapide seven-seat bi-plane, and a delightful aircraft to fly. My first assignment at 2 Delivery Flight at Colerne was on September 24th when I was flown in the Dominie to RAF Digby where I collected a Spitfire to be flown to the maintenance unit at Hamble.

I returned briefly to RAF Harrowbeer on September 26th, a day to remember – to my great pride and with no little embarrassment. Air Vice-Marshal A H Orlebar CBE, AFC (a WWI fighter pilot and the man who had led the famous Schneider Trophy team of the RAF in the 1930s) arrived at RAF Harrowbeer to present some decorations. He also presented the squadron with its crest, approved of by the king of

England and bearing the motto *'Non multi sed multa'* – translated from the Latin as: 'Not many but much', which probably referred to we few Czechs doing a lot of good. The stork emblem in the middle referred to many earlier members of 312 Squadron who had flown in France in the famous Cigognes squadron. Then it was my turn to stand before the great man, to have him pin on my breast the silver Distinguished Flying Medal (DFM) with its white and purple diagonally striped ribbon. There were also other decorations, as five of us had been awarded the Czech War Cross, and a further fifteen received the Czech Medal for Gallantry.

<u>Czech War Cross</u>
Flight Sergeant Frantisek Mares
Flight Lieutenant Karel Kasal
Flight Lieutenant Antonin (Tony) Liska
Warrant Officer S Sotek
Sergeant Josef Novotny

<u>Czech Medal for Gallantry</u>
Flying Officer Josef Keprt
Pilot Officer F Chabera
Flight Sergeant Josef Pipa
Flight Sergeant Z Karasek
Flight Lieutenant Victor Kaslik
Flight Lieutenant Adolf Vrana
Flight Sergeant Jaroslav Dubrovolny
Sergeant Vlada Kopecek
Flight Sergeant Tomas Motycka
Sergeant Josef Kohout
Sergeant Miroslav (Tony) Liskutin
Sergeant Jan Mayer
Sergeant Robert Ossendorf
Sergeant Vaclav Ruprecht
Sergeant Stanislaw Tocaure

We got the works that day. The Czech band gave a concert in the sergeants' mess and then another later in the afternoon in the station gymnasium. In the evening, we held a dance in the airmen's mess, which was a great success. In all – a great day to remember.

Back at RAF Colerne, other flights with 2 Delivery Flight included the transfer of a Spitfire from RAF Manston to RAF Northolt, then taking another back to Manston where the Dominie 'taxi' picked me up. I flew a number of other types of planes and most I was in harmony with, the only one that I detested was the Cygnet. The flights were on a daily basis and continued throughout October regardless of how bad the weather might be. My strong desire to fly one of the Dominie aircraft was satisfied when, on October 10th, I flew X7412 for the first time. My 'payload' was five trustful passengers to do, of all things, a weather test flight. In spite of the worsening weather, I flew almost every day and, on October 25th I experienced another first was when I took up a Boulton Paul Defiant; a torpedo-carrying fighter-bomber with a twin-gun turret mounted over and behind the pilot's seat. By the end of October I had added sixteen hours flying to my logbook total that had now reached 627 hours; some of which had been quite hazardous!

On November 1st, after a very happy spell of Dominie flying, I was flown to RAF Exeter in bad weather to collect an old Hurricane 3151 which had to be delivered to RAF Colerne and from there to its retirement destination. I arrived at Exeter with my parachute over my shoulder but the Hurricane was still being worked on by the fitters and riggers. They were stripping the aircraft of its R/T and other components so I left them to it, asking them to ring the sergeants' mess when the plane was ready. In fact I received a call from flying control advising that the weather had begun to clamp down and that the flight had been called off for the day. Feeling in need of some comfort, I gave control the telephone number of Beth's home where Beth's mother was only too pleased to offer me a bed for the night. When Beth arrived home from work, she too, was very pleased to see me but I could not say the same for her father, who chose to remain disapprovingly distant.

After a very pleasant overnight stay, I returned to the airfield, driven by Beth's mother in her shiney Wolseley 14 saloon car. It was still raining and the cloud base was sagging towards the ground as I climbed the steps of the flying control tower, but I received an optimistic report that take-off should be possible by early afternoon. Sure enough, after lunch in the sergeants' mess, the weather had improved. When I returned to the flying control tower I was told that my departure was scheduled for 3pm. Although the clouds were still rather low I felt confident that it would be OK to fly without radio communication so long as I could maintain visual contact with the ground all the way to RAF Colerne, staying below the rain-laden clouds.

I was given permission to fly and I actually took off at 2.45pm, immediately setting a course that would keep me clear of the Black Down hills on my right, the ground rising towards Exmoor on my left and the Mendips ahead where I aimed to turn eastwards, following the low ground to Frome, then round the back of the Mendips to Bath, thence turning north for the remaining two miles to RAF Colerne. As long as the predicted weather conditions remained unchanged there was no problem flying at 600 feet, and I had a margin of safety. However, on nearing the Mendips, the moisture-laden clouds descended even lower, reducing the visibility to 500 yards ahead and the ground was only visible if I reduced my height to 400 feet or below. These, I deemed, were dangerous flying conditions so I opted for a reciprocal course back to RAF Exeter.

The weather became even more spiteful and after flying for a further three minutes, I encountered a bank of thick mist that was visually impenetrable. Having no choice I turned again onto a northerly course, reverting to my original plan to fly at 400 feet, north-easterly towards Frome – which I found shrouded by a wall-like barrier of fog. I turned left and made the decision to land as soon as possible, before hitting the Mendips or high tension cables that might be ahead. When a small field appeared below, and remembering that the wind direction was from the south, I did a tight left turn onto a heading of about 150° and lowered the undercarriage and full flaps, and made a power approach. When just over a stone wall, I reduced the engine power. Almost immediately I touched down on the grass, applied the brakes, skidded past a haystack and on towards the stone wall at the other side of the field. Before the inevitable crash I switched off the ignition and the fuel. It was a horrendous collision. My back took the full force of the impact. Not content, the Hurricane jumped over a lane and finally crashed through a stone wall on the other side. A deadly silence followed.

Although stunned, my sub-conscious prompted me to climb out of the wreck, my exit hastened by the strong smell of petrol. I had had no choice in attempting to land on a postage stamp sized field but did not expect to demolish two stone walls in the process. The poor Hurricane, once a Battle of Britain hero, was now lying before me, deserving my unconditional apology. If only it could be magically restored and have gone into honourable retirement. I was truly sorry yet grateful that the cockpit section had protected me from serious injury. Having flown countless sorties and fought many battles in Hurricanes I felt it only right that I should salute the sad ending of a brave Hurricane and say: "Thanks pal".

The loud noise of the crashing aircraft immediately brought a farmer driving his tractor to the scene. When he saw me standing by the wreck I think he thought that I was merely an apparition. When I spoke, his eyes widened and nearly popped out of their sockets. After calming down and accepting that I was indeed real, he drove me, with my parachute, to his nearby farmhouse. His wife very kindly poured me a large whisky while her husband phoned the police. I then asked if I could ring the CO of the delivery flight at RAF Colerne.

Two policemen were the first to arrive on the scene – I asked one of them to guard the petrol-soaked wreck while the other, a sergeant, took down some details. My CO, Squadron Leader Williams, then arrived with our ground crew flight sergeant who set about dealing with the removal of the plane. On my return to Colerne, accompanied by the CO, I was expecting to receive a reprimand but it never came. To my complete surprise, his anger was directed at RAF Exeter flying control for allowing me to set off in such horrid weather, especially in a plane with no communication equipment. The following morning I was taken in the Dominie to RAF Zeals from where I flew, in perfect weather, a brand new Spitfire to RAF Church Stanton, later being picked up by one of the Dominies.

On November 25th 1942, I took the controls for the first time of a Lysander, N7543, a type I had escorted in the past on their 'hush-hush' missions to France. It was not a plane that I was familiar with so I felt that I ought to seek out a pilot who had experience with this towering, odd-looking high wing monoplane, to brief me on its behaviour. I was collecting the plane from RAF Harrowbeer where I could find no one around who could brief me except a ground staff rigger. As I was about to start up the Hercules radial engine I asked the rigger if there was anything special I should know about the aircraft. Among other points he said: "Sir, I understand that it is essential to trim the elevator fully forward. Failure to do so may result in the aircraft performing a loop on take-off." I thanked him, and then wondered if it would be wise to accept his tip as a serious suggestion. I did as he suggested, turning the trim wheel fully forward. The rigger had been correct and furthermore, deserved at least a Mention in Despatches! As soon as the wheels of the Lysander left the runway, it required plenty of push on the joystick to prevent the plane climbing like a rocket from a launch pad but it was not long before I got the feel of the aircraft and my confidence in it grew. I happily flew to RAF Colerne and then on to RAF Elstree the next day where I was able to prove that a Lysander could be landed on a sixpenny piece.

For the rest of my attachment to the delivery flight I was kept busy collecting many types of plane, some of which I had not flown before, including a brand new Hawker Typhoon. The notion that being posted to such a flight constituted 'a rest' could not have been further from the truth. Pilots were expected to fly all sorts of aircraft they had never flown before, often without adequate introduction or any explanation of the unknown characteristics. The extreme concentration and responsibility certainly weighed heavily on me. On the more pleasant side, I really enjoyed being 'the skipper' of the Dominie which, by March 10th 1943, I had flown for fifty-three contented hours. I loved flying the Dominie without passengers. I could then throw it about in the air imagining that, if it had guns, I could shoot down a Me109.

It was during my time with the delivery flight that I first encountered Tomas Vybiral, who was then a flight lieutenant but would later be on operations with me as a wing commander. I got very close to him and, of all the Czech officers that I served under, he was the one I knew best.

On one occasion he was the 'taxi' pilot, flying the Dominie. He was known to be a good pilot. Other than Squadron Leader Cermak, who was a real gem, I had the greatest respect for him. After climbing aboard, Flight Lieutenant Vybiral was taxiing along the airfield perimeter prior to taking off, when for some reason unknown to me, he tipped the Dominie up on its nose, bending the props in the process. While I was carefully releasing myself from the seat straps, the thought occurred to me that had I been at the controls, the damage to the aircraft would have weighed heavily on my conscience. Flight Lieutenant Vybiral, however, just shrugged off the incident as one of those things.

On another, more serious occasion, after delivering some brand new Typhoon fighter planes to a Polish squadron, Flight Lieutenant Vybiral collected us in the Dominie. Climbing aboard, as usual, I placed my parachute close beside my seat; the others stowing theirs in the back of the aircraft. No sooner had we taken off when, at about 200 feet, just past the end of the runway, a mighty explosion occurred. From the Dominie window I could see the starboard engine pouring oil and black smoke from under its cowling and the twin-blade propeller motionless. I thought we were doomed. Despite the low altitude, I instinctively grabbed for my parachute but it was not where I had left it. Karel Posta, sitting just across from me, was already strapping it on.

Flight Lieutenant Vybiral was magnificently calm. He managed to climb the Dominie on one engine as gently as he could and as countless training sessions had taught, never turned in the direction of the failed engine. Whilst turning away from the engine belching smoke he nursed the Dominie round and landed safely back on the airfield where the fire crew and the 'blood wagon' stood ready to deal with the emergency. Thanks to the skill of our 'taxi driver' we survived.

After taking a deep sigh of relief, I gave Posta, who still had my parachute strapped on, a few chosen uncomplimentary words, as one might imagine. I knew him as a spontaneously selfish man but a very good pilot. He was five years older than me and was renowned in the Czech Air Force for his daredevil aerobatics. After the war he was invited to perform the most amazing flying display before HM King George VI, the Queen, their children and an entourage of thousands of spectators, including myself. The pageant was held at RAF Farnborough, where Posta took off, flying a specially modified Spitfire. When only a wingspan distance from the runway, he rolled the Spitfire while the undercarriage was still being retracted. When completed, the aircraft was in an inverted position. Remaining at zero feet, he performed a breath-taking and awe-inspiring aerobatic display during which he remained at the grass-skimming inverted position. At the last moment he performed a half-roll to a standing ovation. Brilliant.

After a few days of genuine rest in the company of Beth and her family at Exeter, on March 15th 1943, I resumed operational flying with 313 Squadron which was now based at RAF Church Stanton, located at the northern tip of the Black Down hills between the towns of Wellington and Honiton. Church Stanton (later to be known as RAF Culmhead) was recently built and had three runways and very good facilities. The town of Taunton was some four miles to the north. Church Stanton's station commander was Wing Commander G Blackwood while Wing Commander Karel Mrazek DSO, DFC was still the wing leader. The squadron remained equipped with Spitfire Mark VBs and was commanded by Squadron Leader Jaroslav Himr (who was later to be killed in September 1943). I was assigned to 'B' Flight under Flight Lieutenant Vaclav Bergman.

My first operational sortie with 313 Squadron was the almost inevitable convoy patrol, flying with Flight Sergeant P Kocfelda for 1 hour and 55 minutes on March 19th 1943. On March 26th, I flew another convoy patrol with Sergeant O Spacek. On April 1st Wing Commander Mrazek stood down as wing leader, taking up an administrative post in station HQ; his place being taken by 310 Squadron's former CO, now Wing Commander Frantisek Dolezal DFC.

Since being promoted to the rank of warrant officer, the only noticeable change was that the flight sergeant's crown and three stripes from my uniform, had been replaced by the warrant officer badge which was sewn at a less prominent position lower down the sleeve. Moreover, my flying duties and responsibilities and, above all, my determination to win the war, remained unchanged. Operational flights included escorting eight Whirlwind bombers to attack enemy shipping near Cherbourg on April 9th and three days later we escorted a flight of ten Whirlwinds sent to drop a lethal message on a German airfield adjacent to the French port of Brest. On that occasion the flak was dense and ranged rather too close for my liking. I landed with a sizeable hole in the rudder of my Spitfire and one of the elevator cables was cut by shrapnel, which explained the sloppy controls that I experienced when returning to base.

During the last month of attachment to the delivery flight and since I had rejoined 313 Squadron, my eyes were once again starting to feel uncomfortable, especially the right one. The burning sensation was unpleasant but I kept it to myself. Except for odd days when the weather denied us any flying, operational flights kept the squadron in the air. There were the usual briefings followed by the squadron providing close, low or high altitude, escorts to bombers, ready to tackle any Hun fighters. Shipping patrols or sweeps towards the north-west part of France, made me feel uncomfortable as there was too much of the unfriendly sea beneath me. All it needed was a bullet or piece of shrapnel hitting my Spitfire's engine radiator and I would have to swim back to base.

One of our constant tasks flying with 10 Group was shipping reconnaissance in the South West Approaches. There was a vast amount of sea at this end of the English Channel and the French coast was a long way away, especially for single-engine fighters. In order to hunt for ships over the vast expanse of the South West Approaches, we had to fly reasonably low so, if our engines gave any sign of faltering, we did not have long before having to choose between ditching or bailing out. Over a vast sea out of sight of land, one's ears quickly became attuned to any changes in the Merlin's normally smooth roar!

Four of us went out on a shipping recce on the morning of April 9th – Pilot Officer V Fogler, Flying Officer O Kucers, Sergeant O Spacek and myself (EP606). I cannot recall now if we saw anything or not but perhaps someone did because it led in turn to a shipping strike soon after midday. At 12.45pm, Flight Lieutenant J Muzika led us in escorting Whirlwinds to pre-position for the mission.

We flew outbound at sea level to a point just east of Les Sept-Iles, almost at the French coast, where we jettisoned our long-range fuel tanks. We were well aware that Morlaix airfield was not far away while at Lannion there was a Ju 88 long-range fighter base. At 1335 hours we turned right and carried out a careful search along the coastline west of Ile–de–Batz, then turned north at 1355 hours. We flew either side of the fighter-bombers, ready to help in the anti-flak role but, like so many other sorties, we saw no ships or flak.

We did spot one 'bogey' over France at 2,000 feet, no doubt sent to see what was happening out at sea, but other than intruding on their air space, we were doing no harm to anyone. As we headed home, another 'bogey' was seen behind us and apparently following, making sure we were leaving. It came close enough for us to identify it as a Ju 88 but it left us alone – a very wise move on his part! We left the Whirlwinds at Start Point and flew home.

A similar sortie was flown on April 13th but this time it was evening and this time we had a definite target. Our superiors often liked to order us to 'stir things up' if they had been too quiet and this was one of those days. Rather than just 'sniff' along the French coast, they were sending us to 'poke a stick' at the Luftwaffe by bombing Brest/Guipavas aerodrome. How lucky we felt!

We were away at 2015 hours, setting course once more at sea level and holding this height for twelve minutes before we, and our ten Whirlwind charges, climbed for the French coast. The wing crossed into France at Vierge with us as escort cover at 15,000 feet; a thousand feet above the bombers and their close escort of 65 and 602 Squadrons. The formation turned slightly left in order to swing around and make a bombing run from east to west, which would bring us quickly out to sea once more.

The Whirlwinds bombed in a shallow dive and we could see many hits on the southern dispersal area. Coming out we curved to the right and crossed the coast at L'Ile Vierge where the formation immediately dropped back to zero feet. About fifteen miles into our homeward flight, some Fw190s came up astern of us, one closing to about 1,000 yards, but it did not seem too aggressive and it, and the other three, soon turned back when our Red and Yellow Sections turned up to face them. Four against thirty-six was not good odds at the best of times.

We had taken off at 2020 hours and were back by 2100 hours, myself being in Spitfire AA881. It is surprising how short some of these operations were. In just forty minutes we had crossed to France, flown inland, bombed an airfield, flown out and back again. It often seemed longer but the clock never lies.

April 1943 continued with more shipping recces. One led by Flight Lieutenant V Bergman at midday on the 15th, then a convoy patrol with Jan Skopal the next afternoon. A morning shipping recce on the 25th was followed that afternoon by an 'anti-Rhubarb' patrol with Sergeant Spacek. These sorties were really standing patrols in order to have at least a couple of aircraft in the air in case the Germans mounted a hit-and-run raid on the south coast. These were all the rage at this stage of the war. Fw190s or Me109s would zip across the Channel and lob their bombs indiscriminately at some southern coastal town. I suppose they were trying to do what we did but, at least we always tried to attack something militarily German.

May 1st saw the squadron on a fighter sweep over Brest, as part of a diversion for 10 Group Circus 28 with American bombers. 313 Squadron took off at 9am and made a rendezvous with us and the RAF Perranporth and Kenley Wings. The formation climbed across the Channel and the French coast crossing east of Ushant at 24,000 feet. The huge Balbo formation made a wide sweep to the north-east of Brest and re-crossed the coast at Pointe de Pontusval. We saw nothing – no flak and no enemy fighters. Neither did we see any sign of the American Consolidated B-24 Liberators, which we should have seen north of Ushant. They were part of the diversion; twenty-four bombers that were tasked to fly to the Brittany coast just ahead of seventy-eight B-17 Flying Fortresses that were going to hit the German U-Boat pens at St Nazaire at around 1130 hours.

We returned by 1145 hours and, although we had been out for some time, we had obviously not diverted any of the opposition away from the Americans. But they had their own problems. Poor weather had caused some confusion and one group had drifted too near Brest; a hotbed of flak at the best of times. Three Flying Fortresses went down and a second group, seeing the danger, made a rapid return but in doing so, split up. This was just what the German fighters were waiting for and they came down for the kill. A further four Flying Fortresses were knocked down. The Germans were not fools, they knew we had posed no threat, with no Liberators in sight they just waited around for the Flying Fortresses.

Three days later, on May 4th, it was our turn to assist 11 Group with their Circus 294, by covering twelve Lockheed Ventura bombers bombing Abbeville in the late afternoon. We flew up to RAF Tangmere, had our tanks topped up and then Wing Commander Dolezal led us off at 1845 hours. The Czech Wing formed up over Beachy Head, with the twelve Venturas below and with three more Spitfire wings around us.

We flew across the Channel at sea level for eight minutes, then began the usual climb to the French coast, 313 Squadron leading the wing at 15,000 feet. The Venturas bombed from north-west to south-east and explosions were seen on the northern part of Abbeville airfield. Turning, we re-crossed the French coast, lost height to 10,000 feet and soon Beachy Head was in sight again. We returned to our base, landing at 2045 hours.

On May 14th 1943, we were briefed to attack and destroy a large number of German torpedo boats and barges that had been spotted at St Peter Port, Guernsey. The attack was to be carried out at low level. The firepower consisted of cannons, machine guns and the odd 250lb bomb. Our approach to the harbour was in four sections, line astern, with myself positioned in the third group. On commencing my dive onto the target I saw that the two sections ahead of us were targeted by the merciless low level anti-aircraft shells. The German guns were positioned at the edge of the headlands and were firing downwards, some of the shells ricocheting off the sea.

When it was my turn to unleash the wrath of my guns on the boats, the German trajectory of exploding shells added to the smoke which obscured the burning craft. The duration of our potent attack lasted no more than a minute and, when completed, we made a clockwise turn to hide behind the south side of the island's rocky shore and cliffs. A few seconds later, when I was clear of the German guns and at approximately 800 feet, I noticed a Spitfire trailing smoke from its engine with flames licking the cockpit. Someone switched on his R/T to call the pilot of the crippled plane: "Jump, Jump, Green 2, you are on fire, jump now!" The doomed pilot, Flying Officer Jaroslav Novak, replied with a strained and sagging voice: "I am unable to. Good luck to you," whereupon the plane went into a steep dive and smashed on the sea-whipped rocks below.

With shivers down my spine and my soul aching with grief, I found it difficult to rejoin my squadron which was reforming ahead of me and with a noticeable gap, left by the loss of a very brave patriot. Although we had physically left him behind, submerged by the incoming tide, his spirit inspired us not to forget what our mission was all about. He had laid down his life so that freedom among mankind could be restored. One hour and forty minutes after take-off from Church Stanton, apart from two pilots being slightly wounded and some Spitfires sustaining damage, it was a miracle that only one life had been lost when flying through the wall of death at St Peter Port.

On May 29th, it was my pleasure to be part of an escort to a huge formation of 120 Flying Fortresses whose daylight bombing raids, aimed at blasting the hell out of the German war potential, were flown by the heroic American crews. As on May 1st, the target was the U-Boat pens at St Nazaire. A further thirty-eight Liberators went for the nearby La Palice U-Boat base.

My next operational sortie took place on June 11th 1943 and I found it particularly satisfying. I was participating in an air sea rescue search for a ditched bomber crew. We eventually found them floating in a dinghy and successfully fixed their position. Thereafter we remained on station, in pairs, to protect them until they were rescued. When this was achieved, I could not have been more pleased had I just shot down a German plane.

Once again, I was compelled to visit the station medical officer with my red eyes. The doctor wasted no time in dispatching me to the Princess Mary's Hospital at RAF Halton in Buckinghamshire. Treatment began on the day of my arrival and consisted of drops, injections and probing for splinters of glass. When there was no sign of improvement the specialist looked baffled whilst I impatiently longed to be back with my squadron.

My show of impatience was noted by a visiting therapist who suggested that I become involved in some handicraft to occupy my troubled mind. Given a choice, I decided to learn the art of tooling leather; the materials and tools were provided. I made a sleeve cover for my diaries, which I had been writing since June 1939 – almost four years ago. The craft was interesting – almost on a par with fraternising with the RAF nurses who were taking the greatest care of me. Their therapy proved effective and my 'lusty' red eyes gradually cleared.

It took a whole month before the hospital specialist was satisfied that my eyes were back to normal and then I was given two weeks leave. I left for Wolverhampton to be utterly spoilt by 'Mum', Cliff and their fast maturing daughter, Mary, whose finishing school was transforming her into a desirable young lady. Out of respect for her parents, I loved her as if she were my own sister. The three of them made my stay as relaxing as possible with picnics in the country and a visit to a concert. Cliff made sure that I had not lost the ability to play a good game of snooker. It was upsetting to think that while I was made to feel such a part of their family, my real parents, whom I had left so long ago, were being held by the German Gestapo in prison – their 'crime' was to have a son who believed that truth and freedom was worth fighting for – to the death if necessary.

When the two weeks of my dream-like leave came to an end I drove to London to undergo the scrutiny of an RAF medical board where, after a thorough probing, I was down-graded to 'A2' which meant that I was only fit for non-operational flying duties. The pronouncement hit me like a bullet from a Me109.

In dire need of an injection of spirit, I visited a Czech club situated near Bedford Square where, despite the rationing, a tasty and traditional meal of roast pork, sauerkraut and dumplings could be bargained for. I returned to RAF Church Stanton to collect my kit and posting papers to take up flying duties with 1847 TTU (Target Towing Unit) which was based near St Athan in South Wales.

On my arrival there I was greeted by the CO with much warmth but I deemed the posting an insult to a skilled fighter pilot. I was a reluctant recruit, a feeling I did not try to hide. The CO was very patient and understanding during my eight target-towing sorties in Lysanders and Miles Masters and he did his very best to have me posted to a unit where my flying experience and bloody-minded determination would be of benefit. Thanks to my persistence and his support I was posted to RAF 9 Group and 61 OTU (Operational Training Unit) on August 22nd 1943 to serve as a flying instructor at RAF Rednal.

CHAPTER 19

FLYING ESCORT ON D-DAY

To reach RAF Rednal meant an enjoyable drive across beautiful Wales – heading for the town of Oswestry from where it was easy to locate the operational training unit, situated four miles to the east. The unit was commanded by Flight Lieutenant Janici, a very experienced fighter pilot who was on a 'rest', having completed the stipulated 200 hours of operational flying. He was a very pleasant officer and I was content to serve under his restrained, yet firm command. The camp's wartime facilities were very adequate and the off-duty life quietly sociable. The snooker table in the sergeants' mess provided an opportunity to improve my often-challenged skill.

As an instructor it was my job to train pilots attending courses on how to fly in formation and to shape them into skilled fighter pilots. The specified exercises were carried out in battle-seasoned Spitfires, occasionally with the instructor in a Master when it was necessary to prove any points by demonstration. The sole aim of the instruction was to teach the pupils how to survive during combat with the enemy.

Providing the weather was suitable, I would lead the lessons in formation tactics over the Cambrian Mountains – some peaks being in excess of 3,000 feet. It was a spectacular part of Wales to behold. When it was necessary to carry out the routines in turbulent air conditions, we flew over the areas below 5,000 feet, where unstable conditions would certainly be found.

Whenever I met the Welsh people, in church, in the street or at my favourite pub, they were much like those that I had enjoyed meeting all over England, France, Poland and Czechoslovakia – friendly and peace loving compatriots. Language did not seem to be much of a barrier. During one evening's visit to the pub a man, standing beside me at the bar, addressed me in Welsh and I replied in Czech – the translation of 'good health friend' was provided by the clink of our glasses.

Reluctantly, I began to settle down and come to terms with being downgraded from an operational fighter pilot to an instructor. When I received another posting in early November 1943, to 53 OTU based at

RAF Kirton-in-Lindsey, in Lincolnshire, I knew that there was no point in complaining; nothing could be done. So, without prejudice, I left RAF Rednal with the good wishes of the CO and his staff.

RAF Kirton-in-Lindsey was a compact, smooth-running airfield with three runways and the usual complex of low profile buildings and hangars. The only relatively high building was the flying control tower. The mainly flat Lincolnshire area was ideally suited for the low level navigational exercises carried out by the unit. These were flown mostly in the Master or in the Dominie for group familiarisation flights. There was also a de Havilland Tiger Moth which was fun to fly.

The briefing room was a long wooden hut, which had been meticulously fitted out by the flight commander, Flight Lieutenant Lyeavanti. On each of the four tables was pinned a map, showing clearly defined routes of navigational exercises, each map covered with a sheet of clear plastic. The tables, protected with a linen cloth, were lined up under the windows of the hut and on the other side of the room was a row of chairs. In the middle of the room was a tall cast iron stove, its metal chimney vented through the roof. A navigational exercise was only flown after a pupil had studied and committed to memory, a particular route, no map reading was possible as the flight was to be carried out at a height of 250 feet. The task was to locate a designated target and attack it with a cine-film gun before returning to base. These low level exercises, flown in a Master, with a keen and disciplined pilot at the controls, were a pleasure to take part in, even in bad weather. However, from time to time, when flying with a pupil who disregarded the briefing orders and flew dangerously, I would have preferred to be in combat with an Me109.

To say that I remained passionately keen to return to the forefront of aerial fighting would be an understatement. The Nazi perpetrators of evil crimes against humanity had to have war waged against them until they were permanently defeated. To keep my hand in on the type of flying necessary to achieve this, I volunteered to test fly Spitfires that had been overhauled at the station MU (maintenance unit). They were happy to accept the offer, which enabled me to fly some Spitfire Mark IXs to compare them with the slower VBs that I was used to.

In the middle of February 1944, the weather turned very cold, the rain and the snow made visibility very bad but the theoretical lessons in the navigation briefing hut continued. The maps pinned to the tables were studied carefully whilst the larger versions placed on the wall were used for plotting and calculating different courses to steer. Wind direction and strength were fed into a calculator which could be strapped to the pilot's leg, just above the knee. During the ten-day period of exceptional bad weather, the only flight that I made was a short test flight in a Spitfire Mark IX.

One of my early turns of duty coincided with a particular frosty morning and on my arrival the stove in the centre of the briefing room, which was normally lit much earlier, offered only a luke-warm welcome, and the windows of the hut were decorated with frosty ferns. I decided to summon help to get the stove re-lit and the appointed airman arrived with a can containing a pint of waste oil which he slowly poured over the coals. The airman then departed to fetch some sticks of wood, paper and matches which he stuffed under the coal. Then he lit a match. The explosion that followed filled the room with smoke, the only thing we could make out in the room was the stove glowing red. The 'stoker' and I saw that our airforce-blue uniforms looked as if they had been traded for ones of khaki. My moustache, eyebrows and hair all matched. The other instructors and pupils started to arrive and, to their surprise, they found the two of us still alive. The whole place was covered in black soot but at least no one complained of being cold.

The good old wartime comradeship sprang into action – buckets of water appeared, soap rationing was ignored and the linen tablecloths were washed, rinsed and hung out to dry. An inspired and organised RAF team cleaned the rest of the room. Last of all, just before the CO arrived, the tablecloths were pinned to the tables. His first reaction was to fix his eagle eyes on the precious tables. The linen cloths, although whiter than white, had shrunk, rather like me trying to become invisible. When he discovered the culprit, the warrant officer offered his sincere apologies. The part I had played in the crime became part of the 'lore' attached to me; along with the time I sent six bombers to sink a rock in the sea! It was just one more stain on my RAF character that followed me. The embarrassment was drowned with a few pints of bitter beer.

My attachment to 53 OTU lasted for five months, until mid-April 1944, and was taken up with a busy flying schedule. I spent sixty-four hours in the back seat of a Master trainer, sixteen hours as the skipper of the Dominie, eight hours test flying Spitfires and over three hours juggling the fully aerobatic Tiger Moth bi-plane.

I rejoined 310 Squadron on May 1st 1944, temporarily based at RAF Warmwell, being kept in readiness for the secret D-Day operation. RAF Predannick, west of the Lizard in Cornwall, was also in use and it was here that we were obliged to sleep in tents in a nearby field. The weather was not ideal for camping, it was cold and damp and, before going to bed, we rolled ourselves in our blankets and made sure that our clothes were placed in waterproof bags.

Our superiors had decided to make everyone 'rough it' to get us used to the time when we had to abandon the luxuries of either pre-war purpose-built mess buildings, or even the less luxurious block-buildings, in favour of tents and cold water bathing. Officially, therefore, we were known as 134 Airfield rather than as a wing. This was all part of the preparation plan for those fighter squadrons that would eventually go and operate from France and would be flying from little more than bull-dozed airstrips in the immediate battle area laid out with PSP – pierced steel planking – supplied by the Americans.

When I arrived on 310 Squadron the CO, Squadron Leader H Hrbacek, was away on seven days leave, and Flight Lieutenant V Raba was in charge. Our wing leader these days was Wing Commander Tomas Vybiral DSO,DFC, our 'taxi' pilot at 2 Delivery Unit at RAF Colerne. He had commanded 312 Squadron for most of 1943, having previously been a flight commander, before taking over the wing.

On May 21st, not long after I arrived, the CO went missing, he had crash-landed in France. Flight Lieutenant Raba was promoted to squadron leader and took over. Some of the pilots on 310 when I arrived were: Flight Lieutenant J Hartman, Flight Lieutenant M Divis, Flight Lieutenant K Kosina, Flight Lieutenant K Drbohlavv, Flight Lieutenant O Hruby, Flight Lieutenant J Strihavka (into whose Spitfire I had crashed at RAF Bolt Head almost a year ago); Flying Officers Otto Smik, J Sokol, J Skirka, F Vindis, F Drejtnar (who had returned from breaking his leg on that fateful day in June when shot down near Exeter); and Warrant Officers J Valasek, A Kaminek, Flight Sergeants M Moravec, A Sveceny, J March, A Meier, and Sergeant B Frohlich.

I did not know then that Flight Lieutenant Jiri Hartman would later become the CO of 310 Squadron. He was a good pilot but I remember him best as a gambler that I would happily fly with. He liked playing poker and bet on horse races. I recall he once took a group of us to a race meeting after we had been on a tour of the local brewery. After drinking some very fine beer laid on by the brewery management, Flight Lieutenant Hartman suggested a visit to the nearby dog-race track. He gave tips to everybody and soon, by following his advice, my four pounds was down to ten shillings, each bet I had made proved to be a loser. For the final bet of the day I picked a dog of my own choice and won about £30!

At 2045 hours on June 5th everyone was called to a general briefing, in the officers' mess ante-room and informed by Wing Commander Blackwood that D-Day was planned for the next day. As can be imagined, there was a good deal of excitement amongst us.

At dawn on D-Day, June 6th 1944, flying with 'A' Flight commanded by a very experienced pilot, Flight Lieutenant Divis, we set course, climbing towards the heavily moisture laden, grey clouds. It did not take long to reach a height just under the cloudbank and below us was an armada of sea-going craft of every shape and size. Warships were on the widely spread flanks, nursing the potent invasion fleet towards its destination which was a section of the Normandy beach where the army divisions were to land, scale the cliffs and engage the enemy. With one eye firmly fixed on the events below me, the other spotted a Ju88 piercing the clouds only 500 yards ahead. My gun button was at the ready, so I fired my four cannons, after which salvo the plane quickly climbed into the clouds. From then on, during three more sorties that I flew on that never-to-be-forgotten day, I did not see any other enemy plane polluting the sky above the allied armies and navies making their historic incursion onto the European continent. Even now, as I write this over sixty years after the event, I can still recall the feeling of pride that engulfed me as I viewed the scene from on high, flying in relative safety, protected by the thick layer of cloud above. What enemy flak there was, was ineffective and I was anxious to be down low to fire my cannons at the opposing German forces.

I was flying over the D-Day beaches and witnessed the shells, mortars and bombs exploding among the brave men swarming inland. Casualties were unavoidable and I considered myself somewhat impotent. Heroic deeds were being performed by soldiers and sailors alike. British, Canadian and American forces were fighting, with united determination, the enemies of peace and liberty to drive them to permanent extinction.

It was a scene that became etched in my memory. It was history in the making and I was part of that process – it was exciting to be involved and to this day I can still feel that tingling of my spine, which remains braced with pride.

After the soul stirring flying with my squadron over the bloodstained beaches of Normandy, my CO noticed the redness of my eyes and expressed his concern. He thought that I should undergo some treatment and declared me non-operational. I duly went to see the station medical officer who prescribed a course of medication, which required me to attend his surgery three times a day. When some improvement became evident I was attached, on June 14th, to 84 GSU (Group Support Unit) at RAF Aston Down where I continued to keep myself in practice by occasional flights in a Spitfire IXB. The rest and treatment to my eyes proved effective enabling me to return, on July 1st, to 310 Squadron.

My first operational sortie was a 'Ramrod' 1062, on July 6th, escorting 300 Halifax and Avro Lancaster bombers to their targets ahead of the invasion forces. Their task was to soften or destroy the German positions and fortifications, which stood in the way of our advancing armies.

The following morning, I flew on Ramrod 1069, providing a close escort to another large wave of 350 Lancaster and Halifax bombers on their way to deliver a load of bombs on a target near Caen, northern France. There was no fighter opposition but the flak became unmercifully accurate and very soon started to cost lives. On returning to base our hearts were heavily laden with sorrow.

These Ramrod sorties were carried out from our temporary bases at RAF Lympne, where quite often, during a squadron take-off, a V-1 flying bomb would streak across on its senseless journey to kill people and cause destruction in London. On July 9th, one actually warbled through just as we were airborne and about to participate in Ramrod 1071 – another protection mission. This time we were escorting 300 Lancasters on their way to the Pas de Calais. The bombers were going to attack a V-1 flying bomb launch site near Stracourt and we took off from RAF Lympne at 0730 hours with me in NH692; we were back by 0845 hours. Attacks against the V-1 flying bomb launch sites were codenamed 'No-ball'. The codename for missions against the V-1 flying bombs themselves was 'Diver'. The previous day, Flying Officer Otto Smik, together with Flying Officer Pipa had taken off on a Diver patrol at 2125 hours and had actually spotted the first one three minutes later. Flying Officer Smik attacked and destroyed it near Ashford in Kent. Heading south-west, he then spotted another coming in over the Sussex coast, this one too was destroyed. He destroyed his third flying bomb near Tenterden, Kent at 2200 hours. And what of Flying Officer Pipa? His guns had jammed and he had to sit it out and watch his companion get all three.

Having already flown one sortie on July 9th, a further sortie to escort 57 Lancasters bombing the No-ball site at L'Hey, had me landing at dusk after flying through some very dense and lethal flak. Some of our planes had been hit and never returned to their base. Others were badly damaged and were nursed back to forced landings at the nearest airfields in England. Although I was tired from the long day's flying, my loathing for the continued use of the V-1 flying bombs spilled over and I volunteered to fly another sortie to lay in wait for these devices. After refuelling, I took off with the intention of venting my feelings by shooting down one of these monsters.

The night was dark and when I had taken off I contacted flying control by R/T and was passed to the operations room where an angelic voice took over. She gave me a vector to steer and a height to level off at, giving course alterations as necessary. After some twenty minutes of precise guidance the voice, calm and firm, announced: "I have a 'Witch-craft' for you at 11 o'clock below." No sooner had I received the message, than I saw the flame of a V-1 flying bomb racing towards me – while shouting "Tally Ho", I stood the aircraft on its nose, spiralled through 180 degrees, opened the throttle to its fullest extent, lined up the flame in the gun sight and pressed the button. While the cannons loudly responded, the roar of the Spitfire engine began to cough, then gave up in silent protest.

For a Spitfire lXB to catch up with a 'Doodle Bug', as the V-1 flying bombs were commonly known, the pilot had to have a good advantage of height, be in the correct position and react speedily. Thanks to the expert guidance given by the operations room, such perfect conditions prevailed but, having exploited them a shade too energetically I had disorientated my aircraft's Merlin engine management, thus losing its obedience which meant that I was powerless to blast the thing out of the sky. Just as I began to despair the engine regained its senses, roared into life and I was able to continue with the pursuit of the distant 'witch-craft' flame. With both man and machine revitalised and the cannons spitting out their venom, I willed the shells towards their target. Just as I was declaring my mission a failure, there was a blinding flash and a terrific explosion, which preceded some very severe turbulence. My feeling was one of gleeful satisfaction as I reported my success to the ops room. The gentle voice then guided me through the darkness to a safe landing and a night of dreams about the body and soul that was attached to that angelic voice – I slept really well! My logbook entry was as follows:

> "July 9th 1944 – W/O Mares – Spitfire IX – letter C – take off from Lydd at 2210 hours intercepted a 'robot' between Cap Gris Nez and Dungeness. In a steep dive fired a 7 second burst, when my engine cut out, fired for another 3 seconds. As my engine re-started, continued the chase. The Flying Bomb, while losing speed, exploded when crossing the English coast. Then I saw another Spitfire ahead. Duration of flight 1 hour 20 minutes – 20 minutes of night flying."

During the afternoon, the squadron flew back to RAF Church Stanton (by now re-named RAF Culmhead) for a short break from operational flying but training continued to condition us for even more attacks upon the despised Nazi regime. On August 28th 1944, 310 and 312 Squadrons made a joint move to RAF North Weald, an old established air base, situated on the north-east fringe of London. It reminded me of RAF Northolt where I had been stationed in 1941. Now, three years later, it was like coming home to be among Londoners; the friendliest people one could wish to be with. Their unconquerable spirit was still unshaken, regardless of the merciless V-1 flying bombs and V-2 rockets inflicted on them by Hitler's maniacs. RAF North Weald was like a shrine to Londoners. The airmen were their protectors and the planes were their messengers, delivering reminders to the Nazi hordes that their spirit was unbeatable.

I had no problems in settling in at North Weald. On September 3rd, 310 and 312 Squadrons, including myself, headed for Rotterdam on Ramrod 1258. Soon after take-off at 1655 hours, with the 300 Halifax bombers already heading for the airfield at Soesterberg, we got into 10/10 cloud at 3,000 feet and Warrant Officer Antonin Skach must have become disorientated for he spun out and crashed at Braintree in Essex. He was killed instantly. Our presence was to prove effective, for the few

German fighters that did appear out of the sun were beaten off after a skirmish. It was usual that when the enemy fighters appeared there was no flak to menace our bombers but as soon as they were driven off, the anti-aircraft barrage began. This was always the most dangerous time for our bombers when their fighter escort could not do much about it. During these stressful times I felt unable to protect them. To fight or chase the enemy fighters would have offered me a feeling of satisfaction but, to stand by whilst our bombers were being blasted by the German anti-aircraft guns, induced despair.

Another type of operation, that of armed reconnaissance, code-named 'Rove', now began to appear on our flight rota. In some ways they resembled the old Rhubarbs, except that these were flown in all types of weather and generally with at least four to eight aircraft. With the decline of the Luftwaffe it was deemed less dangerous to fly around the continent at low level in order to shoot up anything that took our fancy. This was all part of keeping up the pressure on the enemy now that the invasion was well advanced. The problem, however, was that while German fighters might have seemed few and far between, the German anti-aircraft guns were, by this stage in the war, very proficient. And why not, they had had more than five years experience!

The squadron flew on one of our first armed recce sorties on September 5th 1944 and fortunately I was not with them. Wing Commander Vybiral led them to Holland and attacked some MT (motor transport). Flying Officer V Kanovosky was hit by ground fire and was seen to pull up to 5,000 feet leaving a trail of white glycol smoke. One did not last long with that sort of problem. If you didn't catch fire, the engine soon seized up and stopped. He entered some cloud and that was the last they saw of him. Sergeant K Lamberton lost his cockpit hood in the attack and it was assumed it had been blown off by more ground fire. Warrant Officer Kaminek just failed to return. If this was going to be one of our future jobs, I was not sure that I wanted to be involved.

We flew again on the morning of September 9th to carry out Ramrod 1264. Wing Commander Vybiral led Red Section, in which I flew (MH878). We took off at 1240 hours. This was a day to be remembered, mostly by the long-suffering ground crews. In order for us to complete these sorties it was necessary to carry long-range fuel tanks, also known as jettison tanks. They came in two basic sizes depending on the depth of our penetrations, either forty-five or ninety gallons.

In the early afternoon the ground crews had been ordered to put ninety-gallon tanks on our Spitfires and no sooner had this been done than the order went out to the dispersals for them to be changed to forty-five-gallon capacity. At 1810 hours, Wing Commander Vybiral led off another armed recce and strafed some barges on a canal. They also reported seeing a six-vessel convoy leaving Neuwe Waterweg, by the Hook of Holland. When they returned the ground crews were then ordered to replace the forty-five-gallon tanks with ninety-gallon tanks. The mechanics were certainly fed up with long-range tanks this day. The morning sortie lasted two hours and fifteen minutes and was followed by yet another escort in the afternoon in order to protect some Halifax bombers on their way to a target near Rotterdam. The afternoon sortie lasted two hours and no enemy fighters appeared. However, being tightly strapped into the seat of a Spitfire for over four hours in one day, was painful on my lower back, the discomfort reminding me of the spine-jarring crash of a year earlier on November 2nd.

The exiled Czech Government, based in London, had reluctantly bestowed an 'honour' upon me. I had been recommended by the COs of 601 and 610 Squadron for a commission but each time it was turned down by my Czech superiors making this present elevation an anti-climax. My new rank would be (from November 1944) that of pilot officer; my service number 787653 would change to 185291.

In order to celebrate my forthcoming new status, two non-commissioned friends and I went to a pub in North Weald. It was a large, three-storey, brick-built building of character which stood alone at the edge of crossroads. On each side, stretching in both directions, were the remains of rows of houses. The pub was the only building to remain standing undamaged within a circle of about 150 yards. Just how the pub survived the blitz, apparently unscathed, was a miracle. On approaching the crowded bar, a space appeared, behind the counter stood a smiling barmaid. I ordered three pints of beer and offered the necessary payment. The smiling lass sweetly announced: "It's on the house". It was not only the free beer that impressed us, the genuine cordiality was truly touching.

Flying from North Weald became a routine for 310 and 312 Squadrons. I was a member of 'A' Flight 310 Squadron, still led by Flight Lieutenant Divis. The CO was Squadron Leader Jiri Hartman – my 'racing' companion and a former regular officer of the Czech Air Force. During the whole of September 1944 we flew almost daily, flying deeper and deeper into Germany, with the Rhur a frequent target.

After the unforgettably complex, heroic D-Day operation, came the land battles that raged continuously. The entire American forces, army, navy and air force, were fully and effectively engaged alongside the British and their other allies. The entire operation was spurred on by Winston Churchill. While the epic drive against the German forces in Europe was maintained, the land, sea and air forces were also engaged in conflict with the Mussolini-fascists, and full-scale operations were being conducted against the Japanese after their sneak attack on Pearl Harbor.

When the flying operations against the German war machine were mounted, the RAF and the US Army Air Force (USAAF) began to carry out 1,000 bomber raids in daylight. For anyone observing such huge swarms of bombers from the ground, surrounded by the might of escorting fighters, it presented a stunning display, rather like a swarm of wasps, determined in their resolve to sting – and sting again. These long-distance flights to the heart of the Ruhr were only made possible if the fighter aircraft had extra fuel tanks fitted to their belly or two separate streamlined pods placed under each wing. When the extra fuel in the tanks had been used up it was possible for the pilot to jettison them. These long-haul missions made heavy demands upon the fighter pilot as no rest was possible throughout the flight. The pilots not only had to keep the enemy at bay but remain alert to avoid mid-air collisions when so many aircraft were in the air.

The next sortie came on September 13th, in the form of another Ramrod 1280. We were involved in escorting 100 Halifax bombers on their way to Osnabruck with a bomb load of 'persuasion', ever hopeful that the enemy would surrender before more of the same medicine was prescribed. The planning of such raids, in such large numbers required a great deal of courage and nerves of steel such as those displayed by the RAF high command. The specific tactics devised and calculated by officers in the operations rooms made a vital contribution to the overall effort. The Osnabruck Ramrod sortie had been carried out with minimum loss of life and damage to our planes. On the way home I noticed that the engine oil pressure gauge on my aircraft began to drop alarmingly which concerned me, as there was still a long way to reach our base. Eventually I landed safely after a round trip of two hours and fifty minutes.

The oil-pressure fault turned out to be relatively minor and was skilfully rectified by the dedicated aircraft fitters, whilst the riggers were busy checking and repairing the airframe. They worked well into the night so that I could fly the same Spitfire the following day when 310 and 313 Squadrons were scheduled to escort a formation of thirty Lancasters to a factory near The Hague in Holland. It speaks volumes for the airmen who serviced my plane that, apart from a small shrapnel hole in the rudder stabiliser, I met with no serious problems on that sortie. That evening, before retiring to bed, I updated my logbook by adding another 2 hours and 10 minutes to my operational flying total.

During the second half of September 1944, the bad weather rendered operational flying impractical but it was just possible to carry out a few training flights.

In need of some recreation I drove to London to oblige our squadron parachute packer, Richard Vavrecka, who asked if I could collect a sewing machine that he had purchased. It was a miserable drizzly morning and after having picked up Richard's prized possession we decided to have a pint and a meal at the Czech club near Bedford

Square. I happened to be stationary at a red traffic-light, when quite suddenly my car was hit in the back by a large khaki-coloured, chauffeur-driven station wagon; in the back of which sat a gold-braided army officer, sporting many medal ribbons on his chest.

After exchanging polite conversation with the uniformed chauffeur and having received his apologies, I was given a signed form absolving me from any blame. Apart from a dent in the body panel behind the bent bumper my car was roadworthy, so I moved on. A minor event of little interest you may say! However, that small incident was destined to herald a life or death situation some two weeks later when I arrived at the London garage to collect the car after its repair.

Richard and I enjoyed a lunch at the club and he told to me that before the war he was a tailor and the recent acquisition of the sewing machine would be the means of a profitable side-line. He was carrying out repairs and alterations to the uniforms of the station personnel, stitching on rank braids and medal ribbons. Richard Vavrecka survived the war and with his English wife returned to Czechoslovakia only to return to England once again after the Communists came to power in 1948. He became a valued tutor of tailoring at Plymouth Polytechnic College.

Upon my return from London I learnt that the Czech Wing had been involved in the ill-fated Arnhem operation when the weather permitted. Wing Commander Vybiral had led an escort mission on September 17th to what had been termed – 'the great airborne invasion of Holland', the wing patrolling a line west of Schouwen-Hertogenbosch. Next day, Squadron Leader Hartman had led the boys to escort another wave of aircraft, experiencing heavy flak over the Schouwen area.

On September 19th the squadron was due to escort reinforcements between Ostend-Ghent-Diset but low cloud prevented penetration of the Dutch coast. Coming back, several gliders were seen down in the sea with air sea rescue launches and aircraft busily trying to rescue the poor soldiers that had failed to make it across. Despite more bad weather the next day, the squadron managed to escort reinforcements.

The day was perhaps a little more exciting for us because of a VIP visit. The president of the Czech Republic-in-Exile, Eduard Benes, paid us a visit along with members of his cabinet. The visiting dignitaries included Dr Jan Masaryk, the Defence Minister, Count Lobkovich, the Czech Ambassador to Great Britain and General Ingr. Air Vice-Marshal J Janousek was also there as well as Sir Roderick Hill, Air Officer Commanding ADGB (Air Defence Great Britain) formerly Fighter Command. They began to arrive at around 1100 hours and there followed the inevitable inspections and speeches but we all welcomed the attention.

On September 21st, another operational sortie was cancelled due to the weather so reinforcements and supplies for the men at Arnhem had to be delayed again. Nor did it improve the next day when we could not fly at all, but the squadron did manage an escort mission in the afternoon of the 23rd. We then moved down to RAF Bradwell Bay and managed, on the 26th to escort fifty-six Douglas DC-3 Dakotas that were to drop supplies around Grave. On the 27th it was back to the old routine flying as an escort to 130 Halifax bombers going for an oil plant at Sterkrade, in the Ruhr, led by Wing Commander Vybiral, along with 312 Squadron. Oil now seemed to be the most important target in the bombing campaign.

It became necessary to make up for the few days of respite and, on September 30th, we carried out two Ramrod missions, 1302 and 1304, escorting our Halifax and North-American B-25 Mitchell bombers all the way to the Ruhr and back, Bottrop being one of the targets, Goch the other. During both sorties we encountered and battled with a few Me109s who unsuccessfully tried to attack our 'flock'. Over the target the bombers flew into fierce flak and, once again, we were powerless to render assistance. Several bombers were hit and one blew up in mid-air, sending shock waves through my Spitfire and touching the deepest core of my heart. In one tragic moment I knew that those dying in the explosion were the bravest, with no choice to reverse the course of their destiny. Later that evening, several of us drowned our sorrow in the back room of our favourite pub. Crate after crate of beer bottles became empties. It was a good thing that my car was still in London; to have driven it back to base would have been decidedly more dangerous than my having a scrap with a Fw190.

On October 3rd 1944, flying my favourite 'F for Faithful' (MH878) Spitfire – Ramrod 1308 lasted an interminable two hours and forty minutes. We patrolled at 20,000 feet, providing cover to wave after wave of our bombers spreading destruction along the Dutch and German coastal regions. When some determined Fw190 fighters tried to penetrate our protective cover, many guns, including mine, blazed away. In the heat of the mêlée I could not see evidence that my cannons or machine guns were inflicting serious damage to the adversary so I made no claim for a kill. There were valid claims for the destruction (or possible destruction) of Fw190s and these were eventually approved.

We escorted Mitchell bombers on October 6th, led by our CO, Squadron Leader Jiri Hartman, while Wing Commander Vybiral led 313 Squadron. The target was oil and petrol dumps at Amersfoort. Someone had obviously reasoned that the Germans could not fight effectively without oil. The mission did not end too well as two of our pilots collided on landing and although both lads were unhurt, their Spitfires were seriously damaged. They were lucky.

Then on October 7th came Ramrod 1317. It was a 1245 hours take-off, led by the CO, to escort a massive raid of 350 Halifax bombers to Cleve. They met intense and heavy flak from the target area, while we fighter pilots had our presence acknowledged by some intense medium flak from the north of the Leopold Canal.

Another impressive Ramrod 1332 sortie took place on October 14th, this time escorting 500 Halifax bombers to Duisberg in the Ruhr. I flew as number two to the CO with 313 Squadron in company. We made rendezvous at Eindhoven, the sky seemed full of aircraft and the bombing seemed concentrated despite heavy anti-aircraft fire.

Although everyone had become used to the frequent sound of air-raid sirens, the V-1 flying bombs were more disturbing. Their warble-like warning and ghostly tail of fire indicated indiscriminate ground destruction was imminent. Equally abhorred were the V-2 rockets which were capable of arriving without any warning at all. Our defences could offer no resistance. What the German bombers failed to achieve with these weapons was to break down the spirit of the Londoners. The civil heroism throughout all these attacks only served to spur everyone on with great determination to go for the jugular vein of the enemy.

Early one morning I was woken by a tremendous explosion, my quarters were shaking, fire engine bells ringing, and I got up to observe the scene from my bedroom window. What I saw was a glow of fire in the direction of the village of North Weald. A while later, during breakfast, I was told that the pub that everyone loved had been hit by a V-2 rocket, killing the landlord and his family. They had died heroically for the same cause that we in the services were fighting for.

Unlike the flames of the pub that were soon extinguished by the firemen, the burning hatred that I still had for Hitler and his Nazi followers intensified. My superstition that important events arrived in threes proved itself once again when a few days later, after the pub tragedy, I went to London to fetch my car from the garage that had undertaken the repairs. It was a low, flat roofed, square building and over its wide entrance was a concrete cantilever canopy under which I was standing, waiting for my car to be brought out. Just at that moment, a blinding flash occurred, accompanied by an eardrum-piercing blast. This was followed by a shower of debris that came crashing down on top of the canopy and over a wide area surrounding the garage. The nearby houses had all their windows blown in by a V-2 rocket which prematurely exploded about 100 feet above the garage. It was a miracle that, on this occasion, no one was killed.

That explosively powerful experience reinforced my admiration for those living in cities who had for so long endured the bombing. During such stressful times, when the sirens sounded at the onset of an air-raid, some protection could be sought in shelters. With the V-1 flying bombs there was enough warning to seek cover but with the V-2 rockets, there was no warning at all. They were messengers of Hitler's despair. During all this the Londoners' heroic spirit became a powerful retaliatory weapon.

Ever since the tragically unsuccessful airborne assault at Arnhem by glider and parachute troops in September 1944, the slaughter on the ground, in the air and at sea had shown no respite. RAF fighter squadrons continued to provide the long-range protection escorts to the ever growing formations of bombers flying deeper and deeper into Germany. They were often flying side by side with the US 8th Army Air Force and their Flying Fortresses that were escorted by their own Mustang fighter planes. One such sortie that remains deep in my memory was Ramrod 1361 to a target in Gelsenkirchen. The Czech squadrons flew as close escort to 639 aircraft, mainly Halifax and Lancasters bombers. On approaching the target, the brunt of the attacking German fighters was taken care of by our high cover RAF Spitfires. The enemy Me109s that succeeded in diving through to imperil the bomber force were 'diverted' by our guns.

When our airfields were shrouded in thick fog and the fuel reserves of the fighter planes were dangerously low, it presented a serious problem. At such perilous times it became necessary for the pilots to communicate with the operations room for advice. Those planes with sufficient fuel were immediately diverted to land at airfields beyond the extent of the fog. Those with almost empty fuel tanks were diverted to an airfield equipped with the FIDO installation. FIDO – Fog Intensive Dispersal Of – was specially constructed on an airfield, which had an extra long and wide runway. Along the edges of the runway, large-bore steel pipes were laid. From the jets spaced along the top of the pipes, vaporised fuel was pumped and lit. The fierce heat that resulted, dispersed the fog along the runway to an average height of fifty feet, to form a clear-air tunnel into which the aircraft was guided along a 'Lorenz' electronic beam with the aid of an 'angelic' voice.

My only training for the use of the FIDO system in an emergency had been on a Link Trainer simulator. Before FIDO was introduced, pilots returning from missions in such desperate situations had no choice but to head their aircraft out to sea before bailing out. The alignment of an aircraft along the electronic 'Lorenz' beam required the skill of one of the highly specialised operations room WAAFs, whose responsibility it was to guide the pilot by radio to align with the beam. When on track a continuous note was heard by the pilot in his headphones which changed to Morse dashes (- - -) if the plane drifted to starboard (right), or dots (· · ·) if the move was to port (left). If the approach was too low or too high the voice would calmly say so. It was the combined skill of the pilot and the vocal guidance to bring about a safe landing.

The moment that the thick wet fog swallowed my Spitfire, my eyes were firmly focused on the artificial horizon and the air speed indicator – my ears strained to receive the vital vocal instructions to which I diligently responded. Lowering the undercarriage and flaps, it was not time for my faith to falter. With the electronic approach beam sounding its continuous note, changing to dashes or dots and the calm, interceding voice announcing: "You are a little too high" or "too low" I saw the half circle of fierce flames into which my Spitfire was aimed. My prayers were answered as the wheels of 'F' for Faithful touched the runway. It was great to be alive and I gave thanks to the lass in the ops room and the one whose presence I was aware of during the flight lasting two hours and fifty-five minutes. There were three FIDO-equipped runways within the south-east sector; RAF Manston, RAF Woodbridge and the one that I experienced first hand, RAF Bradwell. It was not until the morning that the fog began to clear and a twenty-minute flight brought me back to base ready to be briefed for yet another Ramrod mission.

The gradual build-up of a grit-like substance in my eyes was still troubling me despite the daily bathing that I gave them. The burning sensation and the continued appearance of having bloodshot eyes concerned me but I hoped that the inflammation would remain unnoticed. I was also suffering pains in my lower back but this was easier to keep under wraps. When my flight commander questioned my serviceability, he was quick to realise that I would see red if he rendered me unfit to fly, so as an officer and a gentleman, he kept his distance.

Having had a restful morning, in the afternoon of November 8th 1944, our two squadrons were joined by four more, linking up over the Channel and aiming to escort 150 Lancaster bombers on their way to bomb an industrial target in the Ruhr, possibly Homberg. I was wingman to Flight Lieutenant Bernard and the mission was led by Wing Commander Vybiral. The mission was Ramrod 1362 and it lasted two hours and fifty minutes. This time, when over the target, the usually dense flak was out of range, although there was some activity high above and I saw one of the bombers being hit and going down. In comparison with all the other recent raids, this one was less punishing. Once again some of the fighter aircraft ran into a fuel shortage situation and even though there was no fog to hinder us, we diverted to RAF Bradwell to refuel.

When the national press began to headline the news about the RAF and the American daylight 1,000-bomber raids over Germany, the long-suffering British people found the scale of such operations awe-inspiring. However, only a participant, such as myself, could comprehend the might of such aerial destruction. Taking part was mind-numbing and with the sun obscuring the vast spread of aircraft, all trying to maintain a position within a squadron, it felt as if I was an unknown 'twinkle' in a huge cosmos.

I performed an insignificant part amongst almost 1,300 aircraft and

I witnessed the inferno and destruction kindled by the exploding bombs down below. I saw our aircraft, bombers and fighters being hit by dense flak, but was fortunate to escape the carnage and reasoned that, like a herd of gazelles at a watering hole being stalked by a predatory lion, there was safety in large numbers.

A depth of self-examination came as I witnessed the obliteration, not only of the target but of countless others, and the depth of my hate of what Nazi Germany stood for, began to weaken. I was touched by an awareness that these innocent civilians were paying the ultimate penalty for their indifference to what one evil man was loudly proclaiming and organising on their behalf.

My strong wall of hate was cracked by the overpowering and significant impact of such a massive delivery of punishment. A space appeared in my bosom for the innocent Germans that were dying or being maimed. My sorrow and illusion of safety was shattered when on our return, while nursing crippled bombers, four Me109s came out of nowhere, preceded by their tracer shells. Wasting no time, my flight leader and I broke formation and immersed ourselves in an act of vengeance, firing my Spitfire cannons and my bad language too. Once again, the Me109s had the advantage of surprise and speed, and I was unsure if our return to base would be in one piece.

The possibility of further enemy attacks diminished when the English coast came into sight; our mighty returning armada of aircraft had completed their mission. With just enough fuel in my tanks I landed at RAF North Weald where, after a compulsory de-briefing, I laid my aching spine on a bed and rested my eyes.

After the 8th November mission, one week of rest followed, during which I kept my distance from the squadron CO and my flight commander, for fear that my red eyes would be deemed a disability. On November 16th our new wing leader, Wing Commander J Hlado DFC, the former CO of 312 Squadron, led us on a withdrawal support mission Ramrod 1372; this time for 200 Lancasters bombing Heinsberg. One Lancaster was seen to be hit by flak but we only saw three parachutes emerge.

The next flight was Ramrod 1373 on November 18th with Wing Commander Hlado leading us and 313 Squadron escorting 400 Lancaster and Halifax bombers to Munster to deliver their bomb-loads of doom. Once more the occasion sapped my energy and nerves. The flight there and back lasted three hours and was full of action. We were attacked by enemy fighters and our bombers were hit hard by the flak. Our tanks were almost dry when we had to put down at RAF Manston rather than fly back to base. Several were shot down, never to return. As far as I can recall two of the escorting Spitfires were also lost. Of those returning, some claimed victories. All that I managed to do was expend my ammunition which, even if the target had been hit, I could not confirm. My Spitfire received some 'wounds' which took several days of toil by the squadron riggers and fitters to repair. It remained in the hangar for four days.

The stress of the long duration flights over Germany together with enduring the flak barrage made us all tired. The rest from operational flying was very welcome. The extent of our duties for the following few days was test flying our aircraft, in order to pronounce them serviceable or otherwise.

During the lull, I took the chance to catch up with some letter writing and amongst the correspondents remaining was my Pilsen compatriot, Venca Slouf. In his last letter he informed me that his brother Karel had just returned from Canada where he was trained as a fighter pilot. As well as being in good health, Venca revealed that he had been promoted to the rank of flying officer. I also wrote to Beth, who mentioned in her letter that she, along with her mother, was planning a visit to London. My reply assured them that I looked forward to their arrival. To the Cousins family, Net, Cliff and Mary I wrote frequently, regardless of whether I was tired or not, as I liked to keep them well informed. Their last letter to me contained the surprise that Mary had become engaged to a Royal Navy submarine officer. My congratulations were as if I was her brother, wishing her all future happiness.

One afternoon, intending to go to London, I gave my car a check over before setting-off. This was just as well because, although I noted that the petrol tank had been topped up and the oil dipstick was showing plenty of oil, the trip meter indicated that the car had been used a great deal since I last drove it myself. The ground crew had my blessing to make full use of the car subject to their providing the fuel. I noticed that the engine carburettor was stained green which was ample proof that the fuel they used in my Wolseley was 100 Octane aviation fuel. This was, of course, strictly illegal and after issuing a reprimand to them I ordered that the tank be drained, the carburettor cleaned and my car filled with some legally obtained petrol. With self-preservation foremost in my mind, the following evening I drove my fitter and rigger (the culprits) to London to have a meal with me at the Czech club, a gesture they appreciated, particularly after the admonishment that I had handed out. On our way from the club to the car, a V-1 flying bomb's jet engine stopped above us. We dived, in the nick of time, into a shelter that fate obviously provided. The explosion that followed was almost as loud as my previous day's reprimand.

The short, well-earned break from operational flying ended on November 27th. My squadron was detailed for another Ramrod 1379, which entailed escorting a large number of Lancaster bombers all the way to Cologne and back. As with our previous escort sorties there were other fighter squadrons sharing the task. On this particular occasion, and unless we were attacked, we were to climb and remain at

20,000 feet, and prevent any possible attack on the aircraft below us.

During the sortie the anti-aircraft flak began to explode close to the bombers and not too many of the shells were ranged on us. To my surprise, the hell that was let loose on the first wave of bombers suddenly eased, suggesting that the bombs they had dropped had hit the gun positions. On the other hand, the unaccountable lull might just have been in expectation of pending attack by their fighters – possibly the jet or rocket-propelled types that we knew existed. At a height of 30,000 feet, a small skirmish was in evidence and a few puffs indicated that some flak was exploding among our bombers. After two hours and forty minutes airborne, I landed my Spitfire undamaged back at RAF North Weald but, unfortunately, I was not in such good condition. My back felt as if it had been sawn in half and my eyes were burning.

On November 30th we flew Ramrod 1384 and for a duration of two hours and twenty minutes escorted 120 Lancaster bombers to Bottrop in the Ruhr. As a result of the low percentage of losses, this was a successful mission as it served as a pathfinder for the advancing armies. On December 4th we carried out our escort duties for Ramrod 1393. The following day I flew as number two to Wing Commander Hlado on Ramrod 1394, taking off at 1020 hours. We provided target and withdrawal escort for 60 Lancasters bombing a dam near Heimbach. There was some excitement when we spotted what everyone thought to be a Me262 jet fighter. Flight Lieutenant Divis and his Yellow Section were detailed to have a crack at it and peeled away. However the German pilot had seen the danger and although Flight Lieutenant Divis and his boys gave chase, the jet easily disappeared to the south-east despite the Spitfire's air speed of 290 mph during the chase. Each of these sorties lasted for two hours and thirty-five minutes of strenuous and traumatic flying. Fortunately the damage and losses to the aircraft and crew were minimal.

I was in Squadron Leader Hartman's section on the morning of December 11th with Wing Commander Hlado leading the wing to Oberfelt, protecting 150 Lancasters. Due to the problem with my eyes it turned out to be my last operational sortie, Ramrod 1402; an unforgettable two hours and thirty minutes. As if to signal it was my last, the German flak had one last attempt at ending my young life.

We took off at 1000 hours with me in Spitfire MH878 for the last time. As we climbed to the Dutch coast, Sergeant Brazda found he could not jettison his long-range fuel tank and had to abort. He crashed at base but was not hurt. Wing Commander Hlado and Flying Officer Sokol had to drop out due to mechanical troubles and our spare pilot had returned a shade too early so was unable to help replace our shortage. One couldn't really blame him for we had few aborts and it was always a bind knowing that, as spare pilot, one was only wanted to fill a gap. It was only human nature to break off as soon as it seemed prudent to do so and go back to a warm flight hut, or even grab a hot bath, when one didn't really have to fly in a cold December sky to the depths of Germany and get shot at for the privilege.

As we neared the target, the bombers spread out below us, we were greeted by the inevitable flak. One always had to note its presence even though we tried to ignore it. Generally it was just a nuisance but today…Suddenly a shell burst right in the middle of our Spitfire formation. At least two of our fighters were hit; Pilot Officer Slepica went down, jettisoning his long-range fuel tank, and made a rapid forced landing at Antwerpe-Duerne airfield. He was followed in by Warrant Officer Soukup who had developed engine trouble. Flight Lieutenant Divis also righted his aircraft and managed to fly back to RAF Manston in spite of the damage.

Once I had landed from the sortie I was grounded by my flight commander and the CO of the squadron. Their decision was supported by the station medical officer who deemed my eye condition to be very serious, promptly dispatching me to the Royal Masonic Hospital in London. On this occasion I did not rebel against the ruling that had been given for I knew, that unless I underwent treatment, there was a distinct possibility that I would never be allowed to fly again, or even worse, that I would lose my sight.

CHAPTER 20

REST AND RECUPERATION

That I was ready to be pensioned off from flying duties was proving difficult to accept. Had it not been for the pain and the scary look in my eyes that confronted me when I looked in a mirror, I would have appealed against the sentence – if necessary to Air Chief Marshal Tedder or even directly to Winston Churchill. After all, my mission had not yet been accomplished; I still had to see that my parents were freed from their prison camp and living in a liberated Czechoslovakia. No, the war was definitely not over, there was still a lot of fighting to be done before total freedom was regained – this was no time to be lying in a hospital bed.

With God's help, aided by the Battle of Britain pilots and the mighty determination of anyone capable of taking up arms against the common enemy and spurred on by Churchill, Britain had not been invaded. Yet there were still battles to be waged on the ground, at sea and in the air, and many more were to die as a consequence.

My transfer to the Royal Masonic Hospital in Ravenscroft Park took place on December 15th 1944. I had written letters to Beth, the Cousins and Venca Slouf. I asked the ground crew to take very good care of my car, stressing that the tank was never to be filled with 'green' petrol. Assurances were given, together with their good wishes. With my last chores completed, I was reluctantly ready to depart.

The hospital welcome was typically clinical. I did not, at that time, have a clue what Freemasonry stood for. The nurses, a delight to behold, guided me to the ward, I was determined that their handling of me would not be too sterile, in spite of my condition. The matron, about forty-five years old, was of medium stature but shapely and gave me a first impression that she was strictly 'taboo'. There was a twinkle in her hazel eyes and the smiling puckish lips were capable, at the slightest provocation, of becoming tight. She had a gentle but firm voice.

The square-shaped ward held four beds – two on each side, with a large window opposite the entrance which offered a lovely view of a park with a large pond and paths gently curving as if lacing the green expanse and the trees together. The other beds were all occupied by army officers; the one next to me by the window, was a major. He was probably forty-eight to fifty years old but looked younger. At first he seemed somewhat aloof but soon the distance between our beds narrowed. His name was George and he became interested in the mission that I had been pursuing over the past five years. The other two officers who occupied the beds opposite mine were friendly and treated me as an equal, but the major made it his task to take me under his wing. He told me that when we were both sufficiently recovered and allowed to venture outside, he would take me to the Houses of Parliament so that I could witness first-hand, how Britain, the world's cradle of democracy, was governed.

On the day of my admission to the hospital I underwent a thorough examination of my eyes, with a specialist. He probed around and behind the eyeballs, while searching into the depths of my memory about the day that I had sustained the injuries, to discover how soon after the event the infection had set in. Once the inspection was over, he boosted my morale with an assurance that I might fly again. The treatment that followed included rinsing my eyes three times a day, more probing and the application of drops, while my eyes remained bandaged for a week. During that time I learned a great deal from George about the state of British democracy.

During the treatment of the major's injuries, the curtains remained drawn around his bed and I remained in the dark about the extent of his injuries. It took almost a month before he confided that a bullet had passed through his body. He mused that our meeting was worth all the pain. I liked him because he was a typical British officer, an aristocrat with a 'stiff upper lip' and a sense of humour. After I had received a telegram I told George that, as from January 1st 1945, my rank was that of flying officer. He was only mildly impressed.

The way that the dedicated nurses, consultants and the matron took care of me helped to uplift my spirits. After four weeks the other two beds were vacated and new patients arrived. George's wounds, like my eyes, were taking time to heal. He had several visitors who, apart from one very refined, smartly dressed woman, were mainly army officers. There was one other exception to this; a portly man, dressed in a dark suit and carrying a bowler hat. While he was at the major's bedside I could feel the presence of an 'official' scrutiny while they were quietly talking.

One morning I was looking through the window of the ward admiring the thin mantle of snow, lost on a journey of memories that took me through the village of my birth. I felt the presence of my gran, making sure that I was well wrapped up before venturing out to play on the snow-covered slopes on a sledge. My reverie was broken when a familiar voice said: "A lovely sight, isn't it Frank," to my sheer delight it was the major who had spoken and he was standing, unaided, beside me. It was the first time he had managed to get out of his bed without the assistance of two nurses and a wheelchair. He looked excited and added cheerfully: "Perhaps you and I can persuade the matron to let us visit that park and feed the ducks." A nurse then ordered him back to his bed, he complied, with his face aglow and his arm wrapped tightly around her slim waist.

A little later that same morning, during the usual ceremonial routine inspection, I was told that the newly discovered penicillin, in the form of eye drops, would be tried on my eyes. Having read about Dr Fleming's achievement in this field, I hoped that a few magic drops would unite me with my Spitfire in no time at all. A week later when my eyes had not responded to the penicillin, it became another cause for my despair.

The major's excursions from his bed were becoming more frequent and tolerated by that supreme authority – the matron. His strength was gradually building up and plans were shaping up for us to set off on our Ravenscroft Park safari. George, at his most diplomatic, succeeded where I was sure to have failed and was soon able to impart the news that 'She' had graciously given permission for us to have one hour's freedom to go for a walk in the park, providing that we promised not to go astray.

George was supported by a crutch and I was provided with a pair of dark glasses. We set off to the lift, whereupon the opened doors gave a view down the long corridor towards the entrance doors. The bright sunshine outside beckoned us to freedom – the park and some grateful ducks. On this visit the major announced that our next outing would be to the House of Commons at Westminster.

We had to 'mark time' for a few days before our application to the matron to be allowed out for four hours was approved. We set off first thing after lunch, with a taxi waiting outside the hospital front door. The major, having made some telephone calls the day before, told me that at the House of Commons we would meet his Member of Parliament who would make arrangements for us to be ushered into the Strangers' Gallery. George was making good his promise for me to see and hear a debate in the Commons' chamber. "As you are a true democrat, I hope this visit will prove to be interesting and convince you that what you believe in was, and will remain, worth fighting for, as were the sacrifices of the friends you have told me so much about." I was speechless until the taxi pulled up outside the Parliament lobby entrance.

Upon our entry we were met by a uniformed official who offered us a seat on a bench until we were called for. I spent the waiting time transfixed by the piercing eyes of the portraits hanging along each side of the lobby. After a short spell, came a surprise when the same portly man I had seen at the hospital, approached us. The gentleman was a Member of Parliament and it was he who had made our visit to the Strangers' Gallery possible. Had I been told in the past, that one day I would sit on a bench between a Member of Parliament and the Home Secretary, the Right Honourable James Chuter-Ede, I would have thought them crazy.

After the Member of Parliament and my hospital friend had had a brief chat, a welcome to the House was extended to me. An usher guided us up the stairs to the Strangers' Gallery from where there was a broad view of the Commons' debating chamber. On each side of the oblong room were tiered rows of upholstered benches divided by a corridor. At the end of this stood a podium, with a solid carved oak throne-like chair upon which sat a man in black robes wearing a wig. It was explained to me that this man was the Speaker of the House. Slightly below the Speaker, and between the Members' benches, sat several robed and bewigged men at long school-like desks. These were the parliamentary clerks, I was told. Ahead of these gentlemen, between the bottom rows of the Members' benches stood a table upon which the mace was usually placed. I learnt from the major that the mace was a ceremonial staff, borne by the mace bearer who precedes the Speaker on entering for each day's sitting of the House. It is displayed as the symbol of authority; the outward and visible sign of a legislative body. On one side of the tiered benches sat the Right Honourable Herbert Morrison and beside him, the Right Honourable Aneurin Bevan, both of whom I recognised. There were a few more MPs scattered along both sides of the Chamber, the only one that I knew was the MP I had met in the lobby.

I was rather disappointed that Winston Churchill was not in his seat. He was beyond any criticism of mine and occupied a place in the warmest part of my heart. The empty benches were a puzzle to me. Where were the MPs? The war was still raging so there must have been some vitally important matters to be discussed and resolved. Later, when I posed this question to the major, his diplomatic answer did nothing to relieve my concern – however, diplomacy was not my forte.

During the following six days the major made rapid progress towards a full recovery from his wounds and, as promised, acted as my guide to such places as the Tower of London, the Science Museum and Trafalgar Square which preceded a spell of meditation in the church of St Martin-in-the-Fields. Finally, there came a visit to St Paul's Cathedral where both of us were fortified by a moment of prayer. Having climbed under the heavenly dome to the gallery, my wholehearted whispered thanks to George were heard and understood. On the day that the major was discharged from hospital I received a bruising handshake from him – its message was clear and I was glad that I wore dark glasses.

The major's vacated bed was soon supporting another very ill army officer, acquaintance with whom was not yet possible. I began to brood. After nearly two months of varied treatment and impeccable nursing at the Royal Masonic Hospital, I was still not fit for flying. My somewhat shaky optimism that a full recovery was close at hand became undermined when I was told that I was being transferred to Princess Mary's Hospital at RAF Halton. In spite of my very resolute questioning, I received no explanation that I was prepared to believe. All that the matron had to say on the subject was that an official order had been made which could not be countermanded. I had already spent two months at Halton during October and November 1941 during which period I suffered the loss of my tonsils and a tooth, so I began to worry about what sort of radical treatment might be in store for me this time.

The matron of the Royal Masonic Hospital bade me farewell on February 16th 1945. Arriving, this time, as an officer and presumably as a gentleman, I was conducted to a small ward with only three beds. My optimism needed to be resuscitated and this would only come about if my eyes could be restored to their original healthy state. If the charm of the nurses had anything to do with it, the outlook for a speedy return to my squadron looked good. Added to which, I felt my gran was prescribing treatment, which would undoubtedly help in my recovery.

My dreams of being reunited with a Spitfire engaged in shooting down another enemy plane were all shattered when, on March 5th, an order arrived for me to be posted back to the Czech depot at RAF Cosford. Had I actually been on an operational flight I would have let my guns blaze away at the bureaucrat who had conceived and signed the order. Had it not been that the posting would bring me close to my 'family' at Wolverhampton, there might well have been one undisciplined officer being court-martialled and possibly shot.

I left the Princess Mary's Hospital on 5th March to return to RAF North Weald to collect my car which was, thankfully, in fine fettle and the instructions regarding the use of aviation fuel had been obeyed. Issued with some more petrol coupons by the adjutant I set off for Cosford in cool breezy weather. The squadron pilots were airborne so I left unheralded and with a lump in my throat. When I arrived at Cosford there was no fanfare as I drove through the gate; the sentry pointed me in the direction of the Czech depot. The officer in charge was a flight lieutenant, showing no flying qualifications on his uniform and with no ceremony at all he had me ushered by a Czech-speaking airman, to a room of my own. The only order that was given was that I had to report to the station medical officer once a week.

After settling into the single room I took myself off to dinner in the officers' mess. By far the next most important job was to phone my 'family' in Wolverhampton to ask if I could visit them the next day and perhaps stay overnight. Net, who I preferred to call 'Mum', responded with a reprimand as she pointed out that: "You should know by now that this is your home, you can come any time and stay as long as you wish."

It was close to 10am when I pulled up outside their house where, before I could climb out of the car, Mary, closely followed by her mother, gave me hugs and kisses of welcome. Inside the house I was offered the centre of the settee which had cushions piled high. With Mary wedged on one side and 'Mum' on the other, it took some time to answer their barrage of questions, repeated over and over. They followed this with their usual hospitality in the form of tea and an assortment of biscuits, the like of which I had not seen since before the war.

When Cliff arrived home from his factory we enjoyed a superbly cooked lunch matched by some broadly topical and lively conversation. Cliff remained, as were his wife and daughter, very concerned about my eye problem but, after a glass or two of wine, the worries that weighed heavily upon us soon dissipated. I began to believe that I was back home among my real parents, being welcomed as a hero. It was only when we began to reminisce about Albin that my true feelings became evident – that I was beginning to feel insignificant. After the meal, Cliff returned to his factory but not before he had promised that we would play snooker in the evening.

It was a most restful afternoon as Net busied herself around the house and Mary and I found much to talk about. I sought an assurance from Mary that her love and intention to marry a sailor was not a premature decision. It is tragic, that not long after they were married, the submarine that he was serving on did not re-surface and all hands were lost. Against her parent's wishes, Mary made another union which did not last. Many years later she married a retired Royal Naval officer – a man of political importance – which seemed to work out alright.

After a light meal, and with permission granted, Cliff and I soberly departed for a spell of man-to-man talk and a game of snooker at his golf club. He beat me fair and square on the green baize, which pleased him greatly. Cliff was a beer drinker whilst I had scotch whisky and, when it was my turn to pay for a round, I suggested that he had a dram with me. Politely refusing, he placed his arm around my shoulder and said: "Thank you for offering Frank, but if I drink a scotch or two I am ready to fight anybody. If you were near me you might be the first one I would hit. Scotch makes me fighting mad, which is why I do not touch a drop of it." We returned home rather late in an amicable mood, which did not deter Net from looking at us with a very critical eye.

Back in the Czech depot at RAF Cosford, I made it quite clear to the flight lieutenant in command, that being at Cosford was not my choice and that the sooner I could get a posting back to an operational squadron, the better my morale would be. It was quite evident to everyone that I had very hostile thoughts towards whoever had been responsible for sending me to, what I can only describe as, an 'open prison'. The stipulated visits to the medical officer continued and I prayed that I would soon be pronounced fit to fly – thus ending my 'sentence' of being held as a convict at the depot.

One morning when having breakfast in the officers' mess, I caught the eye of the station commander whom I enlightened with my radical point of view. My rebellious tendency was nipped in the bud when, on April 19th, I was transferred to, believe it or not, RAF Halton, whose airfield could be seen from the Princess Mary's Hospital from which I had been discharged on March 5th. At last, I was back among friendly RAF personnel with various aircraft available that my temporary medical grade would allow me to fly. I was no longer of sour disposition. My duties were to ferry civilian or uniformed persons from Halton to various destinations.

Whilst it was immensely enjoyable to captain an assortment of communication aircraft from Halton, my conscience told me that I was betraying the pilots and aircrews currently engaged in fierce battles. The present flying from Halton was in unarmed, mainly small, two or more seated aircraft, and it was to my eternal disappointment that when peace in Europe was declared one bright May day, I was not in the air in the cockpit of my beloved Spitfire and on operational duties. I had now lived in Great Britain for five years. I had fought, loved, worried, grieved, prayed for peace, often felt angry, sometimes overjoyed but above all was the feeling that permeated my whole being which was that I was British.

Yet another order arrived which transferred me on June 3rd to 17 Service Flying Training School (STFS) to undergo a refresher course at RAF Coleby Grange, only a few miles south of the cathedral city of Lincoln. That the RAF could now be so callous as to send me back to a flying school was impossible for me to assimilate. Could it have been a revengeful act by a Nazi sympathiser or an order by a Czech Air Force general sitting on his brain, compiling statistics in a cushy London office?

A very large portion of my self-esteem had been gouged out of my patriotic heart when I arrived at RAF Coleby Grange. I was only a shadow of the once zestful patriot who was about to scare the pants of my instructor. It was merely the spectre of me that drifted about the station or flew in a Harvard trainer. Now aware that Czechoslovakia had been liberated, I left RAF Coleby Grange on June 13th 1945.

CHAPTER 21

RETURN TO LIBERATED
CZECHOSLOVAKIA

In order to accomplish what I had set out to do in June 1939, I flew to Prague in June 1945 in a 'borrowed' Spitfire. I stepped down from my plane at Ruzine airport, which was in the liberated sector of Czechoslovakia. The Russian soldiers and their military hardware were very much in evidence and did not make it feel like a free country. I was at the Prague city railway station, dressed in the uniform of an RAF officer and about to buy a ticket to Pilsen, when the clerk, giving me a good looking over, began to shout at me like a madman: "Ah, you are back again after gorging yourself in England whilst those of us here were starving and being bombed by" – pointing his finger – "You". This hurtful remark left me completely numb with shock; unable to believe that the people standing around me did not twitch a muscle. I made my way to the equally depressing looking, dirty, overcrowded train.

At Pilsen, the reunion with my parents was at their very comfortable apartment, which had hurriedly been vacated by a high ranking Gestapo officer. This apartment had been allocated to them on the day that they had returned, after imprisonment by the Nazis. Their house had been destroyed by a direct hit from an American bomber. Having taken shelter in the deep cellar, they were only slightly wounded. Our reunion was emotionally distant. I had not been forgiven for absconding from our home in 1939, leaving behind my country and associated responsibilities. They clearly believed what the communists were saying – that I was the reason for their imprisonment. Indeed I was not fully forgiven for my sins until some forty-three years later, just before my mother died, when she became aware that the Czech Government had graciously promoted me to the unpaid rank of a retired air force colonel.

During all the battles that I fought in the skies with German Luftwaffe pilots, I was never shot down. What they failed to achieve, my father succeeded in doing when, during our very first reunion, he began to shout and lecture me about the marvels of Communism. It became the first time that I had to bail out. When, in 1948, the Communist regime was at the helm of Czechoslovakia, their brutal totalitarian system was just like the rule that the Nazis had over the country. Whenever I visited my parents I was at the mercy of their police and my father's blind political beliefs remained constant. Even when, in 1946, I became a British subject by naturalisation and had a passport to prove it, I remained a marked man, living dangerously when visiting the far from free, Czechoslovakia.

A second visit to my parents in October 1945 followed fairly quickly and on this occasion I was able to cadge a lift on a bomber of 311 (Czech) Bomber Squadron. This squadron was in the process of transporting all their equipment back to Prague – all in preparation for a ceremonious return to liberated Czechoslovakia. That I was still being looked after by my grandmother was given further proof when, at the last minute, before boarding a Liberator aircraft, I was asked to transfer to another – the one that I vacated took off and crashed.

The horrific news about the crash reached me during the flight and put me in a subdued mood for the train journey from Prague to Pilsen, where I longed to be reunited with my mother. At my home, the chilling atmosphere seemed to have eased – a 'Bailey' bridge had been erected that spanned the past five years – I felt that I had possibly been forgiven for my absence. My stay was determined by the return flight of the Liberator, and mother and I parted sorrowfully. My father looked rather like the statue of Lenin. We flew back to RAF Blackbush, an airfield a few miles west of London, where further details of the crash filled me with more remorse.

Well before my demobilisation from the RAF, I was able to make a third visit to my kinfolk. Still wearing the RAF uniform, the Army of Occupation reluctantly gave me permission to travel by car, provided I abided by some strict conditions. I had to take sufficient fuel for the journey and no stopping was allowed when crossing Germany. I was obliged to follow a set route across France to Strasbourg, then via Stuttgart and Nuremberg to Pilsen. Crossing Germany was a harrowing experience. The destruction of towns and cities was immense. At one stage, having lost my way between Nuremberg and the Czech border and feeling very apprehensive, I stopped when I saw some people working in the fields alongside the road. When I asked them, in broken German, for directions, in spite of me being in a RAF uniform, they were willing to give friendly assistance. I realised that they had not been the enemies that I had fought and hated and I shook hands with them gratefully.

I found my parents in very good health. My mother was particularly excited to see me, immediately spoiling me with food. Her cooking was just as good as I remembered. Whilst the beer flowed, I became a bourgeois, trespassing upon the principles of the Leninist which, I regret to say, my father had become. Nevertheless, my mother was in a mellow mood and our reunion was deeply moving with no words of reproach being uttered. At times, her soft brown eyes glistened with tears during our 'tête à tête'. Before father arrived home from his work at the laboratory in the town abattoir, mother and I sat very close as she gently probed for details of my war experiences and the kind of life that I intended to pursue in the future. She also showed great interest and wanted to know all about the ribbons sewn on under the RAF wings on my uniform. I gave her a brief explanation but she prodded me to expand as her smooth forehead wrinkled and an expression of awe was in her eyes. I was happy when she promised to visit me in England and, to my great surprise, she made the trip several times.

Since returning from their imprisonment by the Gestapo, my parents had both put on some weight. The wounds sustained during the bombing of their house had healed and they were relieved that the war was over. Peace and liberty had been restored. My father would not recognise that my part in the war, although minuscule, had helped to bring about that freedom. According to him, everybody in the land knew that Czechoslovakia had been fought for and liberated by the Russians – the British and allied efforts were dismissed.

On the day before my departure for England and in accordance with the contingency plans that I was required to make at Pilsen, I called upon the American Army depot, which was only two kilometres from my parent's home, to arrange for a supply of fuel to get back to England. The officer in charge of the stores told me that after filling up the tank, I could help myself to as many jerry-cans full of petrol as my car could accommodate. Such a liberal offer was not to be ignored and so I obliged – with thanks. I was not surprised by the generosity of the Americans, even when a pack of 200 cigarettes were thrown in. I had experienced a great deal of contact with them whilst flying their Airacobra fighters. My thumbs were up as I drove out of the camp gates, feeling very grateful.

Having said my goodbyes to my mother – father had left early for his work – I set off for Zamyšel, the village where I was born. At the village church was the cemetery that held my grandmother's grave. I prayed at the graveside and thanked her for looking after me so well during the war years. I always had the strongest of feelings that she rose to all the solemn occasions in my life and that she approved of what I had done. Before leaving her graveside, I also thought of Albin, Tony, Jan and Michel. The memory of Albin in particular, occupied a very special corner of my heart.

At Zamyšel, as expected, I was very cordially welcomed by the Krysl family. The eldest of the family remembered my grandparents whose house had stood close to their farm where I was lovingly cared for and later spent school holidays. Ferdinand and his wife Mary, both about my age, had not forgotten what a nuisance I was around the village until I was old enough to know better. At first I became very emotional while reminiscing with my hosts about those unforgettable years when I was a fledgling, impatiently flexing my featherless wings, that later supported my patriotic mission all the way to Britain.

In the evening, my hosts' overwhelming hospitality was straining the legs of the table, around which sat many other village friends. The celebration rendered one and all, almost legless. In spirit, the pile of empty Pilsen beer bottles became a memorial to the war achievements and sacrifices of those who believed that truth and freedom were worth fighting and dying for.

Later, on the following evening, I sat alone under the star-studded sky, accompanied only by solemn thoughts, and I tried hard to resolve my unease about leaving the country of my birth. With renewed anguish I decided to become a non-participating citizen of Czechoslovakia, believing that the mission I set out to accomplish in June 1939 had been honourably accomplished.

A couple of days later I was ready for the return journey to England – having been generously provided with plenty of food and refreshment. The visit itself was as memorable as any of the highlights of the previous five years. Promises were made to return as soon as possible, as I set off in the direction of my destiny. There was hardly an inch of spare space in my car – it even accommodated my beloved gran who sat beside me. What a soul-filling companion she was. The old car was well overloaded with all the extra fuel. The car's vacuum pump was normally a frequent source of trouble, but the engine purred sweetly all the way to the port where the car was hoisted by a crane and placed into the hold of the ship. Then, it was lifted out on reaching Dover; the gateway to my adopted homeland, beloved England and the British people.

My visits to Prague, Pilsen and to Zamyšel continued at two or three yearly intervals. In 1948 the Communist regime, just like that of the Nazis, had established itself and my visits were not welcomed by the dictators – at times my arrivals were laced with the danger of persecution. The frequency of my trips was now dictated by the longing that I had to be with my mother whose love I sought ever since my birth and greatly missed. Equally strong was my need to be accepted as a patriot by my grandmother as I knelt at her graveside in the cemetery. I would also have liked to be known as a patriot, a true Czech patriot, in the village that had been my home in former times.

On the death of my father from diabetes in 1961, I offered my mother a home with us but because of her commitment to her profession and the need she felt to be among friends and kin at Pilsen, she refused. That she preferred to stay in her own home, and dedicate herself to the paediatric practice was understandable.

When I was demobilised from the RAF in 1946 I added my gratuity payment to my other savings, which, from time to time, had been com-plemented by winnings that had come my way from the games of poker played to pass the time as we waited for the call to scramble. I was now a civilian whose destiny was to become a self-employed businessman.

Many years later, during one of my visits to my mother, who by this time was ninety-six years old, she announced that she had overstayed her life on earth and that it was time for her to die. She was still living independently in the same apartment, having adamantly refused to spend the rest of her life in England. Because her brain was as sharp as ever, and she was not seriously physically impeded, her emphatic announce-ment was all the more startling. I was shocked. She was agile, alert and her adequate pension provided all her needs. That she was about to die was not illusory – she had decided and that was the end to it.

My mother, the daughter of my beloved gran, spoke again – "I've been here too long, I'm no use to anybody – it is time to go!" She died six months later in hospital. At the time I was ill with a bout of food poisoning which I had contracted at a Pilsen restaurant. All family and friends from Pilsen and Prague came to the funeral. I placed the urn with her ashes on the grave that my father rested in and left part of my heart to lie beside my mother's ashes. Was this the time to record the accomplishment of my mission? Perhaps from a patriotic point of view it was as if another destiny-guided mission had begun – my demobilisation had created responsibilities to be shouldered and my attention to these was all important.

In writing this story I have been, at times, encouraged, cajoled and – yes, even bullied into relating the events of long ago, as seen through my eyes. The task now completed, has provided turmoil in plenty, volumes of emotion and a legion of remembrances. I would also like to place on record my own personal appreciation of the country and its people that allowed me to adopt it as my own. To the Royal Air Force who gave me the opportunity to achieve my burning desire to go on the offensive against the oppressors of the country that gave me birth and to the Cousins family in Wolverhampton who provided me with stability and a haven of rest during troubled times. It is only right that I place on record my esteem and admiration of the men and women of this country – from Winston Churchill, whose inspiration I can still recall, to all those brothers-in-arms encountered during the exciting times. My appreciation is also to the skill of the ground crews, whose devotion and long hours kept the planes flying; always available, refuelled, rearmed and ready for the fray. To the women in the WAAF, especially those whose dulcet, cheerful and ever calm voices guided me on many occasions; not only in battle but also, and more importantly, safely and securely back home. The many others whose contribution also gained my admiration include members of the Home Guard, the Royal Observer Corps – the eyes and ears of the air force and those whose diligent and arduous work in the factories kept us supplied with the necessary material to carry on the fight. To those in the other services – the plying of the cargo ships on the high seas bringing precious supplies to these shores, to the fighting men on the ground who were there to finally liberate the war-torn countries of Europe, and to the naval men and women who were ever watchful and provided all the required support in every theatre of war. The indomitable spirit of the British people was a constant spur to continue the struggle, despite all the hardships. The depth of my esteem can be symbolised by the fact that on the cessation of hostilities, I decided to make my permanent home in my adopted country, which has enabled me to enjoy a full family life whilst conducting my own business. In trying to give something back, I have spent many hours providing tuition to the gliding community both at service and civilian level, as well as giving flying experience to the Air Training Corps – it has all been my pleasure to do so. In my retirement years I can look back with a great deal of pride. I am proud that I made the decision to stand up and fight for what I believed in, and proud of the contribution that I could make to the overall effort to gain victory.

After the war, when the RAF Voluntary Reserve was re-instated, I immediately joined and was accepted at Exeter as a pilot. I did not mention anything about the problem with my eyes and nobody asked. We had Tiger Moths to start with and flew at weekends – voluntarily and unpaid. While enjoying myself, I thanked my lucky stars that I was still able to take to the air. 6244 RAF Gliding School was also at Exeter and being curious, I approached the CO, Squadron Leader Hales, who had been with the Air Training Corps (ATC). He suggested I have a flight in a glider and I was taken up in a Slingsby T31.

This first launch scared me more than I had ever been scared during the war. The winch hauled us up at a spectacular angle; far steeper than a conventional aircraft. However, I soon got used to this type of flying, enjoyed it, and eventually joined the gliding club. I was commissioned into the RAFVR(T) and was happy to be dealing with young ATC cadets, imparting my knowledge to them on how to fly. I found it extremely rewarding.

Meantime, Chipmunks replaced the Tiger Moths and I continued flying them for some time, giving air experience flights to ATC cadets too. This continued until I moved with my family to Cornwall, where distance and new business commitments brought all this to an end.

I was away from active flying for eight years but upon moving to Plymouth I was approached by a local team of enthusiasts who were forming a gliding club. They asked me to become their chief flying instructor (CFI), which I gladly accepted. We flew from a field near Kingsbridge but later moved to Bolt Head, my old wartime stomping ground. Later still, the club moved to Davidstow but they went without me. I then joined a new club at Brentor, north of Tavistock, as an instructor and advisor, later to become secretary and vice-chairman. By the time Anno Domini began to catch up with me I had made over 10,000 glider launches. It was a very happy period in my life and it enabled me to remain airborne for far longer than I would have thought possible.

EPILOGUE

After the war, Frank Mares chose to remain in England and for many years carried on a successful business life in the West Country. Now in retirement, he lives his autumnal years only a runway's distance from the former RAF Harrowbeer at Yelverton, Devon. The injuries that he sustained to his eyes and his back have, and still do, trouble him on an almost daily basis. He has not been heard to really complain – he considers the suffering a small price to have paid for the privilege of living in a free country. He fought for it and would have, if necessary, died for it. The story that has unfolded on the previous pages is not only a personal statement, expressed in an intensely personal way, it is also a true one. If nothing else, it demonstrates the demands that were placed upon his courage, setting out on his fight for freedom. To those who have never lost their liberty it may be difficult to understand that there will always be those, to whom freedom in all its aspects is of paramount importance. The country of his adoption has ample cause to give thanks for such devotion.

His mission can be considered well and truly accomplished.

FRANK MARES'S TRAVELS THROUGH EUROPE TO ENGLAND 1939-1940

Europe	Squadrons	Aircraft
Czechoslavakia		
Born 29 July 1919		
Maternity unit at Libětice, Sumava Hills		
Lived in a village (Zamyšel) in Sumava		
Hills close to German border until 6 yrs old		
Pilsen 6-20 yrs old	West Czechoslovakia	WW1 bi-plane
	Aero Club, Pilsen	Praga Air Baby
		(gained PPL 1937)
Hradec Kralove	Czech Air Force	unknown
Route out of Poland – June 1939:		
Prague, Moravska Ostrava, Tesin/Cieszyn (on		
Czech/Polish border)		
Poland		
Krakow (Czech Embassy) – Katovice		
Gdynia (to join cargo ship *Kastelholm*)		
Denmark		
Frederikshavn (port call)		

Europe	Squadrons	Aircraft
France		
Calais (disembark from *Kastelholm*)		
Paris Air Ministry, Exelmans		
Village of Verberie 35 miles north of Paris – escaped from train taking him to the French Foreign Legion		
Paris		
Bourges airfield	Ecole Auxiliare Pilotage de Bourges	Hanriot, Morane Saulnier 230
Avord airfield		Morane 230 Nord
Nachent (airfield) St Igny (base) nr Vilabon – 5 miles SE Avord		
Virson airfield – 14 miles east of La Rochelle		Morane (220 &225), Nord and Dewoitine
Le Verdon-sur-Mer (60 nm NE Bordeaux) to join ship		
Ville de Liège to UK		
England		
24 June 1939 – arrived Liverpool (via Belfast) onboard *Ville de Liège*. Disembark to Haydock Park		

FRANK MARES'S RAF SQUADRONS, AIRCRAFT AND BASES IN THE UK

From	To	RAF Sqn or Unit	Based at RAF	Aircraft
24 June 1940 – arrived Belfast from Le Verdon-sur-Mer onboard animal cargo ship *Ville de Liège* en route Liverpool				
June 1940			Haydock Park	Holding
June 1940			Bridgnorth	Holding
July 1940			Innsworth	Selection tests for RAF
July 1940			Uxbridge	Medical
July 1940			Duxford	Brief visit
Late July 1940	29 Sept 1940		Cosford	Entry to RAF in rank of Sgt
1 Sept 1940 – Rank of Sergeant				
29 September 1940	10 October 1940	Ground School and Flying Training	Benson	Fairey Battle, Avro Anson, Miles Magister
14 October 1940	4 November 1940	6 Operational Training Unit	Sutton Bridge	Miles Master, Hawker Hurricane
10 November 1940	17 December 1940	601	Exeter	Hurricane
17 December 1940	2 May 1941	601	Northolt	Hurricane
25 April 1941 – Awarded Czech Bravery Medal				
2 May 1941	1 July 1941	601	Manston	Hurricane

From	To	RAF Sqn or Unit	Based at RAF	Aircraft
1 July 1941	16 August 1941	601	Matlask	Hurricane
16 August 1941	1 October 1941	601	Duxford	Hurricane, Bell P39
				Airacobra, Hawker Cygnet, Magister, Hornet Moth, Bristol Blenheim
1 October 1941	30 November 1941	Princess Mary's Hospital	Halton	Eye treatment
30 November 1941	10 December 1941	Convalescence	Blackpool	Eye treatment
13 December 1941	4 January 1942	601	Duxford	Airacobra
4 Jan 1942	25 March 1942	601	Acaster Malbis	Airacobra, Magister
				Supermarine Spitfire (from 13 March)
25 March 1942	26 March 1942	601	Digby	Airacobra, Spitfire VB
28 March 1942	1 April 1942	610	Hutton Cranswick	Spitfire VB, Magister
1 April 1942	25 May 1942	610	Ludham	Spitfire VB, Magister
May 1942 – Rank of Flight Sergeant				
25 May 1942	12 June 1942	313 Czech	Fairlop	Spitfire VB, Magister
16 June 1942	15 September 1942	312 Czech	Harrowbeer	Spitfire VB, Magister

2 September 1942 Awarded the DFM and presented on 26 Sept together with the Czech War Cross

From	To	RAF Sqn or Unit	Based at RAF	Aircraft
22 September 1942	15 March 1943 (Hurricane crash 2 Nov '42)	2 Delivery Flight	Colerne	Airspeed Oxford, Boulton Paul Defiant, Hawker Typhoon, de Havilland Dominie, Master, Spitfire, Hurricane, Cygnet
October 1942 – Rank of Warrant Officer				
14 March 1943	14 June 1943	313 Czech	Church Stanton (renamed Culmhead from Dec 1943)	Spitfire V
15 June 1943	13 August 1943	Princess Mary's Hospital	Halton	Eye treatment; 2 weeks sick leave; Medical Board
14 August 1943	22 August 1943	1847 Flight, Target Towing Unit (TTU)	St Athan	Westland Lysander, Master
22 August 1943	9 November 1943	61 OTU	Rednal	Spitfire 1, Master, Dominie
9 November 1943	15 April 1944	53 OTU	Kirton-in-Lindsey	Dominie, Master, Tiger Moth, Spitfire

From	To	RAF Sqn or Unit	Based at RAF	Aircraft
1 May 1944	14 June 1944	310 Czech	Warmwell (temp) Predannick (temp) Lympne (temp) Culmhead (temp) plus several others	Spitfire IXA
14 June 1944	1 July 1944	84 Group Support Unit (GSU)	Aston Down	Spitfire VB [Non-operational flying because of eyes]
1 July 1944	14 December 1944	310 Czech	North Weald Bradwell Bay (temp)	Spitfire IXA
November 1944 – Commissioned in the rank of Pilot Officer			Change of service number from 787653 to 185291	
15 December 1944	16 February 1945	Royal Masonic Hospital	Ravenscroft Park London	Eye treatment
1st January 1945 – Promoted to the rank of Flying Officer				
16 February 1945	5 March 1945	Princess Mary's Hospital	Halton	Eye treatment
5 March 1945	19 April 1945	Czech Depot	Cosford	Holding
19 April 1945	2 June 1945	Communications Flight	Halton	Various communications aircraft

From	To	RAF Sqn or Unit	Based at RAF	Aircraft
3 June 1945	13 June 1945	17 Service Flying Training School (STFS), a refresher school	Coleby Grange	North American Harvard
1945	De-mobbed and joined RAF (VR) immediately			
1945-1961	RAF (VR) – Voluntary Reserve	Air Training Corps	Exeter	De Havilland Tiger Moth and Chipmunk, Slingsby T31 glider
		6244 Gliding School	Exeter	
1961 on ………		Civilian Gliding Club		Kingsbridge and Bolt Head, Devon
		Civilian Gliding Club		Brentor, Devon

FRANK'S JOURNEY FROM
PILSEN TO LIVERPOOL

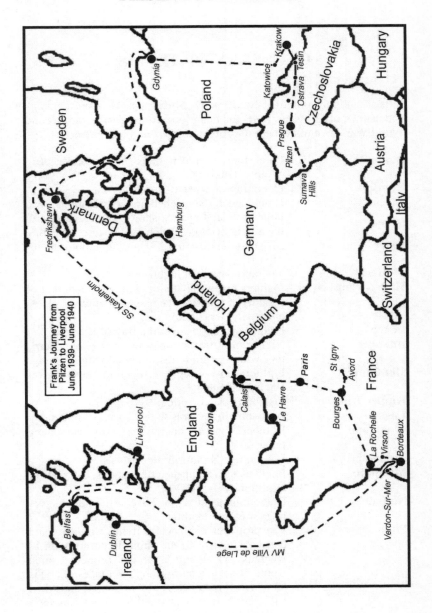

GLOSSARY OF TERMS

This list, kindly provided by the RAF Museum at Hendon, contains codenames used by the RAF for many operations during the Second World War. Several of these are found in *Mission Accomplished*.

Balbo Large formation of fighters such as Bader's Big Wing at Duxford.

Big Ben Operations against V-2 rocket sites.

Circus Combined fighter and bomber operations on a large scale and against short-range targets, with the aim of bringing the enemy air force to battle.

Diver Missions against the V-1 flying bombs themselves.

Flower Operations against night-fighter bases.

High (or top) cover Fighters operating at altitude higher than that of friendly formations engaged below to keep enemy fighters at bay.

Instep Fighter operations over the Bay of Biscay.

Intruder Night-time offensive patrols over enemy territory with the aim to disrupt enemy night flying.

Jim Crow Fighter anti-shipping reconnaissance over English Channel.

Kipper Kites Fishing fleet protection.

Lagoon Anti-shipping patrols with Coastal Command.

Mahmoud Bomber support operations with rear-facing radar.

Mandolin Long-range Night Intruder patrols.

Mosquito Small attacks on unspecified targets, ie targets of opportunity.

No-ball Operations to attack V-1 flying bomb (doodlebug) sites and facilities.

Pitch The propeller pitch while flying would remain constant relative to the strain imposed upon it; whereas, on the ground, the propeller pitch would be set at a narrow angle for take-off and is known as 'Fine Pitch'. After taking off and when sufficient height is attained, the pilot can set a 'Coarse Pitch'. This is done by manually operating a lever and the coarse setting has the effect of achieving an economical engine performance.

Popular	Photo-reconnaissance operations.
Ramrod	Similar to Circus: bomber escort mission by fighters aimed at destruction of a specific target in daylight.
Ranger	Large-formation freelance intrusions.
Rhubarb	Freelance fighter sortie against targets of opportunity. The successor to Mosquito.
Roadstead	Low-level attack by fighters against coastal shipping – at sea or in harbour.
Rodeo	Fighter sweep without bombers.
Rove	Armed reconnaissance over enemy territory.
Sweep	General term for fighters operating over enemy territory with or without bombers. A systematic operation to flush out targets in a given area, eg fighter sweep.

OTHER TERMS USED

Angels	Height in 1,000s of feet.
Bandit	Enemy aircraft.
Bogey	Unidentified aircraft.
Scramble	Immediate operational take-off.
Tally Ho	Engaging visual contact.
Vector	Heading.
Wing	Unit made up of two or sometimes three squadrons.
Witchcraft	Ground controller's call identifying a Bogey as a V-1 flying bomb (doodlebug).
FIDO	Fog Intensive Dispersal Of. Vaporised fuel pumped into pipes and ignited either side of runway to disperse fog.
FTS	Flying Training School.
GSU	Group Support Unit.
MU	Maintenance Unit.
OTU	Operational Training Unit.
R/T	Radio/Telephony.
'V' formation	Aircraft formation in the shape of a "V" usually three aircraft but could be more.

GERMAN TERMS USED

Geschwader	Wing
Gruppe/Gruppen	Group/Groups of squadrons
Jagdgeschwader (JG)	Fighter wing
Jager	Fighter
Stab	Staff
Staffel/Staffeln	Squadron/s

INDEX